Political Theatre during the Spanish Civil War

Political Theatre during the Spanish Civil War

JIM MCCARTHY

UNIVERSITY OF WALES PRESS
CARDIFF
1999

© Jim McCarthy, 1999

British Library Cataloguing-in-Publication Data.
A catalogue record for this book is available from the British Library.

ISBN 0–7083–1523–2

All rights reserved. No part of this book may be reproduced, stored in a retrieval system, or transmitted, in any form or by any means, electronic, mechanical, photocopying, recording or otherwise, without clearance from the University of Wales Press, 6 Gwennyth Street, Cardiff, CF2 4YD.

The right of Jim McCarthy to be identified as author of this work has been asserted by him in accordance with the Copyright, Designs and Patents Act 1988.

Typeset at University of Wales Press
Printed in Great Britain by Dinefwr Press, Llandybïe

To my parents

with gratitude and love
le gra agus go raibh maith agat

Contents

Acknowledgements	ix
Abbreviations	x
Introduction	xi
1 The Emergence of an Aesthetic	1
2 The Development of *Teatro de urgencia*	30
3 Staging the Political Drama	58
4 Attacking the Enemy	85
5 Forming the Soldier	118
6 Training for Victory	147
7 Celebrating the People	178
Conclusion: A Lost Theatre Recovered	206
Notes	214
Bibliography	234
Index	245

Acknowledgements

I am very grateful for the kind assistance offered in response to my many enquiries to organizations and libraries in Spain, Great Britain, the USA and South America. The sheer number of institutions which furnished me with documents, information and helpful lines of further investigation makes individual acknowledgement impossible. My task would not have been possible without their help and I offer them my sincere thanks. I owe a particular debt of gratitude to the late Luis Mussot, a prominent figure in the Civil War theatre, who not only gave generously of his time for correspondence and discussion, but kindly donated typescripts of his plays which had survived the Civil War and its aftermath. Antònia Babí, Derek Gagen, David George and John Hall have all provided incisive academic support throughout the various stages of research and writing. I also wish to thank my friend and colleague Roger Maidment for reading various sections and for support in numerous ways. Similarly, John Worthen, Graham O'Neil and Steve Tett made valuable contributions, not only through their willingness to discuss drama and *teatro de urgencia*, but through their supportive friendship over a number of years. Finally, of course, to V and to R, foremost amongst 'carpenters, electricians, stage managers' – and much more than any of these.

Abbreviations

BIOP   *Boletín de Información y Orientación Política*
           Bulletin of Political Information and Orientation
BOT   *Boletín de Orientación Teatral*
           Bulletin of Theatrical Orientation
CCT   Consejo Central del Teatro
           Central Theatre Council
CNT   Confederación Nacional de Trabajadores
           National Confederation of Workers
GTP   Grupo Teatro Popular
           Popular Theatre Group
JSU   Juventudes Socialistas Unificadas
           United Socialist Youth
TAP   Teatro de Arte y Propaganda
           Theatre of Art and Propaganda
UGT   Unión General de Trabajadores
           General Workers' Union

Introduction

Teatro de urgencia (theatre of urgency) is a subject which has received scant attention from commentators. No detailed study appears to have been published which might allow theatre historians to form a comprehensive judgement based upon the examination of a range of textual material. The reason for this neglect undoubtedly lies in the relative inaccessibility of *teatro de urgencia* scripts. This volume aims to assist in rectifying the shortcoming by offering an analysis of *teatro de urgencia* which derives predominantly from texts recovered through archive research and the generous co-operation of individuals who furnished me with typescripts or rare editions which had fortunately survived the hazards and disruption of the Civil War and its aftermath. To a great extent *teatro de urgencia* is an aspect of Spanish cultural history which vanished after the defeat of the Republic. Sometimes theatrical propaganda was not published, while the atmosphere of post-war fear surely contributed to the destruction of the few editions which were printed. The inaccessibility of archives during the years of the dictatorship also added to the neglect of those plays which had survived. Certain texts of *teatro de urgencia*, for example, were published by military organizations whose records were preserved by the new regime and which became more easily available for consultation in the growing atmosphere of openness in the years following the end of the dictatorship.

The neglect that this kind of theatre suffered is compounded by the widespread dismissal of its worth by those commentators who have lent it their attention. The few who have offered a judgement have found *teatro de urgencia* lacking in dramatic worth. By way of example, García Pavón welcomes its loss, since it is a drama 'que no merece recordarse por respeto al teatro' (which doesn't merit preservation in terms of theatre), while Pedret declares it to be a drama which rarely achieves dramatic quality. For Marrast, *teatro de urgencia* was merely a rather crude sketch-type drama which he found lacking in psychology and which he criticized for its failure to unite the needs of propaganda with the exigencies of art.[1] Such dismissive views arise, I believe, from a misunderstanding of the nature of this kind of theatre. As critical perspectives I would suggest that they fail to take sufficient account of the aesthetic history and purpose of such theatre and, in so doing, they apply aesthetic criteria for its judgement which are largely inappropriate. Such a contradiction is apparent if we compare García Pavón's assertion that *teatro de urgencia* lacked literary merit with Sender's call prior to the war for a new kind of drama which would adopt a resolutely antiliterary stance as a means of freeing itself from the dominant literary culture.[2] *Teatro de urgencia* reflects, as we shall see, many of the characteristics which Sender identified as crucial in this respect. In my view, previous commentators have, therefore, not only lacked a range of *teatro de urgencia* texts, but have devoted insufficient attention to the aesthetic debate conducted on the Spanish Left before and during the Civil War. This debate enables us to see this kind of drama as seeking to escape the dominance of traditional criteria of quality, thus requiring critical assessment of a kind more attuned to its intentions. When Marrast questions the lack of a psychological orientation in the drama he seems to be lamenting the absence of an individualistic art form, complex and subtle in the manner of Chekhov or Ibsen. Such an emphasis would be misplaced since, in *teatro de urgencia*, we encounter a more collectivist art in which concepts such as ambiguity and implication are largely eschewed in favour of factual starkness and an overt desire to instil clarity of understanding in the spectator.

The neglect and critical disregard of *teatro de urgencia* obscures, I believe, the extent to which it can be viewed as a significant but largely unexamined aspect of a European phenomenon, namely, the widespread movement during the 1920s and 1930s of what might best be termed political theatre. In its search for new, non-traditional audiences, its revolutionary zeal and the variety and flexibility of its form, *teatro de urgencia* frequently recalled similar theatrical developments elsewhere on the Continent. The Proletarian Theatre in Berlin, Brecht's *Lehrstücke*, the Living Newspaper in Russia, the Red Megaphones and Unity Theatre in Great Britain share much in common with *teatro de urgencia*.[3] However, while these varied theatrical innovations in other countries have received serious attention, this has not been the case with their Spanish counterpart. During the 1930s a number of Spanish writers and theatre practitioners admired and utilized such experiments in their own work and, in turn, this brought its influence to bear on *teatro de urgencia*. As we will see, therefore, the Republic's political theatre did not appear abruptly in response to the political fracture caused by the events of 18 July 1936. Prior to the Civil War there existed significant theory and practice with regard to political theatre, and this developed along new, sometimes more radical lines during the war. The neglect of *teatro de urgencia* means that no detailed attempt has yet been made to explore the developmental links between these two experiences of political theatre in a Spanish context despite important questions about their similarities and differences. Bilbatúa, for example, one of the most sympathetic commentators on this type of theatre, sees little distinction between León's 1933 play *Huelga en el puerto* (*Strike at the Port*) and Hernández's 1937 *teatro de urgencia* piece *El refugiado* (*The Refugee*).[4] For him both works can be regarded as theatre of political agitation. I suggest the need for a finer distinction based on the closer examination of a wider range of texts. Perhaps as a *result* of its agitational nature, *Huelga en el puerto* was not performed during the war, suggesting that we cannot make an easy assumption that a political theatre will always manifest itself as an agitational one. Hernández's play, for example, has a reflective purpose and tone which seem to contradict the clamorous certainty associated with agitational theatre and demonstrate the need to examine this kind of theatre with greater rigour than has so far been done.

It is for reasons such as this that any discussion of *teatro de urgencia* should seek from the outset to avoid the vagueness which surrounds its precise identity by offering a clear definition of what constitutes a *teatro de urgencia* work. Since my purpose is to analyse an aspect of Spanish theatre which has been marginalized by circumstances and is consequently little known, the term *teatro de urgencia* needs explanation and definition, so that an expression which sounds as though it might have general applicability as a description of any kind of drama with a committed mission, can be understood as describing a specific Civil War phenomenon.

The best-known description of *teatro de urgencia* is that of Alberti which was published in the first edition of the *Boletín de Orientación Teatral* in February 1938 and which, by virtue of its reproduction in the easily available *Prosas encontradas* (*Miscellaneous Prose*), has become widely accepted as outlining the defining qualities of the genre.[5] In fact, Alberti offered his description some three months earlier when he spoke, as Bleiberg recalled, to a packed house at the Teatro de la Zarzuela before a performance of Bleiberg's *Sombras de héroes* (*Shadows of Heroes*) on 12 December 1937.[6] It is an indication of the complicated genesis and characteristics of *teatro de urgencia* that a description of such confident authority, alongside his plea for writers to begin to cultivate what he called this instrument of culture and struggle, should be published so late in the war and after much of the genre seems to have been written:

> Hacen falta esas obritas rápidas, intensas . . . que se adapten técnicamente a la composición específica de los grupos teatrales. Una pieza de este tipo no puede plantear dificultades de montaje ni exigir gran número de actores. Su duración no debe sobrepasar la media hora.[7]
>
> (There's a need for these rapid, intense little works . . . which adapt themselves technically to the specific composition of the theatre groups. A piece of this type can't pose staging difficulties or demand a large number of actors. Its length shouldn't exceed half an hour.)

Alberti's emphasis in the article is upon formal characteristics and tends to assume the creation of a repertoire for mobile troupes. Actors and technical requirements are thus to be kept to a minimum and the plays' running times should be similarly concise. Emphasizing such examples as the recitation of *romances* (ballads) or the publication of war chronicles in broadsheets and posters, he urges rapidity of performance, directness of language and stark clarity of style, whether overtly didactic, satirical or dramatic. Surveying a considerable breadth of *teatro de urgencia* it is now possible to see that, while Alberti offers a useful *description* of the genre, as a *definition* it needs considerable qualification. It could be argued, for example, that if we accept Alberti's speech as offering a definition of *teatro de urgencia*, there are grounds for excluding his own *Radio Sevilla* (*Radio Seville*) from the genre despite contemporary records indicating that this was one of the most popular plays in the repertoire.[8]

Alberti was not alone in suggesting appropriate characteristics of style and purpose. Aware perhaps of Alberti's advice to intending writers, Juventud Campesina (Agricultural Youth) produced a volume of short plays for use by theatre groups within its organization.⁹ In an attempt to encourage a repertoire appropriate to its membership, the editors preface the volume with a request for new works which meet certain criteria. First, the works should be suitable for a youth audience and deal with current topical issues. Second, the production demands should be capable of fulfilment within the limited possibilities of the organization's meeting-places. Third, the works should seek to educate youth. Three of the four plays in the volume are undoubtedly *teatro de urgencia*, but the criteria above will not serve as a satisfactory definition, however much the second requirement is consistent with Alberti's call for simplicity of décor. Orientation to a youth audience or younger performers is obviously limiting as a defining element of a theatre intended to reach all Republican citizens, while the emphasis on *actualité*, attractive in a theatre which often dealt with issues and ideas of great immediacy, would incorporate into the genre works such as de Orriols's *España en pie* (*Spain be Ready*) which was premièred in early 1937.¹⁰ Throughout its three sprawling acts, its military parades, scenes of destruction and the appearance of tanks, troops and Moors, its contemporary topicality is unquestionable. Yet, with its thirty-three characters, technical complexity and its critical reception as crude populism rather than popular art, it cannot be seen as *teatro de urgencia*, nor, thus, can contemporary topicality be seen as an exclusive characteristic of the genre.

Another edition, *Teatro de urgencia*, describes the plays as offering 'enseñanza' (instruction) and allows us to examine whether a definition as 'teaching theatre' will sufficiently encapsulate *teatro de urgencia*.¹¹ It is an appealing definition since it is consistent, not only with Juventud Campesina's third demand, but also with Aparicio's call for commissars to encourage what he called this 'instrumento de enseñanza' (instrument of instruction) through dramatized lessons.¹² In similar vein, an anonymous writer in the *Boletín de Información y Orientación Política* saw such a repertoire as offering highly effective social and political education.¹³ Clearly, a description of *teatro de urgencia* as offering unambiguous political teaching is useful, but, as with the example of de Orriols, it is of only partial assistance in formulating a definition. The Teatro de Arte y Propaganda's Spanish version of Vishnévsky's *An Optimistic Tragedy* in December 1937 offered its audiences exemplary political lessons in revolutionary practice, but it is clearly not *teatro de urgencia*, nor are the various other foreign works of revolutionary theatre which were translated and produced in the Republican zone.[14] Interestingly, both de Orriols's work and that of Vishnévsky would join all *teatro de urgencia* in a common description as anti-Fascist theatre, thus removing even that most obvious label as providing the defining quality of *teatro de urgencia*.

In his study of the magazine *El Mono Azul*, Monleón, however, does attempt a definition of *teatro de urgencia*.[15] Yet, while he makes many useful observations, his assessment of what characterizes the genre seems to be based largely upon direct acquaintance with only three texts, those which were published in the magazine. For Monleón, these three plays are, he suggests, a clear example of the genre, but he also observes that, in the case of many works, only the titles survive. As a result, Monleón's definition does not entirely succeed in containing what emerges in this study as a greater body of the genre. His suggestion, for example, that a characteristic of *teatro de urgencia* is its reaction against 'la tradición conservadora de la mayor parte de nuestros dramaturgos' (the conservative tradition of the majority of our playwrights) (p.102) would exclude two particularly important works, Ontañón's *El saboteador* (*The Saboteur*) and Balbontín's *El cuartel de la Montaña* (*The Montaña Barracks*).[16] The first of these plays was considered such a fine example of the genre that it was published, yet its dramatic form recalls in many ways the traditional melodrama-cum-detective story and, apart from a solitary deprecation of Franco, there is no reason, strictly speaking, to infer from the text that the action is taking place during any specific military conflict. Similarly, Ontañón's other *teatro de urgencia* piece, *El bulo* (*The Rumourmonger*), is described in terms far from radical, as a 'diminuta zarzuela' (little comic opera).[17] Balbontín's play arises from a similarly conventional dramatic tradition, but in its other features we find so many qualities that Alberti would admire that it seems inappropriate to exclude it as *teatro de urgencia*. The play has, for example, a single act played with rapid intensity. There is grotesque humour in its portrayal of rebel officers, and the speed of its composition and rehearsal enabled the author to present on the Madrid stage one of the crucial moments of the uprising only a month or so after the event. If Monleón's definition were to hold, Dieste's *Al amanecer* (*At Dawn*) would face similar difficulties of inclusion.[18] Dieste's play is largely a naturalistic piece. Indeed, Sánchez-Barbudo admired this traditional quality in the play's exposition, the subtlety of the characterization and the manner in which the author's patriotic ardour was expressed 'interiormente' (inwardly).[19]

A further problem with Monleón's attempt at definition is his observation that this kind of theatre opposes what he calls 'los subgéneros' (the sub-genres) (p.102). This is contradicted by one of the most interesting *teatro de urgencia* works, *La evasión de los flamencos* (*The Escapism of the Gypsies*).[20] Described by its author on the title page as 'apropósito cómico-lírico-bailable en un tirón' (comical-lyrical-dancing sketch in a single burst), the play is a sequence of knockabout clowning between two *chulos* (pranksters) whose verbal wit, apparently improvised singing and their flirting with Carmen and Rosa, place them more in the world of Arniches or Muñoz Seca. Here, *teatro de urgencia* is not eschewing less sophisticated forms of popular entertainment but appropriating them in a manner akin to Alberti's appropriation of Cervantes's *El cerco de Numancia* (*The Siege of Numantia*).[21] In this way, the action concludes with a *zambra* (flamenco song and dance) but the verses are given the utmost topicality:

> Marxistas, republicanos,
> juventudes, anarquistas,
> todos juntos como hermanos
> p'aplastar a los fascistas
> lo mismo que a los gusanos. (p.10)

> (Marxists, Republicans,
> young people, anarchists,
> all united as brothers
> to crush the Fascists
> the same as with worms.)

As this somewhat detailed survey has shown, descriptive assessments of the genre require great care, since a definition which lacks rigour can exclude works which were clearly felt at the time to be worthy of repeated performance, and even publication, as examples of the genre whose spirit and style deserved emulation. Ultimately, the difficulty of offering a definition of *teatro de urgencia* arises from the dilemma that, while there is much to include, particularly in terms of stylistic variety, there is also much to exclude. Prominent amongst the latter are the many plays performed in mainstream theatres which received their premieres during the war, which zealously supported the Republic, but did so in a manner more *à la mode*, currying favour with what appeared to be current popular taste. With a historical perspective denied to those who wrote, edited, performed and described the genre from their particular viewpoint, and with the results of detailed research unavailable to Monleón, I would suggest that three fundamental criteria find expression in *teatro de urgencia*. First, the play's content will derive specifically from the Civil War. Second, the *direct* intention of the play will be to encourage in the spectator a 'correct' pro-Republican ideological position. Finally, through the achievement of the second criterion, the play will seek to inculcate values and delineate perspectives which will nurture the spectator as an ideal Republican combatant or citizen.

This definition emphasizes, not characteristics of form, but the relationship between stage and spectator during performance. Dramatized material which has a specific basis in the conflict is ordered so as to exert, with a high degree of focused intention, a particular influence upon the audience which encourages certain habits, certain ways of thinking which correspond to the ideological aims of the Republican camp. This is more than propaganda theatre, for reasons, as we have seen, of what else such a label might include which is not *teatro de urgencia*. For similar reasons it is not, as an anonymous writer declared, just 'breve teatro político antifascista' (short, anti-Fascist political theatre),[22] since this would inappropriately draw into the definition such works as Alberti's *Bazar de la providencia* (*Providence Bazaar*) or Sender's *El secreto* (*The Secret*).[23]

I have dwelt at some length on the matter of definition since, to date, only a highly generalized body of printed commentary is available. This exists largely in Civil War bibliographies, theatre surveys or surviving records, commentary which employs a variety of terms to describe this kind of drama. Terms such as revolutionary theatre, anti-Fascist theatre, theatre of the people, theatre of war, theatre 'a la altura de las circunstancias' (in the spirit of the times) or political theatre, can be misleading and hard to negotiate, since words such as 'political' and 'revolutionary' can be amongst the most difficult in any language. I suggest, however, that the definition I have offered accurately identifies a recognizable genre, enabling necessary distinctions to be made between individual works within the spectrum of 'political theatre' or 'propaganda theatre'.

In the course of writing this study I became aware of the overwhelmingly socialist orientation of *teatro de urgencia*, a feature which raises the intriguing question of the extent to which the Anarchists contributed to theatrical propaganda. The lack of trust between these two Republican factions is well known, as is their struggle for political dominance in numerous areas of state administration.[24] With regard to *teatro de urgencia*, however, the Anarchists do not seem to have played a role, and so an Anarchist aesthetic cannot be isolated and identified in distinctively non-socialist drama. An explanation of this may well be found in the Anarchist antipathy to permanent organizational structures, and it is surely significant in this respect that the impulse to organize and disseminate *teatro de urgencia* very often arose from government ministries, socialist groups and initiatives of the General War Commissariat. The socialist/communist orientation of this latter organization is clear, and it undoubtedly exerted an influence upon the political loyalties of *teatro de urgencia*.[25] The Anarchist dimension of *teatro de urgencia* seems, therefore, to be minimal. It is subsumed into a socialist-inspired emphasis upon a fraternal bond which is forged in the name of Republican unity. References in the plays to both factions are made in such a light, something which avoids images of the bitter division and fierce rivalry which often characterized their relationship.

~ 1 ~
The Emergence of an Aesthetic

The circumstances of its genesis, those of a specific military conflict, and its sole concern to mirror that conflict, enable us to see *teatro de urgencia* as a unique dramatic phenomenon, a highly particular manifestation of revolutionary theatre. Aspects of *teatro de urgencia* were not, however, without precedent, and in seeking to offer comprehensive judgement of the genre it is necessary to outline how, in certain ways, it reflects trends found in earlier Spanish and European theatre. For example, characteristic *teatro de urgencia* vocabulary such as *pueblo, revolución, cultura, proletario* and *tierra* (people, revolution, culture, proletarian, land) is also a significant element of an earlier dramatic language, that found in the dramas of the *cuestión social* (social question) which were prominent in Spain during the first three decades of the twentieth century. In a similar fashion, many of the characteristics of form associated with *teatro de urgencia* recall Russian and German experiments with revolutionary theatre during the 1920s and 1930s, and it is worth remembering in this respect not only that Piscator's influential *The Political Theatre* appeared in Spanish translation in the year following its initial publication, but also that a number of intellectuals subsequently prominent in *teatro de urgencia* were enabled by the Second Republic to travel abroad to study the latest developments in European theatre.[1]

These earlier manifestations of revolutionary theatre played significant roles in the development of a socialist theatre aesthetic in Spain which subsequently brought its influence to bear on the wartime propaganda theatre. There was, for example, a clear perception on the part of many Spanish intellectuals during the 1930s that, given their desire to create revolutionary drama, it would be necessary to seek its aesthetic form beyond Spain itself. María Teresa León declared enthusiastically that in the European theatre 'todo se ha hecho ya' (everything has already been done) and urged similar experiment in Spain.[2] In her view, Brecht's work presented itself as a model, one which challenged traditional structures and approaches and, with more admiration than accuracy, he became for her 'el hombre que había sacado de las manos pequeñas de los empresarios teatrales, de los grupos de élite, el teatro para la multitud' (the man who had removed from the small hands of theatre impresarios and élite groups, theatre for the many).³ With a similar concern to encourage fruitful contact between Russian revolutionary art and that of Spain, *Nueva Cultura* (*New Culture*) published a fraternal letter from Soviet artists urging their Spanish counterparts to apply to their own situation the revolutionary theatre techniques of the early Soviet state:

> la semejanza de la situación os obliga a ir por el mismo camino que fueron los artistas soviéticos, bajo el ruido de los cañones de la guerra civil.⁴

> (the similarity of the situation requires you to go down the same route as that of the Soviet artists, with the roar of the cannons of civil war.)

The role of drama as a weapon, first in the class struggle and later in the Civil War, was debated during the years of the Republic with increasing passion as the political divisions within Spain became gradually less capable of reconciliation. Prior to this, however, similar arguments had occurred amongst socialists who viewed the theatre as one of the agents of profound social change. While it was undoubtedly true that, as León remarked, Spain 'olvida un poco que pertenece al mapa teatral europeo' (forgets somewhat that it belongs on the European theatrical map),⁵ it was also true that, before the advent of the Republic, the Left had sought to utilize the indigenous dramatic tradition as the basis of a revolutionary theatre.

This attempt to use drama to further the cause of socialist change arose because, since the latter part of the previous century, the Spanish Left had conceived of revolutionary transformation in terms which went beyond a programme designed solely to alter economic relationships. Emancipation of the working class could only be achieved, the socialists felt, through culture, a fundamental transformation of the individual through education in the broadest possible sense. Many of the pedagogic activities more frequently associated with Republican efforts to diffuse educational and cultural opportunities had actually been the concern of many on the Left from about the turn of the century. The founding of workers' schools and cultural centres, the promotion of reading, of moral and social debate and campaigns against alcoholism, gambling and domestic violence, had, like numerous socialist initiatives, the principal objective of creating a new model citizen who would prove conscious of the revolution's meaning and articulate in disseminating its message. As Ramos Oliveira remarked: 'un pueblo está tanto más cerca del socialismo cuanto mayor es su patrimonio de cultura en todos los órdenes' (a people are that much closer to socialism the greater its possession of all kinds of culture) and, therefore, 'un obrero analfabeto es un contrarrevolucionario' (an illiterate worker is a counter-revolutionary).[6]

The role which the theatre might take in fomenting revolutionary consciousness was an acknowledged element in this perception of culture as the basis upon which economic change might be achieved. As Miguel Hernández was to describe his contribution to *teatro de urgencia* as 'una de las maneras mías de luchar' (one of my means of combat),[7] earlier socialists, too, called for a dramatic repertoire which would be combative, illustrating radical social ideas and reaching out to audiences with the aim, not only of portraying society, but of suggesting the means by which it might be changed. The purpose of such a repertoire clearly echoes that of *teatro de urgencia* in its need, according to Seisdedos,

> cultivar el espíritu de los trabajadores, distraerlos, hacerlos buenos, es decir, socialistas . . . y propagar, siempre propagar la excelsitud de nuestro ideario.[8]
>
> (to cultivate the spirit of the workers, to entertain them, to make them good, that is to say, socialists . . . and spread, spread at all times the excellence of our doctrine.)

Such language recalls in many ways that of a missionary and anticipates the exalted tone and zealous conviction which characterize much *teatro de urgencia* and earlier examples of revolutionary drama in Spain. Goodness and socialism become synonymous and the theatre adopts a role which is both utilitarian and spiritual, crusade and campaign. There is an eloquent clarity and an assured air about Seisdedos's guidelines which suggest how effective it was felt drama might prove to the socialist cause. However committed the novel or poetry might prove, they would be unlikely to instil revolutionary fervour with the immediacy and impact of the theatre. Implicit in

Seisdedos's comment, therefore, is perhaps an acknowledgement of the visual force of striking dramatic images, of the crucial solidarity which is potential in the audience as collective and the theatre's capacity to overcome the huge obstacle of widespread illiteracy. These were compelling reasons why, in the thirty years or so prior to the Civil War, socialists urged a dramatic repertoire which, in contributing to their cultural programme, would further their broader economic and political aims.

The first attempts to instigate such a repertoire might be judged to have occurred as early as 1895 with the première of Joaquín Dicenta's *Juan José*, but, given the much later date of Seisdedos's call for a revolutionary theatre, we are able to gauge the extent to which the development of a socialist theatre aesthetic in Spain faced considerable problems. García Pavón and Brown emphasize the immediate and enormous popularity of Dicenta's play.[9] A frequently revived attraction of the Madrid theatres during the Civil War, *Juan José* was also widely produced in workers' centres in the quarter of a century after its initial performance. Dicenta's play deals with an orphan, Juan José, who, although he has been reduced to beggary in the past, finds work as a bricklayer and falls in love with Rosa, a prostitute whom he saves from her street life. As the play opens, these events have already occurred and their relationship has soured because Rosa is increasingly susceptible to the attentions of Juan José's employer, Señor Paco. A growing sense of possessive jealousy on Juan José's part leads throughout Act I towards a confrontation between employee and employer. Waiting for Juan José in a tavern, Rosa is invited by Paco to join his group and sing for them. She agrees tentatively, but her song is interrupted by the arrival of Juan José who angrily warns Paco that although he might 'own' his employee, he can never own Rosa:

> Mi sudor, bueno; mi trabajo, bueno también; de éste son porque éste los paga, pero éste (por Rosa) no se paga con dinero; no hay dinero que lo pague en el mundo.[10]

> (My sweat, fine; my work, fine too; they are his because he pays for them, but this (Rosa) can't be bought with money; not all the money in the world.)

For this outburst Juan José is dismissed and, during the second act, he and Rosa are close to starvation. In desperation, and stung by her bitterness at their situation, Juan José takes to a life of crime and is eventually imprisoned. In the final act, on hearing that Rosa is now living with Paco, he escapes and murders both her and his former employer.

This brief summary of the play hints at Dicenta's debt to melodrama and the emotional excesses of romanticism. Yet, not without reason is the play seen as an important landmark in the efforts to create a revolutionary theatre. Principally, ordinary working people and contemporary social issues came to occupy centre stage, becoming the focus of audience interest. Apart from the drama of the seventeenth century the ordinary representative of the *pueblo* had tended to be portrayed only as a simple buffoon, incapable of experiencing or understanding matters of any substance. By contrast, Torrente Ballester suggests that Dicenta's work brought the *pueblo* on to the stage 'investido de derechos' (vested with rights) and that the impulse of the dramatic conflict in the play is found in the 'movimiento proletario del siglo' (the century's proletarian movement).[11]

Dicenta's 'drama de gentuza y oliendo a vino' (drama of a rabble stinking of wine)[12] can be seen, therefore, to reflect the tensions in Spanish society which were apparent around the turn of the century, particularly the spread of socialist and Anarchist ideas. It also seems to have encouraged a range of other writers who were similarly concerned to explore the *cuestión social* through the denunciation of social injustice and the exaltation of the *pueblo*. May Day 1901 in Valencia, for example, saw the première of Arturo Martín's *¡¡Pobres obreros!!* (*Poor Workers!!*), a gripping title which suggests the passion and social idealism which characterized such dramas.[13] Three years later, again in Valencia, José Fola Igúrbide presented his most famous play, *El Cristo moderno* (*The Modern Christ*), a work which suggests much of the spirit of Expressionism and thus reflects the social drama's quest for renewal and the dissolution of the old order in society.[14] Set in Moscow, Fola's play deals with Octavio, the 'Cristo moderno', who, although he is the son of a particularly cruel tsarist governor-general, is compelled by an apparently mystical love of humanity to fight for utopian liberty and social justice. With an unshakeable determination to achieve his ends he is capable of any amount of personal sacrifice. While distributing leaflets he is arrested by his father's secret police and, although offered the chance of liberty through the intervention of his mother, he refuses, allowing himself to be executed instead of Alejandro, a fellow conspirator. The religious parallelism which is suggested, not only in the play's title, but in Octavio's devotion to what amounts to a secular redemption of mankind, is reinforced by the play's division into subtitled scenes such as 'La conversión de la Magdalena', 'Nuevo Judas Iscariote' and 'En casa de Caifás' (The Conversion of Mary Magdalene, The New Judas Iscariot, In Caiaphas's House).

Plays such as Fola's emphasized what they saw as the corruption of the *status quo* and the need for the individual to initiate the struggle by which the workers will, in Octavio's words, 'enseñorearse de la tierra' (take possession of the land) (p.36). García Pavón stresses the widespread nature of such plays prior to 1936 and how they sought to dramatize the socialist or Anarchist view of wide-ranging issues such as poverty, unemployment, land distribution, divorce or clerical power. Typical of such works is Arturo Cortada's *Águilas negras . . . o los misterios de los conventos* (*Black Eagles . . . or the Mysteries of the Convents*) which was first presented in 1931 but which, like a number of these revolutionary dramas, was twice revived during the Civil War because of its perceived topicality.[15] The play is a violent, anticlerical diatribe in which the unhappily married Isabel de Monte Grande is committed to a convent by her husband and family with the assistance of a cardinal who later attempts to rape her. After a series of plot complications the drama reaches a climax in which the cardinal is beaten to death with a crucifix by Padre Luis, a priest who senses the Church to be corrupt and is determined to save Isabel, renounce his Holy Orders and marry her:

> Es la libertad que nos brinda su apoyo. Es la libertad que hermana a los hombres, y acaba con la tiranía. Leyes nuevas que concediéndote un divorcio legal, permitirán rehacer tu vida . . . (*en este momento alumbra la estancia un resplandor rojo que indica que arde la iglesia*). Leyes nuevas que a mí, me abren nuevos horizontes. (p.48)

> (It's liberty which lends us its support. It's liberty which brings men into harmony and makes an end of tyranny. New laws granting you a legal divorce will allow you to rebuild your life . . . (*at this moment the room is illuminated with a red light which indicates that the church is burning*). New laws which, for me, will open new horizons.)

The play's focus on anticlericalism, a much-debated issue both before and during the Republic, draws attention to a characteristic feature of these plays, their concern to dramatize a social thesis in such a way that the audience may draw conclusions as politically certain as those of the playwright and act upon them in the real life beyond the drama. A powerful sense of this is felt, for example, in Álvaro de Orriols's ¡*Máquinas!* (*Machines!*), where the links between industrial production, unemployment, the arms industry and war are explored through events which occur in Señor Norton's factory, a workplace which serves as a paradigm of the complex economic and social relationship between employer and employee.[16] In the first part of the play, subtitled 'Máquinas de paz' (Machines of Peace), El Hurón, an agricultural labourer, is forced off the land and into the factory by economic hardship. Here he joins other workers who are, in effect, machines to be switched on and off as required. When recession forces Norton to make workers redundant, industrial unrest flares, a lock-out is organized and the workers face starvation. In the search for profit Norton switches production to weapons and, at the same time, the dismissed workers seek to resolve their dilemma, in the only way which seems possible, by enlisting in the army. In the second part of the play, subtitled 'Máquinas de guerra' (Machines of War), they must face the prospect of death from the very weapons produced in their own factory. Only El Hurón and another worker, Daniel, speak out against the barbarity of such a system, but the mass of workers, unable to grasp the contradictions of the situation, support the war as a means of offering them a livelihood.

The breadth of the play's thesis, its desire to incorporate as many of the social and economic factors pressing down upon workers as might seem necessary to present a coherent socialist analysis of their situation, is the most striking feature of the work. Such a summary of the play's concerns suggests that it ought to prove highly effective as revolutionary propaganda. In fact, however, the play never rises above the level of an unconvincing melodrama. Written in little more than doggerel, the social thesis has to battle to maintain itself as the focus of the work since, predominantly, the play concerns a love affair between Daniel and Nora who, like Rosa in *Juan José*, increasingly receives the amorous attentions of the factory owner, Norton.

The inadequacy of ¡*Máquinas!* as revolutionary propaganda is characteristic of the social dramas in general. Despite the opportunity to explore class conflict, for example, *Juan José* deals rather more with traditional Spanish dramatic themes of honour and vengeance. The confrontation between Juan José and Señor Paco is less that of worker and master than that of two crudely drawn individuals engaged in a battle for Rosa. Conflict between two opposing groups, a crucial element of any drama interested to propagate the socialist cause at this time, is less apparent than a conflict between individuals, a factor which weakens the general applicability of the play's thesis. Bhattacharya comments astutely that a hallmark of these propaganda dramas is the variety of possible interpretations which can be placed on them, suggesting that, however certain the authors' political views may be, these are often only falteringly apparent in the dramas themselves.[17] Brown remarks in this respect, for example, that Juan José's workmate in the play experiences the same economic and social plight but manages to avoid all of Juan José's problems.[18]

It was not only uncertainty of aim, however, but also confusion of style which characterized much revolutionary drama in the years prior to the Second Republic. With either rural Andalusian or industrial settings such plays tended to obscure their social concerns, constructing themselves around a number of simple plot devices such as the conflict of honour occasioned by an employer's lust for the daughter of one of his employees, or events which follow an enlightened worker's return from the city to rouse his fellow workers and organize a strike. This latter example ought, like ¡Máquinas!, to prove highly successful propaganda material but such plays were rarely able to rise above a mawkish and unconvincing naturalism which undermined the plays' agitational purpose. Although seeking to provide voices of protest and dissent the authors of such plays were inextricably bound up in an outmoded, though still vigorous, theatrical tradition. A play was regarded as a 'slice of life', although this did not prevent works, both in language and acting style, from falling into melodramatic excess. The three-act division remained dominant, although one can sense in *El Cristo moderno* and *¡Máquinas!* that in the authors' use of *cuadros* (scenes), sections and subtitles they are straining to be free of traditional dramatic methods of story-telling.

Dominant theatrical conventions were, therefore, a significant obstacle to dramatists who wished to present on-stage a socialist critique of Spanish society with the aim of urging the audience to change it. In their tentative structural experimentation with subtitles Fola Igúrbide and de Orriols hint at that liberating distinction Brecht was to provide for playwrights when he suggested a dramatic structure based on 'one thing after another' rather than the traditional three-act pattern of 'one thing out of another'.[19] Unable to resolve the problem of dramatic form, however, in plays such as *El Cristo moderno* and *Juan José*, the precise nature of the social question remains shrouded and the audience is consequently hindered in the search for an answer to it. The explanation of such failure lies in the unsatisfactory combination of individualism, romanticism and naturalism which is typical of the social dramas. These theatrical traditions and characteristics were not successfully reinvigorated or extended despite being so clearly at odds with the writers' desire to offer a more dogmatic and general analysis of social injustice.

Perhaps the most illuminating insight into many of the revolutionary dramas is that they were considered successful by the very people they sought to oppose, the fashionable, upper- and middle-class audiences which comprised the overwhelming majority of the theatre-going public. Here again one senses the constricting nature of the dominant theatrical tradition. Neither Dicenta nor Fola Igúrbide could have expected productions of their works if they did not appeal to this narrow audience, a factor which created a further obstacle to radical writing. The apparently 'impregnable bourgeois vulgarity'[20] of theatre audiences was certain to hinder writers concerned to present matters of social or political importance in a genuinely challenging manner. Rodríguez Alcalde refers, for example, to the 'exigencias bien escasas' (very limited demands)[21] of audiences in the earlier part of the century and Brown to their 'frenzied appetite for entertainment'.[22] The narrow, privileged section of society from which audiences were drawn would not, according to Brown, admit 'any attempt to puzzle or worry'.[23] The demands of such audiences were insatiable, with plays receiving only short runs before their replacement by some novelty. Spectators also enjoyed considerable power since, although Madrid during the early part of the century had a mere half-million inhabitants, its theatre-goers could choose from some eight theatres. It was above all necessary for theatres to offer entertainment of the widest possible appeal in order to ensure financial survival. Such a situation was certain to exert a strong influence on the form and style of dramatists' work and, thus, while writers such as Dicenta, Fola Igúrbide and de Orriols extended the concerns of drama beyond the leisured and untroubled world of, for example, drawing-room comedy, they did not effect a comparable change in the structure of their works. Following an established set of conventions, what resulted was a rather clumsy hybrid quality to plays which sought to fuse dramatic fashions in vogue at the time with a political anger which was in direct opposition to almost every aspect of the financial and social apparatus of the traditional theatre.

While, in general, the Left had indicated its belief that the theatre could contribute significantly to its cause, the reaction of socialist intellectuals to the social dramas was varied. A principal concern was that, since such works were presented in professional theatres, workers were largely excluded from attending by long hours of work and the relatively high cost of tickets. Such practical considerations were, of course, important in terms of the effective diffusion of socialist ideals through drama. However, in the columns of *El Socialista*, a more theoretical debate took place regarding aesthetic aspects of revolutionary theatre. A number of intellectuals on the Left were concerned to discover precisely what might be meant by socialist art, in what ways it might differ from the more easily recognized bourgeois art and what aesthetic criteria should apply when judging the merits of plays whose commitment to revolution would seem to imply a rejection of many inherited notions of quality. It is hardly surprising that Spanish socialists should have found these questions troubling since, as late as 1923, Lunacharsky, as commissar of enlightenment, admitted candidly that even the Soviet state had little clear idea of what constituted Marxist aesthetics: 'the ideology of art from a Marxist viewpoint . . . has received little consideration. Our mentors have hardly touched upon these questions, and we have far from established an orthodox Marxist view of art.'[24] The deep-seated nature of the Spanish socialists' problem can be felt in Araquistáin's declaration in 1925 that drama ought not to be labelled socialist, ought not to define itself by siding with a political tendency. Socialism, rather, should 'hacerse literario' (become literary).[25] For Araquistáin, therefore, the dramas of the *cuestión social* were on a par with the escapism of Muñoz Seca or the Quinteros's romanticized portrayals of Andalusian life, further evidence of what he saw as the overwhelming artistic mediocrity of the Spanish theatre. Aesthetic merit should be found, he suggests, in a work's ability to rise above the daily struggles of society, seeking to affirm universal, poetic qualities rather than act as a political platform or a mass meeting. Reflecting a reformist rather than a revolutionary viewpoint, Araquistáin's argument rejects a theatre of the masses and favours instead an élite vanguard of dramatists whose works would fuse 'lo popular' (popular traditions) with traditionally understood notions of artistic quality. Placing himself firmly against a socialist theatre aesthetic, he declared that revolutionary drama

> generalmente interesa poco, incluso a los obreros . . . el teatro es mala tribuna de propaganda: no convence a nadie, porque no es una misiva, y de rechazo desprestigia al propio teatro.[26]

> (is generally of little interest, even to workers . . . the theatre is a bad propaganda platform: it doesn't convince anybody because it isn't a missive, and, in turn, it brings the theatre proper into disrepute.)

The logic of Araquistáin's position is a minority theatre, exclusive rather than élitist, one which would turn its back both on the commercial imperatives of the mainstream theatre and on what he saw as the facile slogans of revolutionary drama. The outcome of such a stance is vague, a belief that works of high quality would filter down to the masses and contribute to the improvement of their lot through the moral conviction and truth of art.

Araquistáin's essentially liberal position found a strenuous response in the views of Seisdedos who, also in *El Socialista*, outlined a view of socialist theatre derived from a recognition that if economic and political struggle arose from two opposing ideologies, then there must be two kinds of art: bourgeois and socialist. Seisdedos does not so much answer Araquistáin's position as seek to ignore it. By rejecting bourgeois art he hoped neatly to sidestep the dominant culture's ability to impose criteria of quality on marginal cultures. For Seisdedos traditional notions of good art and bad art were to be jettisoned in favour of the single-minded pursuit of socialism through art whose quality would be determined by the extent to which it furthered the cause of revolution. In an interesting analogy, Seisdedos likened the situation to the differences between 'high-quality' bourgeois newspapers such as *ABC* which drew upon extensive financial and material resources, and the humble workers' daily, *El Socialista*. The latter could not compete with the former, yet this did not deter socialists from buying the newspaper, learning from it and disseminating its views to fellow workers. So too with the theatre, suggested Seisdedos, quality and merit were less important than that works should be 'impregnadas de socialismo' (saturated with socialism).[27]

Underlying the polarized reactions of Seisdedos and Araquistáin to the revolutionary theatre is the issue of aesthetic form and how both men are reacting in different ways to plays which sought to be *à la mode* by addressing matters of political significance but which were, ultimately, hackneyed, unconvincing melodramas. Araquistáin's response is their outright rejection but Seisdedos's reaction, for all the crude certainty of his views, is more complicated. In attempting to ignore the aesthetic questions raised by Araquistáin he betrays a desperation to offer positive support to any repertoire which assists the socialist cause. Rejecting bourgeois art, Seisdedos contradicts himself by sanctioning the use of its theatrical forms if these can serve the revolution. Lacking a coherent socialist aesthetic which might serve as a model for dramatists, the attempt to create a repertoire of revolutionary drama was therefore threatened by a crisis of form. Unable to overcome what they perceived to be the monolith of bourgeois theatre practice, writers of social dramas found themselves able to do little more than ape its exhausted, discredited dramatic forms and then find their plays judged inadequate by criteria which, in any case, seemed unsuitable yardsticks of their work. Added to this crisis of form was the related crisis of performance space. As has been noted, the narrow social composition of audiences in the mainstream theatres and the consequent commercial factors which governed the production of plays, further hindered radical experiment with dramatic form. Yet, without such experiment it would prove very difficult to develop an aesthetic free of bourgeois concerns which might prove effective as socialist propaganda.

The profound social crisis with which Spain entered the 1930s sharpened political divisions, which in turn made their influence felt in the sphere of drama. The questions raised by Araquistáin and Seisdedos were posed again, but with a radical spirit perhaps derived from the recent demise of a dictatorship and the establishment of a liberal Republic. Sender, for example, furthered the debate about a socialist theatre aesthetic, moving it on to far more radical ground than Seisdedos, when he called for the rejection of all bourgeois theatre forms: 'no hay que barrer los caminos andados y emporcados, sino destruirlos y echar a campo traviesa abriendo bajo los pies las nuevas rutas' (one mustn't sweep the well-worn and dirty tracks, but rather destroy them and break new ground, opening new routes beneath one's feet).[28] Sender's energetic dismissal of, in effect, almost all previous theatre practice was accompanied by a much clearer theoretical notion of the aesthetic form of a socialist theatre than anything yet to have emerged in Spain and, as Vilches de Frutos suggests, his ideas had a profound influence on his contemporaries' efforts to clarify new thinking about drama.[29] In certain central ideas expressed in *Teatro de masas* (*Theatre of the Masses*) we find important principles which underpin experiments with revolutionary drama which took place, not only during the peacetime years of the Republic, but also during the Civil War. This experimentation, by writers such as Aub and Alberti, superseded the dramas of the *cuestión social* by seeking forms based on entirely different assumptions about drama. These assumptions were as fundamental as what a play might be, what were the criteria for judging effectiveness and what kind of audience was most suitable for a particular work.

Sender raises three crucial issues about revolutionary theatre which, when applied in practice, break the mould of the three-act structure as the traditional form for revolutionary drama and question the role of conventional theatre buildings as the performance space for such drama. First, he denounces the traditional theatre for ignoring what he suggests is in fact the principal element of the theatre, the spectator. The audience's role is passive and undemanding, worn down by a repertoire in which 'lo único original . . . es el teatro de tarjeta postal de los Quintero' (the only originality . . . is the picture postcard theatre of the Quinteros) (p.30). Second, Sender calls for a theatre 'sin literatura' (without literature) (p.67) in which the text would be reduced to a secondary role, a work becoming the result of collaborative craft between authors, directors, designers and audiences. The text would, thus, become a set of guidelines for 'la obra definitiva que ha de conseguirse en la escena' (the definitive work which must be achieved on the stage) (p.67). Third, he demands that the spirit of the new drama be found in what he calls the 'verdadero teatro nacional' (genuine national theatre), the bullfight (p.15). In this latter demand Sender seems to echo Brecht, who had earlier advocated the boxing match as an aesthetic model for epic theatre and the behaviour of a sports crowd as that of the ideal spectator.[30]

These three issues were key areas which, if explored, would establish revolutionary theatre along entirely new principles and, applied in practice, produce very different works from the previous decades. Particularly significant is Sender's analysis of the function of the audience. Earlier revolutionary drama had, for example, accepted the traditional role of the spectator – seated in the dark of the theatre, required to participate silently, if at all, and watching actors who maintained the pretence that the spectator was not present. In identifying the viewer's function as critical lies the possibility of propaganda directed with a greater sense of purpose, not only within the theatrical event itself, but in the search for the ideal spectator. Having marked out a significant role for the audience, a subsequent question is what kind of spectators should comprise this audience and where might they be found. For Sender they are the *pueblo* who, as Unamuno had previously recognized, 'abandona el teatro y se va a los toros' (abandons the theatre and goes to the bullfight).[31] In the alert, critical crowd of the bullfight Sender saw the possibility of a new aesthetic relationship between audience and drama, declaring that, 'un buen aficionado taurino . . . es material excelente para el teatro moderno de multitudes' (a good bullfight fan . . . is excellent material for the modern theatre of the masses) (p.25). Implicit in Sender's words is the difference between the idea of 'teatro para el pueblo' and 'teatro del pueblo' (theatre for the people, theatre of the people). The essentially liberal humanist stance of the former, represented at this time by groups such as La Barraca and the theatre section of Misiones Pedagógicas (Educational Missions), was criticized by León who saw their rural tours as, by and large, ineffective since the groups' relationship with their audience lacked a 'sentido político de lo que estas aldeas debían y querían ver' (political understanding of what these villages ought to see and wanted to see).[32]

Sender's analysis clearly derived from close knowledge of developments in the revolutionary theatre of Russia and Weimar Germany. Experiments with agitational and propaganda drama in these two countries during the 1920s and early 1930s provided influential models and suggested new approaches which were absorbed by those Spanish writers, such as Sender, who studied abroad through the financial support offered by the Republic's Junta de Ampliación de Estudios (Studies Extension Council).[33] Those areas outlined by Sender as essential to the creation of a revolutionary theatre can be clearly felt in German and Russian examples. In Russia in 1923, for example, the National Union of Journalists formed a group of actors known as the Blue Blouse which dramatized texts taken from leading articles. This was not only an effective means of transmitting news to a largely illiterate population but also, since the majority of workers were not revolutionaries, enabled political exhortation and discussion to take place. The Blue Blouse worked through caricature to illustrate in short scenes personal characteristics and behaviour which were felt necessary to the continuing success of the revolution. The effectiveness of its work was considerable since, in 1924, the Trade Union Council of the Moscow Department of Culture established regular troupes with a standard pattern of performance known as the Living Newspaper. The format of performance was common to all groups and involved an initial parade before the audience after which the actors would perform short scenes illustrating the substance of a lecture. Each scene was linked by a commentator who, before the singing of the 'Internationale' at the conclusion of the performance, would offer an analysis of the political meaning. Each troupe consisted of about twelve performers who worked with few props or costumes but depended instead on the expressive powers of the body through gesture and gymnastic movement. Workers' clubs and factories were principal performing spaces, but the Blue Blouse's visit to Berlin in 1927 served as the principal means by which its aims and methods were disseminated to England, Germany and the United States.

In Germany somewhat similar developments centred on the work of the director Erwin Piscator, whose Proletarian Theatre, founded in 1920, established a structure and format for agitational theatre which became widespread both in Germany and elsewhere. As with so much Spanish propaganda drama of the 1930s, very little similar German material has been preserved. Not only did the Nazis destroy many traces of communist agitation, but the improvised nature of these activities themselves contributed to the absence of records. Of the plays performed by the Proletarian Theatre only one has survived, *Russlandstag* (*Russia's Day*), a short sketch staged in the autumn of 1920 in working-class districts of Berlin.[34] The play is a loosely connected series of short scenes intended as an act of homage to the new Soviet workers' state and as a passionate call to German fellow workers to rise up in violent revolt. That the revolution could only be made through violence was reiterated throughout the play. In the opening scene, for example, three workers in turn approach a sociology professor to ask his advice about how to combat the 'White Terror'. He suggests parliamentary democracy as a solution to their fears, but in a subsequent scene this is shown to be no more than a weapon of society's repressive forces. Following this lesson that moderate compromise has no place in an extreme political situation, the repressive forces themselves are introduced, represented by caricatures of an army officer, a diplomat and a priest. These are seen as the servants of a particularly grotesque caricature, World Capital, who is addressed as 'Your Majesty' and presented as a fat money bag wearing a top hat. These four figures explain that through their control of social institutions they intend to maintain workers in ignorance and enslavement.

In the following scene one of the workers reads aloud from a book on socialist theory and class reconciliation which he has been given by the professor. Meanwhile, three workers cross the stage and, in accordance with the principles expounded in the book, surrender their weapons. They explain that their actions are in keeping with the demands of world order, but the point is made that world order is determined by world capitalism. At this point the war wounded and war widows enter to blame world capitalism for their plight. Their complaints are heightened by the Voice of the Russian Revolution who, speaking through a megaphone, exhorts the German workers to end the 'terror' by the violent destruction of capitalism. Even more victims of war and counter-revolution enter and, in vivid terms, add to the catalogue of massacre and rape for which capitalism is blamed. In the final scene, as their cries reach a climax, the servants of World Capital re-enter and admit their powerlessness in the face of historical forces, declaring that the future lies only with the masses. On this note the German workers storm the stage and the figures of Diplomacy, the Church, Capital and the Military are driven away.

I have dwelt in some detail on Piscator's production since Sender's admiration of the director's work was very high, and also because it enables us to glimpse how Sender's three key areas worked in the German context. As Sender recommends the abandonment of the conventional theatres for the atmosphere and crowds of the bullfight, so Piscator had in practice sought new audiences in the working men's clubs and beer halls of Berlin. Sender's sense that the traditional function of the spectator needed reassessment in order to place him or her in a more active relationship with the events on-stage, can be seen in the forceful means by which the propaganda impresses itself on the audience, provoking realization, commitment and action. The text, too, has become, rather, a working script which can be amended or expanded as circumstances dictate. The narrative sequence of the three-act drama has given way to a loose anthology whose scenes might conceivably be played in a different order without obscuring the overall purpose of the play. What had been achieved by Piscator and the Blue Blouse was at least the basis of the socialist theatre aesthetic which had escaped the Spanish dramatists of the *cuestión social*. Unable to unite revolutionary content with bourgeois form, these earlier writers had failed to produce works which had the utilitarian effectiveness they desired. In the Russian and German experiments, however, a new aesthetic, largely independent of previous forms, fuses revolutionary content with a form appropriate for its expression. What had been achieved was a radical shift which, as the German director Jakob Geis observed, enabled the theatre to be seen as craft rather than art.[35]

Articles in *Octubre* (*October*) and *Nueva Cultura* demonstrate the extent to which this aesthetic impressed itself on the Spanish Left. Piscator's work was, Aub wrote in *Nueva Cultura*, the 'visión de un mundo futuro' (vision of a future world) which arises from a 'nueva arquitectura teatral' (new theatrical architecture)[36] to proclaim the imminent ruin of contemporary society. In similar fashion, Piscator's agitational form can be felt in the rules of a play competition announced in *Octubre* in late 1933. Thus, while entries might offer material which recalls the social dramas, dealing with 'sucesos revolucionarios o problemas que interesen a los trabajadores' (revolutionary events or problems which might interest workers), crucial controlling factors exert themselves in terms of dramatic form through a demand for a single, uninterrupted sequence of action, great rapidity of style and clear ideological conflict.[37]

Cobb describes how, in Spain's politically charged atmosphere during the 1930s, many on the Left with an interest in cultural matters embraced: 'con tanto entusiasmo toda referencia a Piscator o Meyerhold o al teatro de "agitprop"' (all references to Piscator or Meyerhold or to 'agitprop' theatre with very great enthusiasm).[38] Yet, precisely how such interest translated itself into practice is much less clear. The *Octubre* play competition, for example, was intended to provide a repertoire for a theatre group committed to the same political ends as the magazine, but it is uncertain whether the company was actually formed. Cobb's work in the area of Republican culture, has, however, facilitated a more detailed picture of the Madrid theatre group Nosotros (Ourselves) and from this company's work between 1932 and 1934 a representative impression can be gauged of how agitprop groups functioned.[39] What emerges is a picture of feverish activity to write appropriate original dramas, to borrow, translate and adapt the political repertoire of Germany, Russia and other European countries and to disseminate works to similar groups elsewhere in Spain. The testimony of Irene Falcón would suggest that work was often carried out after performances:

> por la noche, trabajando, escribiendo a máquina, repartiendo los papeles, también a máquina, y las obritas que nosotros mismos escribimos pues también las hacíamos así, pensando: ahora habría que hacer esta cosa y nos sentábamos y lo hacíamos. (p.271)

> (throughout the night, working, typing, distributing the roles, also by typing, and the little works which we wrote ourselves we also did them like that, thinking: now it would be necessary to do this thing and we sat down and did it.)

The loss of many of these short works makes it less easy to see how the agitational form in its Spanish context might have worked in detail or translated itself into performance. Falcón indicates the air of improvisation and immediacy attached to a script's composition, the writers' lack of interest in perceiving their work as belonging primarily, if at all, in a bound volume and how, rather than any interest in posterity, current political circumstances were the writers' sole concern. However, either through the author's care or because they were printed in political magazines, certain scripts have survived. The latter is the case with Parrado's proletarian sketch ¡Guerra, a la guerra! (*War, to War!*) which, printed in *Nueva Cultura*, offers a detailed indication of how some of these new aesthetic ideas may have emerged in script form.[40]

Parrado's sketch was included in the magazine as part of *Nueva Cultura*'s editorial policy of publishing works by unknown writers and ordinary workers whose concern was 'la cultura en el mundo y la sociedad nacentes' (culture in the world and the society which are being born) (p.18). Like de Orriols in *¡Máquinas!* Parrado is concerned to explore how workers can unwittingly subscribe to war by failing to recognize what the author perceives as the destructive relationship between capitalist economics, bourgeois politics and military conflict. Unlike de Orriols, however, Parrado maintains a ruthlessly simple focus on this issue, a focus which arises from an awareness that, for his projected audience, a subject with such complex ramifications must be presented unambiguously. This is achieved through what is, in effect, a question-and-answer format, first in the dialogue between Antonio and some male workers and, later, between Antonio and the workers' wives and mothers. Unlike his fellow workers, Antonio refuses to obey the order for males to present themselves for military manœuvres, exhorting them to see that such activities are in fact preparations for war. In response to the workers' uncertainty about who will care for their families while they are away, Antonio asserts energetically that hunger will care for them since the men's actions will inescapably bring war and all its attendant suffering. Their claims that he exaggerates the significance of some innocent manœuvres, failing to see the lasting strength of world peace through the League of Nations, the Treaty of Versailles and disarmament conferences, bring spirited denunciation of their inability to recognize 'la máscara de los imperialismos' (imperialisms' subterfuge) (p.18). Similarly, the workers' hope that, if war does come, Spain will remain neutral is undermined by Antonio's explanation of Spanish capital's logical and ardent desire to foment, and profit from, war. Won over by his articulateness the workers seek guidance as to the best course of action, finally leaving the stage to demonstrate against mobilization and war. In the second part of the sketch the men's wives and mothers enter to bid them farewell as they leave for the manœuvres. Their plight at being deprived of their breadwinners increases as Antonio likewise warns them that military exercises are a prelude to war, the 'única salida a la crisis capitalista a costa de sangre proletaria' (only exit for the capitalist crisis at the expense of proletarian blood) (p.18). Unlike the men, the women's reaction is immediately resolute and, to prevent the men departing, they leave the stage with cries of protest. As the play ends, with the men and women united on-stage carrying banners and placards denouncing war, Antonio speaks from a soap-box to address the audience, urging them to prepare for revolution just as the bourgeoisie is preparing for war. To cries of '¡ni un solo hombre para la guerra!' (not a single man for the war!) and '¡viva el gobierno obrero y campesino!' (long live the workers' and peasants' government!), the play ends with the singing of the 'Internationale' (p.23).

The similarities between Parrado's work and that of the Proletarian Theatre and the Blue Blouse are striking even from a summary of ¡Guerra, a la guerra! The stark political lesson enacted by representative figures, the strict focus on its unambiguous communication despite its inherent complexity and the rapid, energetic momentum of the dialogue recall both *Russlandstag* and the format of the Living Newspaper performance. Particularly interesting is the manner in which Parrado utilizes a kind of socialist iconography, turning away, like Piscator, from traditional notions of theatrical realism. The setting of the play is a barricade which plays no direct part in the action and is not referred to during the sketch. Its role is a symbolic one, a prominent and evocative image upon which the spectators' minds can focus and which offers a sharp visual contrast to the submissive attitude of the workers whom Antonio challenges. A similar iconographic intention is felt in the newspaper from which Antonio reads aloud, reporting, apparently at random, facts which are later seen to support his argument that the military manœuvres are part of an orchestrated prelude to global war. The newspaper, evoking strongly the crucial link for the socialists between reading and social progress, symbolizes access to history, knowledge and, as a result, revolutionary action.

When Cobb, after offering an exceptionally thorough account of the 1930s group, Teatro Proletario, regrets that its repertoire cannot be discussed in any substantial detail given the 'inexistencia de los textos' (non-existence of the texts),[41] the survival of Parrado's sketch is seen to have considerable significance, providing primary evidence of at least elements of the range of material thought appropriate for presentation by revolutionary theatre groups. Brief and striking, Parrado's sketch has that quality which Ontañón declared to be so admirable in aspects of the Civil War's art: its capacity to 'gritar' (shout).[42] The final tableau of barricade, banners, soap-box and the united, purposeful mass of workers chanting *vivas* brings the street and the theatre together in the manner of an invasion as the icons of revolution become the materials of set design. In his use of the term 'sketch' to describe the work Parrado indicates, too, the extent to which, in the quest for robust political effectiveness, dramatic form must be rendered flexible and imaginative. The freedom of the sketch format lends itself with ease to Parrado's political purpose: to outline a political lesson which can, vigorously presented, then be summarized in an easily memorized slogan at the end of the performance. *¡Guerra, a la guerra!* becomes a fine example, therefore, of Piscator's recommendation of 'trivial forms' which have the merit of clarity and the possibility of being understood by all.[43]

The use to which such forms were put in the immediate pre-war period enables us to see, in the work of Aub and Alberti, the increasing flexibility and expressive power with which the agitprop aesthetic continued to develop. Parrado's term 'proletarian sketch', for example, can be revealingly compared to the very different terminology employed by Aub and Alberti with regard to their contributions to theatrical propaganda during the 1930s. When Aub describes his *El agua no es del cielo* (*Water doesn't Come from the Sky*) as an improvisation he too suggests experimentation and, as with *Russlandstag*, structural freedom to organize the work's content in whatever format is demanded by the intended political analysis of the drama.[44] However, although Aub's admiration of Piscator is undoubted, *El agua* demonstrates how, unlike Parrado who tends to imitate a basic model, Aub transmutes that model into a form which is distinctively Spanish rather than borrowed. As opposed to the term 'sketch', with its sense of rough outline, improvisation suggests lively unpredictability, actors' inventiveness and, as in the *commedia dell'arte*, development of a basic scenario. Alberti, too, emphasizes his intention to utilize a popular theatre form in the title of his *Farsa de los reyes magos* (*Twelfth Night Farce*).[45] Both these works represent significant achievements in developing the form of the agitational sketch, enriching its language and refining the structure's ability to present a more complicated narrative while remaining lucid and unambiguous. These two works must rank as the ideal for which Seisdedos hankered when he called for socialist propaganda to combine distracting entertainment for workers with forceful ideological clarity.

El agua deals with the purchase of a river by the Banker who then imposes a charge for watering animals of five pesetas per hour. The disbelief of local villagers at the loss of their traditional watering rights is received impassively by the Banker who suggests that 'el agua no es del cielo' but must be paid for. The local Teacher, who has been summoned before the Banker and his associates, the Priest and the retired Commander, to explain why the local children are singing radical songs, outwits the Banker by declaring that he has bought his factory, the sky:

> Acabo de pagarlo con agua de los hombres, con sudor. Cuando venía hacia aquí, amarrado al pobre tonto de don Comandante, vine mirando al cielo y lo compré, mamotreto; sentí que era mío, mía el agua de su vientre gris, mío su hálito azul, mía la fuerza indomada de su vientre. (p.236)

(I've just bought it with the water of men, with sweat. When I came towards here, hitched to the poor fool of a Commander, I came gazing at the sky and I bought it, you gross buffoon; I felt it was mine, the water from its grey womb, its soft blue air, the untamed strength of its womb.)

The play ends with the Teacher taking the Banker by the scruff of the neck and pulling from his costume objects associated with his financial power so that the villagers can see that

> un banquero está hecho de teléfono, de recomendaciones de la Ceda, de bulas del beato Chapaprieta . . . del dinero de los demás: de tablas de multiplicar: $1\times1=3$; $2\times2=5$; $3\times3=12$; $4\times4=26$. De madera quebrada; (*saca una pistola.*) de ruido. (p.239)

> (a banker consists of telephones, of right-wing recommendations, of dispensations from the pious hypocrite, Chapaprieta . . . of other people's money; of multiplication tables: $1\times1=3$; $2\times2=5$; $3\times3=12$; $4\times4=26$. Of flimsy wood; (*he takes out a pistol*) of noise.)

The idea of revealing the essential function of the character so that the villagers may perceive not the individual but his role in a financial and political structure forms part of a wider metaphor of insight in the play which centres on the figure of the Blind Man, a ballad singer whose off-stage recitation opens the action. His satirical verses at the expense of the right-wing electoral coalition land him in trouble with the Banker and the Commander who warn him that 'te espera la cárcel' (jail awaits you) (p.232). Towards the end of the play, however, the Blind Man's sight is restored when he washes his eyes in the river and, as though reborn, he begins to identify that which had been only indistinctly imagined:

> este es un banquero, este es el cura. Nunca creí que las cosas que no se ven, se parecieran tanto a las cosas imaginadas. (p.238)

> (this is a banker, this is the priest. I never thought that the things one can't see could be so similar to the things one imagines.)

Similarly, the villagers' metaphorical blindness, and perhaps by implication that of the audience, is ended through the insight offered by the Teacher who urges them to see, for example, not the intimidating power and authority symbolized by the Commander's uniform, but 'chatarra . . . cruces, galones y falsas estrellas, espuelas, pomadas y un poco de brillantina' (scrap-iron . . . crosses, braid trimmings and fake stars, spurs, pomades and a bit of polish) (p.240). The action closes with the literal deflation of the reactionary figures as the objects of their power are plucked from their costumes, enabling the villagers to see their enemies and, thus, the world anew.

The figure of the Banker may have his origins in Aub's article on German theatre when, admiring Piscator's method of characterization, he suggests:

> lo que interesa hoy de un banquero no es el individuo, como pudo ser en tiempos de Balzac, sino el banquero en cuanto a su función. (p.7)

> (what's of interest today about a banker isn't the individual, as it could be in Balzac's times, but the banker with regard to his function.)

Unlike Piscator in *Russlandstag,* however, Aub introduces his three reactionary figures, the Banker, Priest and Commander, for comic effect which assists his political strategy in the play. The opening establishes the farce-like style required of the actors, performing in huge costumes stuffed with the properties required later in the play. Outraged on hearing the Blind Man's ballad, the Banker races to the window to summon the Priest and the Commander before falling into his chair in shocked collapse. The commanding force of the play's opening, the feeling of pantomime or puppetry in the exaggerated dimensions and emotions of the Banker, arises from the wit and energy of Aub's language:

> ¡Señor Curaaaaa! ¡Don Comandante! ¡Vengan, corran, acudan, pronto, de prisa, volando, creo que traspaso, siento cómo se me revuelve la sangre. ¡Ay! (p.231)

> (Mister Prieeeest! Mister Commander! Come! run, gather, hastily, speedily, flying, I think I'm injured, I feel as though my blood's churning! Oh!)

This broad comic style undermines the status of the Banker in the audience's eyes so that a figure whose power had seemed both threatening and 'natural' is deflated and becomes an object of ridicule. When the Banker intimidates the villagers, therefore, with his apparently limitless knowledge of the world, their humiliation and confusion is in contrast to the audience's enjoyment and in the strength of collective laughter lies class confidence and unity:

¿Sabéis cuál es la capital del Afghanistán? ¿Sabéis cuantos quesos embarcan semanalmente en Holanda? ¿Sabéis la altura de la torre Eiffel? . . . 'Comment allez-vous? Bon jour. Bon soir. Mes pantalons sont trés courts.' ¿Habéis entendido? (p.234)

(Do you know the capital of Afghanistan? Do you know how many cheeses they ship out of Holland every week? Do you know the height of the Eiffel Tower? . . . 'How are you? Good Day. Good Evening. My trousers are very short.' Have you understood?)

The sense of fun with which Aub invests the play is important to its effectiveness. The light-hearted pace of the action, the humorous word-play of certain of the speeches and the irony of the play's central theme and title, blend powerfully with the anger and clear resolve of the Teacher. The play is successful also in uniting within its brief structure a variety of social and political issues, showing in this a greater sophistication than Parrado's sketch. Aub is able, for example, to evoke a range of the conflicting forces operating in a small *pueblo* so that these can be presented in turn to rural audiences, encouraging them to see in the play the determining structures of their own community. This is strongly felt in the Teacher's role as an articulate conscience and guide for the villagers when confronted by the Banker's legalistic explanations of the loss of watering rights, or the Priest's suspicion of the Teacher as a subversive force in traditional village life.

Similarly incisive social insight is also displayed by Alberti in the *Farsa*, a play which, even more than Aub's, combines political topicality with dramatic origins in earlier forms of popular theatre. In basing the play upon the earliest known vernacular dramatic text in Spain, Alberti seems to draw on that rich tradition of drama found in the *pasos* and *entremeses* (sketches and interludes). The religious drama of the *autos sacramentales* (allegorical religious plays) with its symbolic figures, miraculous occurrences and perennial struggle between good and evil might also have provided a fruitful source of dramatic ideas which could be transposed to serve the purposes of revolutionary propaganda. Clearly, Alberti enjoys the irony both of using the Epiphany text for anticlerical ends and juxtaposing the term 'farce' with the solemnity suggested by the Magi. Whereas Sender had called for a theatre which eschewed literature as unlikely to assist current political struggles, Alberti, by contrast, takes a highly literary source and uses it to extend the agitprop form into areas of such spirited humour, consistent verbal inventiveness and zany clowning that the play assumes something of that 'alto valor universal' (high universal quality) with which Falcón described elements of the Nosotros repertoire.[46] Lucidly expressed, one finds in the *Farsa* the life of the *pueblo* which the dramas of the *cuestión social* had strained to articulate, presented in a dramatic form which recalls not so much the agitational sketch as Brecht's comic works of this period such as *A Man's a Man* and *The Elephant Calf*.[47]

The *Farsa* gradually unites two strands of narrative separated by an interlude in which caricatures of civil guards perform a slow, threatening dance, creeping in formation about the stage in search of suspected Bolsheviks. Prior to this the audience has been introduced to the story's two elements, a group of workers who plan to trick the local Boss and the Priest, and a poor family of villagers who are awaiting the arrival of their son on army leave. The play opens in darkness as, in low voices, the workers plan to lie in wait for their victims and play a trick which will ensure that 'esos dos sinvergüenzas van a acordarse para siempre del Nuevo Testamento' (those two scoundrels are going to remember the New Testament forever) (p.20). As they hide themselves, the lights reveal the family's poverty-stricken home. His legs wrapped in rags, the Grandfather is seated at the table, while the Wife arranges candles around a crib. The family's young Daughter gazes vacantly into space while her Father moodily surveys the Wife's devout activities. Scorning religious celebration when the family are starving and cold, the Father is outspoken even to the Priest who arrives to celebrate the Epiphany. Threatening the Father with the condemnation of his soul, the Priest warns the family that such sentiments, if heard by the Boss, would mean eviction. With the Boss's arrival, somewhat drunk, the Father leaves, ignoring the Priest's warning that Bolsheviks are reputedly roaming the countryside.

The Priest's fear of the rumoured Bolsheviks increases when the Daughter demands to see the promised green star of the Magi. The Priest's plan that the Sacristan should raise a star on a stick above the 'mountain' at the back of the stage has backfired and, after whistling desperately at the 'cabrón de sacristán' (cuckold of a sacristan) (p.25), a red star appears. In an effort to save face, and terrified that the Bolsheviks have arrived, the Priest and the Boss rush inside the house for safety, declaring that a miracle must have occurred. Anxious to understand more about the Magi, one of a group of shepherds asks whether the Priest has actually ever seen the kings. The Priest's reply that they can be seen in the early hours bringing presents to the poor spurs the Daughter's demand that they visit her family that night. Anxious to maintain the family's superstitious belief, the Priest, Boss and Sacristan plan to dress up as the Magi but are overheard by the workers who suddenly play their trick: a giant puppet scarecrow in the image of a Bolshevik swings down and blocks their path. As the Bolshevik demands their clothes the Priest and the Boss surrender their trousers, reduced to 'ridículas e impropias enaguas blancas' (ridiculous and unbecoming white underpants) (p.30). While they stand half-dressed the puppet is suddenly reversed to reveal 'un grande y gordo señor' (an imposing and fat figure) (p.41), the Governor, to whom the Priest and Boss express their outrage and plead for help. The assistance of the Civil Guard, however, is offered only at a price and, as the Boss pleads his poverty, the puppet turns again and the Bolshevik returns to threaten them with his sickle. In panic and fear the reactionary figures flee and the three workers, joined by the Father who has watched the proceedings, celebrate their success and now plan to upset the family's deception by the three 'kings'.

After the interlude the Magi enter, dressed in exotic costumes. As they bow reverentially to the infant in the crib the child's face is suddenly removed and the hand of a soldier reaches out to snatch the mask from Melchior's face. The Soldier, the son of the family, has met his Father and joined in the plan to discredit the three villains. As the play ends, the Priest, Boss and Sacristan are given a comic beating by the family and the shepherds while the Magi's green star engages in a battle with the eventually triumphant red star.

The *Farsa*, along with Aub's play and Parrado's sketch, offers varied illustrations of the socialist theatre aesthetic which emerged, predominantly under the influence of European models, during the peacetime years of the Republic. It would be wrong, however, to imagine that either the *Farsa* or *El agua* was merely an imitation of such models. Both writers, for example, stress humour in their plays far more deliberately than Piscator did, and tend to dispense entirely with the repetitive, emotional exhortations which featured strongly in the early German productions. Rather than being essentially static tableaux, both plays have a sense of narrative development and, in this respect, the *Farsa* is particularly sophisticated, demonstrating the extent to which Alberti had cultivated the 'trivial' forms which Piscator had recommended.

Most striking, however, is the way in which Aub and Alberti move beyond the notion of a formulaic approach to dramatic construction. Whereas Piscator had called for a wholly factual style, one which can be seen in Parrado's sketch, and the Living Newspaper had adopted a common format for performance, both Aub and Alberti pursue unique individual styles. Contrary to Sender's and Piscator's belief that the author can be replaced by collective writing, Aub and Alberti demonstrate how powerful socialist propaganda can emerge from conventional approaches which utilize popular forms and even Christian literary sources. Piscator also has an intensely earnest, dogmatic tone in his theoretical writings which was reflected in the Proletarian Theatre's performance style. At the centre of the *Farsa* and *El agua*, by contrast, is Brecht's sense of *Spass* (fun) as the essence of the theatrical experience.[48] The dramatic impulse behind both plays is the idea of fun, each having the atmosphere of a *fiesta*, although without either play lapsing into self-indulgence or losing sight of the seriousness of the issues under analysis. A light-hearted tone is predominant, with music making a significant contribution to the considerable variety which characterizes the performance. In keeping with its role as electoral propaganda, *El agua* starts with satirical verses denouncing the 'gil-cedistas' (right-wing authoritarians) and, once the village's watering rights have been restored, crowds enter and conclude the performance with celebratory singing. Interestingly, given Alberti's concern in the play to denounce religious superstition, the *Farsa* opens with a hymn sung by the Daughter and the shepherds. Far from being anti-religious, its touching innocence casts the characters in a sympathetic light and throws into relief the hypocritical religious attitudes of the Priest.

That the success of the *Farsa* and *El agua* as propaganda resides essentially in their humour and spirit of fun is felt most clearly in the relentless lampooning of reactionary characters such as the Banker, the Boss and the Priest. Occupying a substantial proportion of each play, the bullying antics of these ridiculous figures contrast with their physical cowardice and obsessive fear of the Bolsheviks. The comic opportunities which this presents for actors are numerous and the swaggering manner of such characters is constantly undermined. In the *Farsa* this is achieved most notably when, in their desperate efforts to placate the scarecrow, the Boss and the Priest are embarrassingly reduced to their underwear. Characters such as these assume a central role, becoming clownish, grotesque figures subject to cruel physical punishment. The Boss and the Priest, for example, are severely beaten at the end of the play, while Aub's Banker ultimately has his 'insides' ripped out. Yet, since the arrogant excesses of the reactionary figures are so great, the humorous tone remains intact throughout the plays' final moments and it was possible to inflict such punishments without rousing the misplaced sympathy of the spectators. Indeed, because such figures are like puppets the punishments are not so much 'real' as symbolic gestures through which social types and institutions are ridiculed and denounced. Humour, therefore, becomes the audience's route to revolutionary understanding, which emphasizes not only the oppression of working people but their capacity to overcome it. At the close of the *Farsa*, for example, the family is united not only in understanding the deceit by which the Boss and the Priest have maintained their acquiescence, but in taking action to punish it. The family, and by extension the *pueblo*, discovers its power, conquering the reactionary elements by which it had been tyrannized. Such revolutionary optimism was rarely a strong characteristic of earlier theatrical propaganda, in which, rather, a dominant and angry theme was the resignation and continued suffering of the *pueblo*.

The evidence of *El agua* and the *Farsa* indicates that, by 1936, the role of drama in socialist propaganda had attained levels of considerable originality, skill and sophistication. The lucid structures, flowing action and the resolute certainty of the plays' political message are in marked contrast to the social dramas' earlier attempts to create a socialist theatre repertoire and perhaps suggest the mood of optimistic confidence on the part of the Left that, by 1936, a working-class seizure of power was inevitable and perhaps imminent. The rejection of bourgeois politics by many writers at this time was often accompanied by a commitment to the new concept of proletarian literature, and this led to a deep interest in European experimentation with political theatre from which, as we have seen, a unique Spanish brand of revolutionary drama came to be fashioned.

New playing spaces, new relationships between actors and audiences and new emphases in acting styles contributed to the creation of a new aesthetic which released, particularly in the case of Aub and Alberti, the 'graciosa ingenuidad de la farsa' (the witty ingenuity of farce).[49] It is interesting to speculate about how this socialist theatre aesthetic might have developed had the Civil War not broken out. Would, for example, the principles of dramatic construction which underpin such works have paved the way for experiments with theatrical realism in works of greater magnitude? Would this popular, agitational style have found its way on to the main stages under a liberal Republic's encouragement of a non-commercial National Theatre such as that proposed by Aub in 1931?[50] As events turned out, the political theatre aesthetic was forced by circumstances to redefine its task, moving away from an oppositional, attacking role to embrace instead a responsibility to defend the Republic. Perhaps uniquely in European theatre, therefore, this resulted in Spanish propaganda drama assuming both a pre-revolutionary and post-revolutionary aspect. It is this latter aspect which has been hitherto neglected, and our focus must now turn to a detailed examination of the little-considered area of how the agitprop form fared once hostilities had broken out.

~ 2 ~

The Development of Teatro de urgencia

In his discussion of the education policies of the wartime Republic, Cobb notes a tendency on the part of scholars to impose firm chronological divisions when discussing the history and culture of Spain between 1931 and 1939 so that 'the wartime period has somehow been set aside as an entirely separate order of things'.[1] This has also to date been a noticeable feature of certain studies of modern Spanish theatre. García Pavón, for example, sees the wartime period as an interlude before 'normal' theatrical activities resume in 1939.[2] Yet, if we consider the socialist theatre aesthetic discussed earlier, an aesthetic which had largely been forged during the troubled peacetime years of the Republic, and compare it to *teatro de urgencia*, it is clear that in form and intention the two are linked by common features. The earlier agitational form was a flexible one and faced, therefore, with the demands of a wartime situation, it easily adapted to new circumstances and became a drama at the service of the state rather than one which opposed it.

Gorelik's observation that 'theatre exists for the sake of its audiences' is intriguing and challenging, especially in the context of political theatre.[3] In particular it enables us to see the attempts to create a revolutionary theatre in Spain during the 1930s as a continuum rather than a phenomenon interrupted by war. The questions of dramatic structure explored earlier, for example, indicate the extent to which dramatists on the Left had increasingly sought a form which, embracing concepts and models from elsewhere in Europe, was purposefully directed towards a mass audience. The examples of Irene and César Falcón, Aub and Alberti clearly suggest that their theatrical work during the 1930s was impelled, above all, by a desire to reach audiences outside the conventional theatres, audiences which it was felt must be reached since in them lay the prospect of the revolutionary transformation of society. The popular forms of sketch, puppet play, farce and revue which were prevalent in various European countries during the 1920s and 1930s testify to this desire to play to audiences which, for cultural, financial and geographic reasons, were unlikely to be found in mainstream theatres. Increasingly, drama was viewed as a weapon in the class war, a means to empower the working class, to make it conscious of its strength and encourage the use of that strength in what was perceived to be the imminent seizure of revolutionary power. In identical fashion, the wartime *teatro de urgencia* also sought a preeminent role for the spectator. Frequently the subject of the drama, he or she was always the plays' direct propaganda target since, either through instruction or entertainment, the purpose of *teatro de urgencia* was to present its audiences with appropriate models of Republican behaviour. Similarly, we have noted the Left's desire in earlier propaganda to create the new model citizen or the active revolutionary. In both pre-war and wartime propaganda theatre, therefore, the audience is persistently felt as the determining factor of many elements of the drama. In the case of *teatro de urgencia* the playing space, for example, was enormously influenced by the varying locations of audiences. León recalls a performance by the Guerrillas del Teatro in an iron foundry in Sagunto,[4] while Dieste saw a performance of street theatre 'al paso en alguna plaza o encrucijada de Valencia' (passing by some square or crossroads in Valencia).[5] Mussot's stage was described as 'la propia tierra combatida' (the battleground itself) since the groups for which he was responsible during 1937 worked without any kind of formal staging.[6] The content of plays, too, often derived from the writers' commitment to reach a particular audience in order to communicate specifically with that audience. Mussot's 'Mi puesto está en las trincheras' (My Place is in the Trenches), for example, was written in great haste at the request of brigade commissars to explain the restricted availability of home leave for soldiers.[7] By contrast, de la Fuente's *El café... sin azúcar* (*Coffee... without Sugar*) is intended for an urban audience, warning against the dangers of defeatism and the presence of fifth-columnists amongst the ordinary populace.[8]

The particularly significant role allotted to the audience was a shared assumption both of pre-war agitprop and *teatro de urgencia* and the similarities of dramatic form which emerge as a consequence enable us to see the socialist theatre aesthetic as having continued to develop after July 1936, emerging as *teatro de urgencia*. Perhaps more so than before the uprising, audiences were to be found in a variety of non-theatrical locations and the easy adaptability of the agitprop form ensured that only the content of the drama needed amendment and not its essential structural features. Class war's replacement by civil war as the dominant issue in performance was, effectively, the only modification required.

Given its origins as a 'poor' theatre it is surprising, however, that the first *teatro de urgencia* was presented in mainstream Madrid theatres. Mussot's '¡No pasarán!' (They Shall Not Pass) opened at the Teatro Fontalba on 23 September 1936,[9] while two days later Balbontín's *El cuartel* was presented at the Teatro Maravillas.[10] Almost a month later Nueva Escena (New Stage), the theatre section of the Alliance of Anti-Fascist Intellectuals,[11] presented Dieste's *Al amanecer* and Alberti's *Los salvadores de España* (*The Saviours of Spain*) at the Teatro Español.[12] At the Teatro Lara from 22 October the cultural propaganda organization Altavoz del Frente (Loudspeaker of the Front) offered a play dealing with the first crucial hours of the military rebellion, Luisa Carnés's *Así empezó . . .* (*It Began Thus . . .*).[13] With the exception of Balbontín's play, all of these productions formed part of more extensive programmes but were the only offerings specifically written in response to the war. It is ironic that this *teatro de urgencia* should have been presented in such circumstances since, as we have seen, during the earlier years of the Republic radical writers had tended to discount the possibility that their work might be presented on the mainstream stages. They had, furthermore, consciously sought an audience beyond the predominant social spectrum of the Madrid theatres. The presence of the agitprop form on the stages of the capital's theatres is, thus, a remarkable phenomenon which invites speculation as to how a clearly marginal dramatic aesthetic came to occupy the performance spaces of the dominant culture. *¡No pasarán!*, for example, was written for improvised acting areas at locations in the Somosierra region. Yet, produced in Madrid, it finds itself on the stage of the most luxuriously decorated theatre of the capital. The mismatch is striking and raises significant issues concerning performance dynamics, the play's effectiveness as propaganda and the nature and role of the audience. In particular, the question arises of how a kind of drama committed to audiences which, experience had shown, were to be reached on their own ground, found itself performing on the bourgeois stages which the Left had so vigorously denounced. Barely two years had passed, for example, since the *Octubre* group had published the announcement of a group of unemployed actors who intended to form a theatre company which, by virtue of its commitment to the *pueblo*, 'no puede estar subordinada al régimen actual, al mismo régimen que ha determinado la crisis de que somos víctimas' (cannot be subordinated to the current regime, the same regime which has created the crisis of which we are victims).[14]

Teatro de urgencia first appeared, therefore, in performance circumstances which seem alien to it as a dramatic form. This is largely explained, however, by the upheaval during the late summer of 1936 of the traditional repertoire of certain of the Madrid theatres. Events here reflected the wider social transformation occasioned by the military rebellion and, in attempting to account for the development of *teatro de urgencia* as an element of wartime propaganda, it is necessary to outline the radical changes which were made to the working practices of the capital's theatre industry. During the crucial days immediately after the attempted coup, as official channels were ignored or disrupted, effective political power came to rest in the *ad hoc* committees which sprang up under UGT or CNT control in order to restore the framework of industry, commerce and transport. Throughout late July and August 1936, in an atmosphere of improvisation, working life was reorganized on a co-operative basis as workers' councils replaced employers who had perhaps been shot, had surrendered their businesses to their former employees or had fled to areas in which the uprising had been successful. According to Narciso Julián the sense of upheaval was

> incredible, the proof in practice of what one knows in theory; the power and strength of the masses when they take to the streets. All one's doubts are suddenly stripped away, doubts about how the working classes are to be organized, how they can make the revolution until they are organized. Suddenly, you feel their creative power; you can't imagine how rapidly the masses are capable of organizing themselves. The forms they invent go far beyond anything you've dreamt of, read in books. What was needed now was to seize this initiative, channel it, give it shape.[15]

Since the rebellion occurred in July when many theatre companies made their provincial tours, most of the Madrid theatres were closed during the early weeks of the war. This did not, however, shield them from the far-reaching changes which Julián so graphically suggests and which were being effected in all areas of society. As in other industries, the trade unions and various political groups responded to the social uncertainty by taking over the theatres and establishing control committees. It would seem that groups simply claimed or were offered the theatre of their choice if they were able to command sufficient trade union support for their actions. The Sindicato de Artistas Teatrales (Theatre Artists' Union), for example, who took over the Teatro Alcázar, did so having first decided unanimously to merge with the Anarchist CNT. At the Teatro de la Zarzuela the company of Miguel de Molina and Antonio Isaura became the Compañía de Variedades Socializadas (Nationalized Varieties Company), a part of the socialist UGT. Although such measures seem to have been independently adopted, it would be correct to assume that the trade unions were intent on bringing the theatres into their sphere of control. The constant and at times bitter rivalry between the CNT and the UGT ensured that each was determined to control more theatres than the other.

The testimony of Luis Mussot, an actor by profession and later director of the Grupo Teatro Popular, offers an impression of the initial simplicity of the take-overs and of the unstable atmosphere in which they took place when he recalls the events which took place at the Teatro Fontalba on 23 July.[16] According to Mussot, members of the Communist Party, carrying weapons, entered the theatre during the night and claimed it on behalf of the GTP, a revolutionary theatre group which had been formed in 1935 but which had performed irregularly since it did not possess a permanent base. The theatre, legally the property of the Marqués de Fontalba, was then renamed Teatro Popular. The Marquis was later shot, although Mussot claimed this bore no relation to events in the theatre.[17]

The take-overs led to a restructuring of the finance and administration of the theatres in line with the political viewpoint of the trade unions. Ironically, despite their hostility towards each other, there is no evidence that theatres controlled by the CNT operated a different administrative system from those controlled by the socialist confederation. Details of how the new administration functioned can perhaps be gauged from a newspaper article concerning the Teatro Martín which, written some four months after the start of the war, serves as an indicator of likely developments in other theatres.[18] Following the take-over, a mass meeting was called of all those who had worked in the theatre during the previous season, and a cooperative system of management was agreed upon. A workers' council was then elected with representatives of each section involved in production. Two actors looked after the interests of performers, while, in similar fashion, the orchestra leader, a chorus girl, a carpenter and a dance master represented their particular fellow employees. There was also a union representative but it is unclear from the article whether he or she was an employee of the theatre or a delegate from the central organization. Perhaps surprisingly, those not represented on the workers' council are those described in *Mundo Gráfico* (*Illustrated World*) as receiving a low wage and working elsewhere in other jobs, such as the cleaning staff and the stage hands. The workers' council was responsible for the economic management of the co-operative. At the Teatro Martín the wages system was reorganized on the basis of a daily payment of ten pesetas supplemented by profit-sharing. The bonus, however, was calculated on a salary scale rather than in an egalitarian fashion. In some theatres this expenditure policy was complemented by a restructuring of the ticket system in order to attract a more broadly based audience. Discounts were offered to union members or the fixed entrance fee was entirely dispensed with, the theatre relying instead on the donations of spectators.

The fundamental nature of these changes is illustrated by a report in the newspaper *ABC* which draws attention to the CNT's expressed desire to transform the theatre industry not only in terms of employment patterns but also in terms of a spiritual regeneration. Thus, 'de él va a desaparecer toda obscenidad, vulgaridad y grosería' (all obscenity, vulgarity and coarseness is going to disappear from it) as the new theatre sought to reject those elements which confuse 'las tablas de la escena con los mercaderes del mercado o los prostíbulos' (the stage boards with market traders or brothels).[19] Such a rhetorical tone is characteristic of many press reports concerning the planned future of the industry. Phrases such as 'teatro sano', 'purifiquemos la escena' and 'necesidad imperiosa de renovar' (wholesome theatre, clean up the stage, the powerful need for renewal) are commonplace and reflect the desire to force a complete break with past forms and traditions. The groups which presented the first *teatro de urgencia* works shared this widespread enthusiasm, believing that a revolutionary theatre was the inevitable concomitant of a revolutionary society. Mussot's company, for example, planned to use the ex-Teatro Fontalba for productions which included translations of Rolland's *Fourteenth of July*, Wolf's *Professor Mamlock* and Podogin's *The Aristocrats* as well as new adaptations, presumably with added contemporary relevance, of *El alcalde de Zalamea* (*The Mayor of Zalamea*) and *Fuenteovejuna*.

Similarly ambitious plans to stage revolutionary classics and examples of 'la más viva literatura dramática' (the most dynamic dramatic literature) are found in the projected schedule of Nueva Escena.[20] Works by Rolland are promised, clearly in an effort to bring Spanish theatre into tangible contact with the European political drama introduced to those writers and artists who had studied abroad during the early 1930s. O'Neill's *The Hairy Ape* as well as works by Shaw and Lorca were under consideration, and a production of Alberti's *De un momento a otro* (*From One Moment to the Next*) was planned. A policy was announced, in the longer term, to invite leading foreign directors such as Tairof to direct the company on specific projects. The sense of innovation in many aspects of Spanish life at this time must have fuelled the powerful feeling of ambition which is felt in Nueva Escena's plans, a confidence which was undoubtedly enhanced by the group having been granted the use of the Teatro Español for its work.

If the planned repertoire of the GTP and Nueva Escena had come to fruition it would indeed have signalled a regeneration of the Spanish theatre in keeping with the confident press announcements of the late summer of 1936. Yet, as has been noted, the opening programmes of both companies were much more limited and the short *teatro de urgencia* pieces which were presented seem to indicate that both companies encountered significant problems which frustrated their more ambitious projects. The GTP's production of *Fuenteovejuna* became instead a selection of scenes from the third act which accompanied a recitation of Alberti's *El Gil Gil*, Segismundo's monologue from *La vida es sueño* (*Life's a Dream*), Sender's *El secreto* and Mussot's *¡No pasarán!*[21] The programme of Nueva Escena likewise indicates that initial plans were scaled down as the enormous nature of the undertaking became clear. Another short Sender play, *La llave* (*The Key*), was thus pressed into service for the company's opening performance on 20 October, alongside Dieste's and Alberti's *teatro de urgencia* pieces, *Al amanecer* and *Los salvadores*. In conversation Dieste recalled that the Nueva Escena company had existed since the beginning of 1936 and that, in the initial weeks after the military rebellion, various writers had agreed to participate in a plan of Alberti's by which each of them would write a play within a week. Since only Dieste, with *Al amanecer*, met the planned deadline it was extended to a fortnight. It would seem that Alberti's and Dieste's plays resulted from this plan and that these two works became the mainstay of Nueva Escena's opening repertoire.²²

Dieste's play is a twenty-minute piece, described as a 'farsa-reportaje' (farce-report), dealing with a treacherous plan to ambush a group of *milicianos,* while Alberti's *Los salvadores* was termed *ensaladilla* (little medley) by the author. Both works seem to be substituting for more ambitious productions. Similarly, ¡*No pasarán!,* which lasts approximately ten minutes, requires no set and deals in a stylized fashion with the need for soldiers to see their collective strength in the face of the tyrannical hierarchy of the officer class, is quite the opposite of the group's desired repertoire. An explanation of this confusion is found in the mistaken assumption on the part of both groups that since a revolution had occurred in the ownership and working practices of the theatre industry it was inevitable that a revolution would follow in the repertoire of the theatres. The sheer scale and complexity of the problems involved were underestimated. The result was somewhat incoherent, as conventional proscenium theatres, in which it was hoped to present full-length productions of European political and classic theatre, were utilized for works which depended on quite different environments for their effectiveness. An illuminating example of this problem is Mussot's recollection that his group had planned a production of Rolland's *Danton*, but that this had gradually become less feasible as the company was a group of *aficionados* and large numbers of extras were needed in crowd scenes. For a 'poor' theatre working in equivalent circumstances, adequate solutions present themselves. The GTP, however, was attempting to produce the play on a large, conventional stage which demanded technical, financial and human resources which the group did not possess. Similar problems seem to have occurred at the Teatro Español, and Dieste recalled some urgency about the date of the opening performance in order to accumulate a box office float to finance the group's activities. The ambitious production plans announced to the press seem to have been made without serious assessment of the financial implications of their projects.

It is perhaps understandable that in the euphoric atmosphere which seems to have characterized Republican Spain at this time all things must have seemed immediately possible to writers and artists of the Left who had for so long fulminated against the perceived inadequacies of the Spanish theatre. In the space of a few weeks the entire apparatus of the theatre industry had been transformed and, theoretically at least, it had been delivered into the hands of the people. This was, however, a double-edged sword. It inevitably became clear that possessing the theatres in the name of the revolution was easy, but that utilizing them in the revolution's name was fraught with difficulties since a revolutionary theatre of the magnitude initially announced depended crucially on an administrative and artistic infrastructure which could not be instantly conjured up. The examples of the GTP and Nueva Escena suggest that the first *teatro de urgencia* works arose almost by default as the preferred repertoire failed to materialize. Had the Nationalist siege of the capital in the opening week of November 1936 not led to the closure of the theatres it is interesting to speculate as to what would have happened to the repertoire of Nueva Escena. When Collado, for example, refers to the leasing in late 1937 of the Teatro de la Zarzuela to Nueva Escena's successor as the theatre section of the Alliance, the TAP, he warns that they are 'decididos nuevamente a repetir la catástrofe de entonces' (newly determined to repeat the earlier catastrophe)[23] and it is clear that he is thinking in financial terms since he quotes Cabero's article in the *Heraldo de Madrid* denouncing the fact that the TAP 'en dos semanas de actuación se llevan perdidos más de siete mil duros' (in two weeks of operation they carry a loss of more than seven thousand *duros*) (p.240). Collado's views on these matters encapsulate the general trend in the Madrid theatres once the immediate dangers of the siege had passed and the theatres reopened in January 1937. The reassertion of the traditional commercial repertoire was, more or less, complete and the experimentation, however limited, which had followed upon the take-overs became 'los nuevos modos y el lenguaje inhabitual' (the new methods and the unaccustomed language) which were declared incomprehensible to spectators 'mal educados artísticamente' (badly educated artistically) (p.159).

The initial *teatro de urgencia* works were aberrations from the characteristic theatre offerings and resulted from highly exceptional circumstances. With hindsight it is possible to see that an aesthetic of this kind clearly did not belong in a conventional theatre, that it was merely filling the gap between the clamour for a vigorous political repertoire and the immense problems of achieving it. *Los salvadores*, for example, subsequently entered the repertoires of the *guiñol* (puppet theatre) of the Seventieth Mixed Brigade, the puppet theatre La Tarumba and the *guiñol* of the Seventh Division, as well as being part of the repertoire of the Guerrillas del Teatro of the Army of the

Centre (Theatre Guerrillas).²⁴ The frequency of references to its performance testifies to its effectiveness, and one has the sense that, however much it may have pleased audiences at the Teatro Español, as a short piece of satirical lampoonery its playing style was that of popular entertainment and unlikely to accommodate itself to the stalls and circle of the Teatro Español. The Alliance learnt from this experience since, when it returned to the theatres in September 1937 as the TAP, it was with a more sustainable repertoire on a scale appropriate to the stage intended for its performance.²⁵

What had occurred, in effect, between September and November 1936 was that those who had been engaged in revolutionary theatre activities during the earlier years of the Republic and whose overriding concern had been to reach a popular audience rather than a theatre-going one were, understandably, lured towards occupation of the theatre buildings which represented, for them, the monolith of bourgeois theatre practice. The lack of an achievable repertoire presented itself as an immediate problem, but far more significant for those who had founded groups such as Nueva Escena and the GTP was that in entering these buildings they left behind many of the spectators whom they had so consciously sought to cultivate. The assumption which had been made, that a revolutionary theatre was the logical result of a social revolution, was compounded by the assumption that a revolutionary audience would automatically present itself if it were offered a revolutionary theatre. The example of Soviet theatre might, on reflection, have offered evidence that this was not easily the case. *Teatro de urgencia*, like its agitprop predecessor, was crucially interested in the *pueblo*, and all experience had demonstrated that, for the purposes of working-class empowerment through propaganda, the theatres had to be rejected as unable to offer the appropriate relationships between the drama and the spectator. That audiences were not significantly different in their social composition during the war is clear from the overwhelmingly conservative, indeed frivolous nature of the repertoire which, despite its specific mission in this respect, the Consejo Central del Teatro (Central Theatre Council) was unable to curtail.²⁶ Collado, with characteristic brusqueness, draws attention to the difficulties of changing audience tastes when he suggests that to create 'una moderna generación cultural por decreto parece una burla' (a modern cultural generation by decree seems a joke) (p.256).

It might have proved possible for *teatro de urgencia* to find an appropriate niche in a revolutionary theatre centred on traditional buildings, but that was certainly not the case at this stage of its aesthetic development. The word 'urgencia' must, rather, be kept in mind since it had never been more crucial for the Left to reach audiences of the *pueblo*. The previous work of groups such as Nosotros provided a more appropriate model for *teatro de urgencia* than the proscenium theatre and we find that, as the war settled down into a pattern of attrition and the Popular Army painfully formed itself from the militias, *teatro de urgencia* appeared more confidently, maintaining a strict focus on an audience which was no longer simply the *pueblo* but the *pueblo en armas* (people under arms).

Such a focus was, however, achieved only gradually and, rather than ideologically direct propaganda, the initial emphasis with regard to theatrical performance for soldiers lies predominantly on entertainment. As early as 29 July 1936, *ABC* reported an improvised *fiesta* given in the Somosierra region by 'aficionados al "cante jondo"' (fans of 'gypsy song') and announced its own plans to organize a theatrical event at the battlefront. The dominant tone of the performance is clearly intended to be recreational since 'nuestros valientes luchadores merecen que sus horas de descanso sean alegradas por los mejores artistas nacionales' (our valiant combatants deserve to have their rest time enlivened by the best national artists), and perhaps its essential character can be felt in the newspaper's call for the most famous stars to demonstrate their goodwill and commitment by placing their work 'al servicio de los camaradas en armas' (at the service of the comrades in arms).[27] By 30 July it seems that unconditional offers of support had been received from outstanding theatrical figures, including the popular Madrid duo, Loreto Prado and Enrique Chicote:

> El hilo telefónico nos trae la voz emocionada de D. Enrique: 'aunque seamos viejos y sirvamos para poco, Loreto y yo queremos que sepan Vds que nos tienen incondicionalmente a sus órdenes. Todo nos parecerá poco para cooperar a distraer el breve descanso de los defensores de la España liberal y digna.'[28]

> (The telephone line brings us the emotional voice of D. Enrique: 'although we're old and useless, Loreto and I want you to know that you have us unconditionally at your orders. Everything will seem as nothing to co-operate in enlivening the brief rest of the defenders of worthy, liberal Spain.')

A powerful feeling of sentimentality pervades what one might suspect to be nothing more than a variety show in which performers become missionaries 'para solaz del espíritu de los heroicos soldados' (to comfort the spirits of the heroic soldiers).[29] That the structures and performance styles of the traditional theatre are being mobilized to replicate themselves for an afternoon in improvised circumstances would be understandable were it not for the newspaper's report that the actors of Club Anfistora have expressed their desire to join the *ABC* theatrical campaign. Presumably, the group intended to present those classic works which had left, according to *ABC*, a 'recuerdo imborrable en las fiestas de conmemoración de Lope y del romanticismo' (an indelible memory in the anniversary celebrations of Lope and of romanticism).[30] Similarly, the Teatro Escuela de Arte (School of Theatre Arts), founded by Rivas Cherif, 'nos hace patente que se pone por entero a disposición de *ABC*' (makes clear to us that it places itself entirely at the disposal of *ABC*).[31] This latter offer is particularly interesting since some two weeks after pledging its support the group is reported to have approached the newspaper with a suggested repertoire which is apparently in rehearsal. Particularly striking is that, alongside Lope's *La tienda de los gestos* (*The Shop of Appearances*) and Calderón's *El dragoncillo* (*The Little Dragon*), is the plan to perform a 'comedia de actualidad' (play about current events) written by Antonio Ayora, the group's director, *Triunfo de Julianita y muerte de Don Petimetre* (*Triumph of Julianita and Death of Don Petimetre*).[32]

Since no further newspaper references to the planned *ABC* performance occur after 18 August it is unclear whether it actually took place but, if it did, it seems likely to have been an unusual mixture of periods, styles and intentions. Of particular interest is the possible inclusion of Ayora's play. No references to this play occur again but it was clearly more than a planned project since *ABC* refers to it as being in rehearsal. The play's title teasingly invites the supposition that the play was an allegory of the Civil War, but it would be unwise to speculate too far even though another lost play, *El vengador* (*The Avenger*), was in the repertoire of the Guerrillas del Teatro of the Army of the Centre in 1938 and is attributed to an author named Ayora.[33] What does seem clear, however, is that in attempting to foster performance material centred on the idea of *deleite* (entertainment) rather than *doctrina* (instruction), *ABC* was continuing the spirit of pre-war organizations such as the Teatro del

Pueblo of Misiones Pedagógicas which had approached its audiences in the belief that 'acaso aprendáis pocas cosas de nosotros; pero quisiéramos ante todo y sobre todo, divertiros noblemente' (by chance you might learn a few things from us; but, over and above everything, we would like to entertain you nobly).[34] It was this gentle, essentially romantic outlook which León had criticized in the Teatro del Pueblo and La Barraca since, without a clear ideological attitude towards their audience, their work lacked a hard, political edge. *ABC*'s notion of a performance before soldiers, while it certainly involved a move towards the *pueblo*, was offered, therefore, in a spirit which mingled celebration with a sense of cultural charity.

The transition from this kind of troop entertainment to propaganda aimed more purposefully at its audience is not an easy moment to isolate since the initial stage of the war was a time of great upheaval and improvised activity in which initiatives tended to overlap. Sender records, for example, that the organization Cultura Popular had undertaken a mammoth task of educational and propaganda work almost immediately the war started: 'Work began at seven in the morning with making up parcels of printed material for hospitals and barracks, and continued all day with arranging lectures, cinema exhibitions, plays, and the formation of travelling libraries to be sent to the fronts.'[35] The precise nature of the plays performed by this group is not known but they were clearly of an anti-Fascist nature and presented by at least one mobile company. Similarly, *ABC* records that on 29 August 1936 in Toledo the group La Tribuna (The Platform) had initiated a series of performances before *milicianos*.[36] Again, the exact nature of the company's work is unknown but it is surely significant that the group's name is similar to that used by the first Piscator theatre group. More substantial evidence, however, of the manner in which theatrical propaganda began to focus on reaching audiences in locations dictated by the conflict is found in the work of Altavoz del Frente, a cultural propaganda organization under the control of the Communist Party, whose theatre section operated from the ex-Teatro Lara. The central involvement of César Falcón in this group undoubtedly brought sufficient agitprop experience from the days of Nosotros to ensure that the take-over of the Teatro Lara was accompanied by the establishment, not just of a company to work in the theatre itself, but of two touring groups al servicio y exaltación del pueblo, con una concreta tarea antifascista de agitación por el pronto y total aplastamiento de la rebelión fascista.[37]

(at the service and exaltation of the people, with a concrete anti-Fascist task of agitation for the early and total crushing of the Fascist rebellion.)

These two groups performed on the back of a lorry which could be converted into a stage. The vehicle was also intended to double as a means of delivering hundreds of radios to battle fronts, thereby permitting reception of Altavoz del Frente's broadcasts. The clarity of the group's propaganda purpose is in striking contrast to the performance envisaged by *ABC,* and Altavoz's initial repertoire of six plays included both agitational material written before the war and two lost *teatro de urgencia* pieces, Iglesias's *Los hombres al frente* (*The Men at the Front*) and Romillo's *Singladura roja* (*Red Voyage*). Presumably as a result of the siege of Madrid in November 1936 the Altavoz organization seems to have left the capital and based itself in Valencia. Here, from 4 January 1937 a group of five actors and five musicians gave a dozen performances daily, not only at front-line locations but also in streets and cafés, under the name Retablo Rojo (Red Stage). Dieste recalled that 'muy probablemente fue una actuación de esas guerrillas la que vi al paso por alguna plaza o encrucijada de Valencia' (very likely, it was a performance of those guerrillas which I saw when passing by some square or crossroads in Valencia).[38]

The work of Altavoz del Frente illustrates how, as the military situation suggested a drawn-out conflict was likely, drama's role emerged as an element of diverse cultural, educational and propaganda programmes.[39] The theatre section, for example, must be considered alongside the organization's other aspects, such as music, broadcasting, exhibitions, cinema and political education conferences. The common aim of this and similar groups emphasizes again the central role of the spectator in the development of *teatro de urgencia*. Their purpose was, in Mussot's words, to transform 'un pueblo retrógado, analfabeto y fanático en otro culto, decente y digno' (a backward, illiterate and extreme people into an educated, reasonable and worthy one).[40] To this ambitious end it was inevitable that theatre groups should not only seek their audiences at locations within the wartime community itself, but that the performance material presented should offer unambiguous explanation of the conflict as a spur to individual effort, commitment and understanding. What gradually emerged, therefore, as a notable characteristic of *teatro de urgencia* was not just the use of improvised performance spaces, but of plays whose impulse often arose from single issues. Through concentration on a specific issue aimed at a specific audience, theatrical propaganda proved itself able to respond to exigencies of the moment and, in terms of style, this entailed a development beyond either generalized exaltation of the *pueblo* or satirical ridicule of the enemy. With propaganda of this highly focused nature the audience's role is quite the reverse of that intended by the theatre group of Misiones Pedagógicas. Rather than seeing an educative strategy as central, the hope of the Teatro del Pueblo was largely to offer distracting entertainment. By contrast, *teatro de urgencia*'s development is, to a great extent, marked by its interest in establishing a clear teaching role and, inevitably, this demanded that the spectator's function should take on the critical role identified by Sender in *Teatro de masas*.[41]

A particularly useful example of this kind of propaganda is *Cuatro batallones de choque* (*Four Shock Battalions*), which was performed at various street locations in Madrid by the Compañía Teatro Popular (Popular Theatre Company) during the first days of November 1936.[42] The purpose of the play was to encourage recruitment within seven days of 2,000 men and women for the defence of the capital in the face of the impending Nationalist attack. This single-minded propaganda task was explored through the use of six actors who, performing on the back of a lorry, represented undesirable civilian notions about the war which were then challenged by the Obrero Alistado and the Obrera Alistada (Enlisted Male Worker and Enlisted Female Worker). From the audience which was gathered around the lorry, these two characters denounced the civilians' lack of fervour for the struggle before ascending the stage to encourage the spectators' immediate enlistment. The well-aimed efficiency of the Communist Party as propagandists is felt, not only in the publication of the play by the Fifth Regiment, but also in the prologue to the edition which illustrates the degree of focus with which the propaganda task was approached and the work fashioned. The script, written 'en unos momentos, atendiendo principalmente a su eficacia' (in a few moments, attending primarily to its effectiveness) (p.3), works in the manner of a propaganda poster, sharply etching recognizable contemporary attitudes to the conflict such as that hinted at in 'el burgués gordo que se ha quitado la corbata y asoma un pañuelo rojo en el bolsillo de la cursilería' (the fat bourgeois who has got rid of his tie and displays a red handkerchief in the pocket of his absurdly affected outfit) (p.4).[43] An intriguing and revealing inclusion in this respect is the figure of the Artist who is ironically described as 'elaborando' (fashioning) a new work and unable to lend more active support to the war effort since, to stimulate his creativity, he needs 'el silencio y la tranquilidad de la paz' (the silence and tranquility of peace) (p.4). The ridicule to which this figure is subjected draws attention to the widespread sense among artists at this time that active political commitment necessarily involved the embracing of those forms which are represented by *Cuatro batallones* itself. Through the inclusion of the character, the author or authors of the play seem to draw attention to that abandonment of traditionally understood notions of art or artistic creation which was much debated throughout the time of the Second Republic.

The confident sense of purpose in the play as propaganda is enhanced by the work's knowledge of its dramatic origins. The idea of street performance for political ends is thus described as having been both widespread and effective in the Soviet Union, offering a model with which Spanish groups might develop their own Living Newspaper technique for wartime ends. Central to the propaganda success of the play, too, is the desire to monitor its effectiveness. Obviously, a crucial factor here is the level of enlistment in the battalions which was, apparently, in excess of the planned target as citizens registered to acquire weapon-handling skills outside their daily working hours.[44] Of great importance also, however, was the work's recognition of Gorelik's assertion concerning the meaning of theatre. The spectators are explicitly acknowledged, therefore, as 'el elemento principal' (the principal element) (p.3) and are described, significantly, not as the public or the audience but as 'el pueblo' (p.3). Bearing in mind that the edition is itself propagandistic and possibly exaggerated when it describes audience response, it is still highly useful in terms of evaluating the intended reaction which was sought from the spectators. The sense is one of active response rather than merely passive observation and, as though recording an experiment, the writer reports the audiences 'reaccionando admirablemente a la intención de la obra' (reacting marvellously to the intention of the work) (p.3). Photographs of the play in performance were fortunately included in the edition and show spectators who seem physically close to the action and attentive to the performers. It is worth mentioning in this respect that Mussot, in conversation, was at pains to stress quite emphatically that the reaction of front-line audiences to the plays presented by his groups was never anything but wholeheartedly enthusiastic.

In considering *Cuatro batallones* one senses why, amongst the variety of labels attached during the conflict to this kind of theatrical propaganda, *teatro de circunstancias* (theatre of circumstances) recurs frequently. Written, with immediately clear aims, as a rapid response to overcome deteriorating military circumstances, the play was an effective demonstration of drama's potential to furnish propaganda oriented thoughtfully towards achieving sharply delineated educational, training or cultural objectives. Complementing the increasingly certain focus on the *pueblo* as the audience for *teatro de urgencia*, what emerged from early 1937 onwards was a trend on the part of the various military and civil organs of state to define and encourage such works. Within the army, for example, the General War Commissariat declared that all military units should aspire to the formation of groups to perform the 'breve teatro político antifascista' (short anti-Fascist political theatre)[45] which, it suggests, is the most appropriate definition of the kind of theatre it wishes to encourage for the education of soldiers. Whereas *Cuatro batallones* had arisen almost spontaneously in response to the Nationalist assault, the Commissariat, by contrast, sought to institute a strategy for the development of *teatro de urgencia* as 'un magnífico aparato de propaganda y de educación social y política de una eficacia extraordinaria' (a magnificent propaganda system and an extraordinarily effective social and political education) (p.23).

The Commissariat's strategy to achieve such development centred on the creation of mobile groups to tour front-line locations with works designed to enhance the educational and training tasks undertaken by brigade and battalion commissars. Mussot's experience is particularly significant in this respect since, in early 1937, he had been appointed inspector of the *grupos artísticos* of the Army of the East and was responsible for establishing six troupes of performers who rehearsed at the Teatro Principal in Valencia prior to undertaking tours which lasted a fortnight.[46] Apart from supervising the rehearsals and administering the groups, Mussot's task was also to provide the groups' repertoire, and he recalled writing seven plays of which four have survived 'a pesar del esmero que tuvo la dictadura franquista en hacerlas desaparecer' (in spite of the care which the Francoist dictatorship took to make them disappear). Despite Mussot's claim that the theatrical focus of the plays was the general one of assisting the 'nuevo régimen contra el enemigo tradicional' (new regime against the traditional enemy),[47] one of the works in particular, *Mi puesto*, demonstrates a more tightly defined propaganda task. Subtitled 'crítica de los permisos' (critique of leave passes), the play invites the audience to pay close attention: 'prestad al espectáculo el máximo interés porque en provecho vuestro y nuestro trabajamos. Recoged sus enseñanzas, sus ejemplos, sus palabras' (lend maximum attention to the performance because we're working for your and our advantage. Take in its lessons, its examples, its words) (p.3). The subsequent action demonstrates a number of lessons whose assimilation is presented as crucial to military success. In this manner, the audience is encouraged to understand the war as an invasion, to show unquestioning obedience towards officers, to view service leave as a luxury rather than a right, and each soldier is invited actively to combat his own illiteracy.

Theatrical propaganda of this nature was felt by the Commissariat to have a significant role in the huge task which confronted the Republic of forging a capable military machine from the remnants of loyal professional forces and the Popular Militias. Writing in 1938, for example, Aparicio acknowledged the effectiveness of *teatro de urgencia* amongst soldiers when he described the Commissariat's efforts amongst troops of the Eighth Division to teach the need for intense fortification of the entire military sector.[48] Lectures, talks and articles in company broadsheets played their part in raising consciousness, suggests Aparicio, but particular tribute is paid to a lost sketch entitled *Fortificación* (*Fortification*) which acted as an 'ejemplo vivo extraído de las mismas trincheras' (living example drawn from the trenches themselves) (p.280) and whose language and action were felt by Aparicio to have a direct relevance to the soldiers which enhanced the teaching strategies of the drama. A number of plays such as this, illustrating issues considered of particular importance to be impressed upon combatants, were written under the auspices of the Commissariat and performed either by groups such as Mussot's or by the performance troupes which seem to have been established within military units themselves. An extremely important example of such work is *En las trincheras* (*In the Trenches*) since, consisting of four short pieces, it also provides the lines to be spoken between each play and therefore assists in the evaluation of the nature of performance and its intended atmosphere.⁴⁹ Three of the pieces present images of Nationalist Spain, seeking to explain the Republican soldiers' task as a new *reconquista* (reconquest), while the final piece stresses the notion of Republican unity as a prerequisite of victory. The deep ideological divisions within the Republic underlie the play's optimistic image of followers of Marx and Bakunin sharing 'un abrazo de fuego' (an embrace of fire) (p.15). Socialist and Anarchist differences are denounced as beneficial only to the common enemy and a fraternal pact is urged. Although the title page of *En las trincheras* bears no author, the final element at least was the work of Pedro Garfias since, in an extended form and entitled *¡Que nos quitan nuestra tierra!* (*They are Usurping our Land!*), the play was published by Juventud Campesina in 1938 as part of an anthology intended for performance by youth groups.⁵⁰

The dissemination of Garfias's work in this manner demonstrates a further aspect of the Commissariat's strategy in relation to *teatro de urgencia*. From the activities of the mobile troupes and other performance groups it was intended to nurture a repertoire which could, in printed form, provide performance material for an increasing range of groups and audiences. To this end the Subcommissariat of Propaganda initiated the series 'Teatros del Frente' (Front-Line Theatre), cheap editions printed on flimsy paper, which sold for twenty *céntimos* to provide funds 'a beneficio de la formación cultural del Ejército del Pueblo' (for the benefit of the cultural education of the People's Army).⁵¹ To this series belongs García Narezo's *¡Hacia la victoria!* (*Towards Victory!*), which sought to teach the correct response for soldiers when, under enemy fire, retreat seems the immediate reaction, and Herrera Petere's *Torredonjil*, which urged soldiers to respect the inhabitants of rural communities as fellow combatants.⁵² Plays such as these stress the educative role of drama which, by publishing plays, the Subcommissariat sought to emphasize. Yet, it seems likely that a number of factors intervened to limit the success of the Teatros del Frente series. As late in the war as December 1938, for example, Aparicio reports that a bibliography of *teatro de urgencia* would be very brief and, despite his close involvement with the Subcommissariat, he omits to mention the Teatros del Frente series. What Aparicio is at pains to urge through discussing a possible bibliography is that publication is the principal means to disseminate plays and encourage further writing. Implicitly,

Aparicio is suggesting a repertoire which has failed to flourish; hence perhaps his view that 'convendría que se editara cuanto de teatro de urgencia ha sido escrito' (it would be appropriate to publish as much theatre of urgency as has been written) (p.282). The Teatros del Frente series, therefore, probably amounted to little more than *En las trincheras*, the works by Herrera Petere and García Narezo and an anonymous piece entitled *Guadalajara-Italia* which celebrated Republican successes in March 1937 at Trijueque and Brihuega.[53] The sheer difficulty of arranging publication of work when paper was a scarce resource must also have acted to inhibit the Commissariat's intentions in this respect. By the time Aparicio wrote his article the price of a daily newspaper had risen to twenty-five *céntimos* and, increasingly, the press failed to appear because paper was unavailable.[54]

The strategy evolved by the Commissariat was reflected by one of the civil organs of state when the Ministry of Health and Public Education created the Guerrillas del Teatro by a ministerial order of December 1937.[55] These mobile groups were charged with a similar task to that carried out during 1937 by groups such as those of Mussot, but seem to have performed a repertoire which more fully incorporated civilian audiences. Their appearance at a rather advanced stage of the war is potentially misleading since it suggests that work of this kind was initiated only at this point. In fact, groups such as Altavoz del Frente and El Búho (The Owl) had presented plays in various improvised locations almost since the outset of the conflict.[56] The creation of the Guerrillas troupes must be seen, however, as a further indication of the increasingly organized sense of audience focus. An examination of surviving texts demonstrates how the broad anti-Fascist task of the earlier groups is further refined so that certain of the Guerrillas are found targeting, to a greater degree, particular elements of the population with theatrical propaganda fashioned to offer highly specific teaching about current aspects of the war. The German annexation of Austria on 11 March 1938 becomes, for example, the subject of *España no es Austria* (*Spain is not Austria*), performed by the Guerrillas del Teatro of the Army of the East in the streets of Barcelona from 25 March.[57] Prominent in the text is the idea of accommodation with the enemy, the play seeking to posit an ideologically correct view for spectators which challenges the growing mood of compromise amongst the Republican population:

¡No! Nuestro compromiso, el compromiso de todo el pueblo español y de su gobierno es éste: aplastar a Franco y enterrar a los invasores en la tierra que quieren robarnos. ¡Ese es el compromiso nacional: el de la victoria absoluta y terminante! (p.47)

(No! Our commitment, the commitment of all the Spanish people and of its government is this: crush Franco and bury the invaders in the land which they want to rob from us. That is the national commitment: that of absolute and decisive victory!)

A similar concern to maintain morale and clarify the value and meaning of the struggle is found in *Lección y escarmiento del derrotismo* (*Lesson and Warning about Defeatism*) which was presented in street performances from 15 March 1938.[58] The increasing gravity of the military situation gives the play a tone of desperation and there is a violence, not only in the urgency of the language, but also in the dragging from the stage of a suspected defeatist by an assault guard who, as far as the audience can judge, appears not to be an actor but a genuine member of the security forces. In both examples urban civilians are the target group, the plays seeking to rally Barcelona in the face of repeated Nationalist success. The attempt to bolster flagging enthusiasm for war or to reiterate the conflict's purpose is also found in *Tres soldados en una batalla* (*Three Soldiers in a Battle*) which was presented by the Guerrillas at the Ebro battle front in the spring of 1938.[59] The time's military desperation is similarly felt, here reflected in the figure of the wounded soldier who urges a fleeing comrade to turn back and remember that

el día 6 de noviembre teníamos en Madrid un solo lanzabombas que nadie sabía manejar. En el Jarama, por cada cañón nuestro disparaban diez cañones alemanes. En Guadalajara esta inferioridad era mayor. ¡Y resistimos! (p.90)

(on 6 November in Madrid we only had a single artillery launcher which nobody knew how to use. At the Jarama, for every one cannon of ours ten German cannons were firing. At Guadalajara the disadvantage was greater. And we resisted!)

Significantly, these three examples suggest how the groups' repertoire seems to have differed from the plays which emanated from the

Commissariat. For the latter, theatrical propaganda tended to emphasize aspects of training. These plays of the Guerrillas are characterized by the energy of anger, and stress resistance at all costs. There is a sense, too, that the plays are responding to immediate issues, challenging or supporting perceptions almost as soon as they manifest themselves. Hence its assessment of itself as a kind of theatre which 'se ha asomado en la ciudad en uno de los momentos más duros para Barcelona' (has appeared in the city at one of the harshest moments for Barcelona) and has taken itself to the front line 'cuando las divisiones italianas rompían momentáneamente el frente de Aragón' (when the Italian divisions temporarily broke the Aragon front line).[60]

The feeling of *actualité* is intense in those works which have survived from the repertoire of the Army of the East's Guerrillas del Teatro. One has the sense of a group working in the manner which Irene Falcón recalled when describing the creation of the Nosotros repertoire[61] and, especially since no authorship is acknowledged for these Guerrillas plays, it would seem perfectly reasonable to assume a communal authorship. By contrast, the other Guerrillas del Teatro established by the government ministry, that of the Army of the Centre, presented a somewhat different *teatro de urgencia*, focusing less on aggressive, slogan-like work than on satire and rather more conventional examples of the one-act play. That this should be so is undoubtedly due to the leading role of the Alliance in the creation of the Guerrillas del Teatro. The establishment of the groups, for example, by ministerial order in December 1937, was to some extent focusing and extending the work of mobile companies which had, for some months, operated as part of the theatre section of the Alliance, the TAP. The testimony of the actor Edmundo Barbero indicates that the operational base of the Guerrillas was Marqués del Duero, 7, the nerve centre of the Alliance and the wartime home of Alberti and María Teresa León.[62] Not surprisingly, therefore, the most frequently performed works by the Guerrillas del Teatro of the Army of the Centre were *Radio Sevilla* and *Los salvadores*, along with Ontañón's *El saboteador*. Unlike Alberti's grotesque caricatures, Ontañón's piece is a one-act play in a realistic vein and setting which deals with the cunning machinations of a treacherous Republican officer who seeks to delay a troop convoy, thus causing it to be blown up while crossing a bridge. To this repertoire was added a version of Chekhov's *The Duel* and Calderón's *El dragoncillo*, as well as two *teatro de urgencia* pieces, de la Fuente's *El café* . . . and Aparicio's *Los miedosos valientes* (*The Brave Cowards*).[63] From the image of sugarless coffee and the complaints about wartime shortages of three well-dressed, middle-class Madrid citizens, de la Fuente stresses how the morale of the rearguard depends 'en la medida en que seamos implacables con la quinta columna' (on the extent to which we deal implacably with the fifth column),[64] while Aparicio's sketch presents a persistent theme of *teatro de urgencia*, the fears of the non-enlisted overcome by the persuasive arguments of the committed *miliciano*.

The inclusion of works by Chekhov and Calderón indicates the Alliance's wider cultural concerns and, as Barbero recalls, the repertoire of the groups was supplemented by Golden Age *entremeses* as well as further *teatro de urgencia*. The presentation of short plays from the seventeenth century is easily understood in terms of a *teatro ambulante* (travelling theatre), but the Chekhov play is an intriguing illustration of how the Guerrillas del Teatro which operated from Madrid were an element of a broader policy of the Alliance's TAP. The essence of this policy derived from the incorporation into the group's title of the concepts of art and propaganda. Alongside works designed to serve immediate political ends, a more traditional repertoire was intended to introduce audiences to classic authors. In effect, an education policy was in operation which, ironically perhaps, given León's view of the theatre section of Misiones Pedagógicas, could be seen to differ only slightly from the earlier group. Chekhov's work had entered the repertoire of the TAP at the Teatro de la Zarzuela from 15 April 1938 and its inclusion in the Guerrillas repertoire seems to suggest a conscious decision to utilize the mobile groups as more than just a means of Republican propaganda. Such a view is strengthened when one notes the presentation by the Guerrillas del Teatro of a translation of Molière's *The Imaginary Invalid* at the Alliance's headquarters in November 1938.[65] Had the military circumstances of early 1939 enabled this production to tour front-line locations it would have been a very sophisticated development, a move towards the combination of 'poesía y acción' (poetry and action) which, in the early weeks of the war, Nueva Escena had announced as its theatrical goal.[66]

An article in *El Mono Azul* indicates that the Guerrillas of the Army of the Centre gave 119 performances during 1938 and the total number given by the group could not have been much in excess of this.[67] Barbero's testimony is reasonably specific about the location of performances in the cinemas and theatres of small towns as well as at more improvised locations. Various tours were made to military zones as far as Andalusia to the south and Extremadura to the west but, given the difficulties of communication and transport, the majority of performances took place in the Guadarrama region. The focus of the repertoire is surprisingly close to that of Misiones Pedagógicas and La Barraca and suggests, interestingly, that the supposedly fierce radicalism of the Alliance members might have been exaggerated, perhaps by unguarded attention to newspaper and magazine sources of the time whose propaganda interests have been insufficiently regarded. The similar troupes which operated in the Army of the East, for example, or some of Mussot's plays, indicate work with a much harder political edge, greater *actualité* and, as we have seen, a more actively interventionist attitude to the audience. By contrast, León's description of a performance by the Guerrillas in Sagunto might easily be mistaken for an account from one of the expeditions of La Barraca or Misiones Pedagógicas:

> por todos los lugares libres se instaló un público con las manos sucias y las caras sudorosas y los trajes de faena, engrasados . . . para oír los graciosos versos de Lope de Vega y las afortunadas ocurrencias de Chejov, de Alberti, de Santiago Ontañón.[68]
>
> (in every free space sat an audience with filthy hands and sweaty faces and greasy overalls . . . to hear the witty verse of Lope de Vega and the entertaining incidents of Chekhov, Alberti and Santiago Ontañón.)

A number of explanations might account for the differences which can be felt between the repertoires of the Guerrillas in the distinct military sectors. First, at the time of the groups' creation, the Ebro sector was emerging as a critical military area in a way which contrasted with the relative stability of the central fronts, and this would in itself have determined the kind of theatrical propaganda deemed necessary.[69] Second, the Alliance clearly had a broader vision of the meaning, possibility and purpose of theatre which arose from the long argument concerning the regeneration of the Spanish theatre. This topic, if anything, was debated more widely and with greater energy during the war years. The commitment of intellectuals on the Left to the popular cause led them, as is well known, to embrace new concepts of art and literature. Given their status as intellectuals, perhaps indeed by virtue of such status, the dissemination of traditional culture also seemed crucial. Common to the plans of Nueva Escena, the TAP and the Guerrillas del Teatro of the Army of the Centre, is an effort to develop a repertoire which is felt to be worthy and intrinsically important in conjunction with one felt to be contingent and necessary. It is in such a light that the Molière and Chekhov productions need to be understood, as well as León's unfulfilled ambition for the Guerrillas to present a translation of Maeterlinck's *The Miracle of Saint Anthony*.[70]

Although the above indicates how Republican theatrical propaganda was undoubtedly a diffuse phenomenon, an examination of how it developed during the war would have to acknowledge the principal role of the Commissariat and the Ministry of Health and Public Education as the means by which *teatro de urgencia* was nurtured. These state organs established structures which not only created mobile theatre groups but encouraged the establishment of performance troupes amongst political groups and military brigades. The socialist Juventud Campesina, for example, sought, as we have seen, to provide an appropriate repertoire for theatrical activities in its clubs and meeting-places by establishing Ediciones Juventud (Youth Editions) with the aim of disseminating *teatro de urgencia*.[71] The introduction to what seems to have been its only such anthology recalls in large measure the tone both of the ministerial order which established the Guerrillas and Alberti's speech to the CCT concerning the need to expand the available repertoire of *teatro de urgencia*.[72] Alberti's recognition, for example, that such plays must not pose staging problems is reflected in the advice of Juventud Campesina to intending authors that they must bear in mind 'las posibilidades escasas de llevar a la práctica, por falta de medios económicos y técnicos, ciertas realizaciones' (the prospects, limited by lack of economic and technical means, for putting certain production ideas into practice).[73] Although no details exist concerning the performance of any of the works in this volume, another socialist group, the Juventudes Socialistas Unificadas (United Socialist Youth) is recorded as having performed in Guadalajara and the surrounding area during August 1938 with a repertoire including *El saboteador* and, in the only known wartime performance of any of his *teatro de urgencia*, Hernández's *El refugiado*.[74] Reflecting such civilian initiatives, the work of the Commissariat in utilizing drama as a means of propaganda encouraged theatrical activities in various brigades and battalions. Aparicio claimed in *Comisario* that 'actualmente, ¿qué División, qué Cuerpo de Ejército no cuenta con un grupo de esta clase?' (currently, what Division, what Army Corps doesn't rely on a group of this type?) (p.279). In conversation, Dieste felt such a claim was exaggerated. Marrast, however, records a number of such groups, including the presentation, remarkable in itself, of a translation of Ibsen's *A Doll's House* by a Signals Corps's cultural organization in the Albacete region during October 1938. These groups were probably *ad hoc* creations offering infrequent performances without a particularly clear propaganda focus. In June 1937, for example, the theatre group of the Second Battalion's Sixty-Seventh Brigade presented Sender's *El secreto*, a work which is also recorded as having been performed in September of the same year by the Third Division's Thirty-Fourth Brigade. This latter performance was also accompanied by Arniches's *La real gana* (*The Bloody Bother*) and the same month also saw a performance of Casona's *Nuestra Natacha* (*Our Natasha*) in a festival performance organized by the Chemical War Unit.[75]

The role of these performance troupes in propaganda work is the least-known aspect of an extremely complicated history. The titles of other works which such groups might have performed are unknown and, with a theatrical form such as *teatro de urgencia*, it is possible that examples of the genre were simply never recorded. In correspondence, for example, Tomalin recalled writing a sketch for performance before fellow brigaders satirizing Franco's apparent boast that he would enter Madrid on a white horse.[76] Using the pantomime convention of two actors forming the horse, the performance was sufficiently sophisticated to have used an improvised horse costume, but the script, presumably the only *teatro de urgencia* written in English, was discarded. Anecdotal evidence such as this can safely be amplified to indicate a wider picture of a festive performance culture behind military lines whose details are unlikely ever to be known, the more so given that even the structured efforts of centralized organizations are difficult to reconstitute. Dieste recalled, for example, that at the request of Ehrenburg, he wrote at great speed a puppet play, possibly called *El toro antifascista* (*The Anti-Fascist Bull*), reacting to news which had filtered through to the Republican zone concerning a Nationalist massacre carried out in the bullring at Badajoz.[77] All traces of the play have disappeared, although it was, Dieste remembered, performed in Sonsona, forming part of a repertoire of three puppet pieces of which only one has survived.[78]

Despite such a fragmented history, sufficient *teatro de urgencia* texts survive to demonstrate a sense of shape with regard to its development during the war. What emerges is a dogged attempt to co-ordinate and develop along two broad lines, military and civilian, aiming to provide a mixture of education and recreation within the overarching anti-Fascist endeavour which Altavoz del Frente described as its essential purpose. In order to achieve this task it was necessary, after the initial euphoria of occupying the theatres of the major cities, to seek audiences which had often been uprooted from their customary circumstances in order to address them concerning the urgent issues thrown up by the war. Although factual details can sometimes be uncertain, *teatro de urgencia*'s role can readily be perceived by scrutinizing its relationship with its audience. In this way we find that acting spaces are flexible, as is the plays' content, because the determining factor of performance is the urgency with which the spectator's reaction is viewed. The audience is frequently involved as the subject matter of the drama and, sometimes, involved in the action of the drama itself. Such a concern with the audience continues the similar preoccupation with which pre-war groups viewed the spectator and, just as these groups continually faced a shortage of suitable dramatic material for performance, *teatro de urgencia*, too, was always felt to be in short supply. A further persistent aspect of the development of theatrical propaganda, therefore, is the frequency of calls for its composition. Reports and articles in newspapers reflect this concern, but its expansion was principally encouraged by the numerous competitions which were organized, building perhaps on that initiated by *Octubre* in 1934.[79] The creation of the Guerrillas del Teatro, for example, was accompanied by the establishment of a permanent competition for works which met the requirements of form set out by Alberti in his speech to the CCT. Identical repertoire problems faced Piscator who outlined in his Proletarian Theatre manifesto the nature of the plays desired by the group but was unable to encourage writers to compose them. Ideological and structural advances in the theatre made demands which playwrights seemed unable to meet.[80] Similarly, the Proletkult in Russia sought to overcome its repertoire difficulties in a manner akin to that of *teatro de urgencia*, by recycling them to various groups through cheap printed anthologies.[81]

When Marrast concludes his survey of the Republican theatre he suggests that the Nationalist soldiers, on entering Madrid and seeing the offerings of the theatrical repertoire, would not have found a great difference from that presented before July 1936. From this Marrast concludes that the attempts to revolutionize the theatre largely failed. While this is certainly true in terms of Madrid, in making this judgement Marrast ignores much of the radical dramatic experiment which, in general, occurred beyond the capital. This *teatro de urgencia* extended some of the important lines of theatrical debate on the Left which had taken place before the war, particularly, as we shall see, with regard to the function of the audience during performance. What resulted was a unique and surprisingly varied drama as *teatro de urgencia* persisted in efforts to reach a military and civilian community whose commitment to the struggle was tested by increasingly difficult obstacles. Its aim was a more urgently perceived version of the earlier socialists' desire to create the new citizen, and its commitment in this respect is felt in its rapid withdrawal from the conventional theatres at the close of 1936. Having made little progress there, *teatro de urgencia* gained that sense of purpose which had characterized the work of groups such as Nosotros – a belief derived from Rolland's notion that if you wish to create a people's art, you must first create the people.[82] Rolland's emphasis upon the role of the people as the focus of a new aesthetic was, of course, an important aspect of much European experimentation with political theatre during the earlier part of this century. A central consideration in this respect was the performance's intention with regard to the spectator, a factor which, in the case of a wartime propaganda theatre, assumed perhaps even greater significance. The relationship which *teatro de urgencia* sought to establish between spectator and performance offers evidence of important innovation in this regard and, given the genre's orientation towards a self-conscious communication with its audience, it seems appropriate at this point to continue with an examination of its intentions and achievements in performance.

~ 3 ~
Staging the Political Drama

A prominent feature of the discussion thus far has been the manner in which the creation of a new model citizen was a persistent characteristic of left-wing cultural activities throughout the Civil War and the preceding decades. Emancipation was viewed not only in traditional Marxist terms, namely the overthrow of the state by the masses, but also through more obviously gradualist means such as the moral and social education of the individual. In terms of the theatre, this socialist desire to construct what has been described as 'un nuevo modelo de persona' (a new-model person)[1] manifested itself as a concern with the spectator and the means by which the *pueblo* might be influenced through an appropriate repertoire of revolutionary drama. The increasing sense of clarity with which writers and artists on the Left viewed this task prompted the development of a theatre aesthetic which, contrasting sharply with traditional assumptions about drama, found forceful expression in the wartime propaganda theatre. Central to this aesthetic was a fundamental dislocation of conventional dramatic structures which led, from pre-war agitprop experiments through *teatro de urgencia*, to a radical shift away from the conventional role of the audience. As the development of *teatro de urgencia* demonstrates, such a shift involved new playing spaces and distinctive performance dynamics, and encouraged drama which, for purposes of training, education or entertainment, frequently made the spectators themselves the objects of the spectacle.

Given the paramount consideration lent to the audience, critical dismissal of *teatro de urgencia* as fundamentally undramatic is, therefore, surprising. Templado finds 'escaso valor' (little worth) in the drama, while Ruiz Ramón laments its failure to find 'la fórmula teatral adecuada para expresar los contenidos que se desean comunicar' (the adequate theatrical formula to express the content it wishes to communicate).[2] Templado's assertion recalls those issues of literary merit which had so vexed commentators such as Seisdedos and Araquistáin, while Ruiz Ramón's emphasis on a unifying structural formula is at odds with a form of drama much of whose strength derived from a chameleon-like ability to assume forms determined by the varying natures and needs of its target audiences. Both Templado and Ruiz Ramón seem out of sympathy with Sender's demand discussed earlier that, in order to rediscover its relevance to modern society, drama should be resolutely 'anti-literario' (anti-literary) and seek its spirit in the alert enthusiasm of the bullfight crowd.[3] Such a viewpoint, seeking to diminish the conventional literary status of the text, shifts the emphasis towards its realization in performance. The relative unimportance of the author and the contrasting centrality of the spectator increase the emphasis on the dramatic event itself and, by reconstructing the technical apparatus and likely practice of the performance troupes, and by examining the evidence of surviving scripts, we can assess the effectiveness of the relationship *teatro de urgencia* sought to establish between spectator and performance.

Initially, of course, *teatro de urgencia* was presented in the newly socialized Madrid theatres and these early plays offer an illuminating example of the contrast between the propaganda drama's desire to celebrate, agitate and educate, and the obstacles which traditional auditorium design placed in the way of appropriate communication between actor and audience. Sender had drawn attention to this when he observed that, unlike the 'círculo perfecto' (perfect circle) of the bullring, extending the architectural lines of conventional auditoria ensured that 'el escenario queda fuera' (the stage remains apart) (p.27). Such a problem can be felt in practice in Balbontín's *El cuartel*, one of the earliest theatrical responses to the military uprising, which was presented at the Teatro Maravillas in late September 1936.[4]

Balbontín's play is intended as a collective celebration of the failure of the army rebellion in Madrid.[5] Its single act, divided into fourteen scenes which play without interruption, is set in the patio of the Montaña barracks where a group of officers and Falangists are outwitted and defeated by a combination of loyal soldiers and ordinary citizens. The play's predominant tones are those of humorous irony which derives from the audience's knowledge of the actual rebellion's failure, and a heroism which glories in the achievements and new-found potential of the *pueblo*. For the seditious General, whom Balbontín presents both as cruel fanatic and simple buffoon, in the rebellion 'se trata sencillamente de un paseo militar hasta la

Puerta del Sol' (one is simply dealing with a military parade to the Puerta del Sol) (p.13), while for the sole loyal officer it offers, in language typical of the play, a bond with the masses which will 'engrandecer la hoguera esplendorosa de la España que nace' (augment the radiant blaze of the Spain which is being born) (p.22).

The conclusion of the play, however, offers a striking illustration of how *teatro de urgencia*'s early sojourn in mainstream theatre buildings erected, in effect, a barrier between stage and audience. The final moments of the play see the stage fill with flags as the citizens of Madrid storm the barracks and the loyal soldiers are liberated. To the Republican tricolour is added the red and black flag of the Anarchists and the red banners of the socialists until 'se funden en una sola' (they fuse as one) (p.23). A gradual increase in celebratory clamour is intended as different groups enter, unfurling their banners to shouts of '¡Viva el Frente Popular!' (Long live the Popular Front!). As the curtain falls the crowds exit, repeatedly chanting '¡U.H.P!' (Unite, proletarian brothers!) and giving the clenched-fist salute. The sense of a meeting or demonstration is intended, but this is at odds with the style of the play, which is rooted, both in design and acting, in naturalism. Identification with the psychological experience of the characters is fostered, much in the manner of the *cuestión social* dramas, and, as with all naturalist acting, audience intervention is excluded. It is highly probable, of course, that in the emotionally charged circumstances of the time, various speeches and moments such as the final scene would have elicited the excited approval of the audience. Yet this is in spite of the play's form rather than because of it. The audience, rather, has been forced to adopt the position which was such anathema to Brecht, that of 'sitting in front of a keyhole'.[6]

Balbontín's play does have force as Republican propaganda but this seems to owe more to the celebratory significance of the historical event it purports to describe and less to the success of the author's propaganda intentions. The spectator's undynamic role in the performance links weakly to the on-stage action and consequently diminishes propaganda effectiveness. Certain deficiencies of the play's structure are also significant in reducing the power of the play, but of greater importance is the inappropriateness of the playing space for which it was written. The similarly large proscenium stage of the Teatro Fontalba must have exerted an equally negative influence on the relationship between action and spectator in Mussot's *¡No pasarán!* despite the clarity of its structure and intentions as propaganda. For all that the actors might declaim, exhort and seek to bond with their audience the footlights demarcate two worlds, one in light, one in darkness, which are mutually exclusive.

Early *teatro de urgencia* such as Balbontín's arose from the political upheaval which had delivered the mainstream theatres into the hands of groups which viewed their ideal audience in terms very different from the passive, unacknowledged non-participants decried by Brecht. The disposition of proscenium theatres to focus action inward towards the actor and the stage was, of course, ideally suited to that kind of naturalism which sought to erect an invisible glass wall between actor and audience, but it did little to serve the ends of a kind of drama desiring to fuse spectator and performer in the heroism of the collective struggle. In effect, the theatre itself threatened to defeat *teatro de urgencia* since it could not, conventionally defined, provide the audience relationship demanded by a propaganda drama which perceived its task with increasing urgency. The search for such a relationship necessarily involved the search for a more appropriate playing area, and a marked feature of the evolving performance of *teatro de urgencia* is the eager experimentation implicit in Gatti's intriguing observation that 'in order to create theatre, it is necessary to leave it behind; and so the first thing to do is to find another place where the theatre can express itself'.[7]

This other place was not a single location but many. Shifting its interest from the traditional theatres of the capital, *teatro de urgencia*'s response to the exigencies of war was, as has been noted earlier, to emerge as a flexible element of Republican propaganda by presenting drama in a wide variety of locations through mobile troupes comprising a small number of actors. Mussot recalled that streets, railway stations, hospitals and trade union headquarters were predominant performance venues in the rearguard and that 'de cara al enemigo: trincheras, parapetos y puestos de mando militar' (facing the enemy: trenches, parapets and military command posts) were utilized by the various groups which were formed for the purpose of consolidating what Mussot describes as 'las fuerzas e ideales republicanos' (the Republican strengths and ideals).[8] These Guerrillas del Teatro consciously sought to build upon the tradition of travelling theatre which forms a significant part of Spain's dramatic heritage by performing wherever an audience might gather. The imminent formation of the Guerrillas del Teatro of the Army of the East, for example, is enthusiastically reported as the theatre's return to 'el siglo de oro de nuestra literatura' (the Golden Age of our literature).[9] The surviving scripts written and performed by this group in the streets of Barcelona offer a picture of *teatro de urgencia*'s attempt to establish a model for performance free of the proscenium's restraints, and the resulting approach might safely be assumed to reflect the working methods of the numerous other 'guerrilla' groups to whom references can be traced but few details furnished.[10]

The playing area used by the Guerrillas del Teatro of the Army of the East was a portable stage transported by lorry and sufficiently mobile to enable it to be erected by the professional actors who formed each troupe. The play *Dos divisiones de la juventud* (*Two Youth Divisions*), initially performed on 3 April 1938, makes it clear that a stage of this kind was used since, in a moment which displays a stylistic flexibility quite unlike anything found in Balbontín's work, two of the performers consciously acknowledge the presence of the spectators:

CONCHA ¡Mira, mira qué gentío!
ADELA   Es para ver las 'Guerrillas del Teatro', que van a actuar. ¿No ves el tabladillo?[11]

(CONCHA Look, look, what a crowd!
ADELA   It's to see the Theatre Guerrillas who are going to perform. Can't you see the stage?)

Effective sightlines would suggest that the height of this stage was approximately the head height of the spectators, but an earlier stage direction in the same play referring to the presence of 'la escalerilla derecha' (the right-hand steps) (p.54) tends to confirm that the playing area was indeed some considerable height from the ground. Consideration of the stage's height is important since it enables an impression to be gauged of the dimensions and robustness of a structure which, as the plays indicate, had to support the weight and movement of approximately five actors. A photograph in the *El Sol* newspaper article referred to earlier shows two actresses performing traditional dances, offering further evidence that the Guerrillas' stage was a substantial construction built to withstand heavy use.

The same photograph indicates the presence of curtains arranged in a slightly decorative manner, not as a proscenium but acting as a backdrop for the performers. None of the plays performed by the group demands anything other than actors' entrances from the sides of the stage and so the implication might be that, apart from their ability to lend focus to the playing space, the curtains are intended to create a preparation and changing area for the performers. Make-up, for example, seems to have been used, since *El Sol*, lauding the group's enthusiasm for its task, refers to the actors carrying 'en una mano el martillo con que levantar el tablado; en la otra los colores que animarán sus rostros' (in one hand the hammer to erect the stage; in the other the paints which will enliven their faces) (p.13). In *Defendemos la Tierra* (*We Defend the Land*), which the group performed in the Gandesa region, the suggestion occurs that screens might also have formed part of the stage setting since the opening directions request the 'simulación de una próxima tierra labrada' (impression of nearby cultivated land), and costume of some degree is called for in the actresses displaying 'la amplitud graciosa de la falda aldeana' (the pleasing fullness of rustic dress).[12]

The keynote of simplicity which is felt in this kind of staging did not, however, preclude a degree of sophistication. Alberti's *Radio Sevilla*, for example, frequently performed by the Guerrillas del Teatro of the Army of the Centre, utilizes screens and curtains to excellent satirical effect.[13] The play's opening scene between a young girl and a Nationalist conscript is played, according to the stage directions, in front of curtains. A loudspeaker's announcement that Radio Seville is about to broadcast alerts the soldier who advises the girl to listen carefully:

> Veremos aparecer,
> entre vinos y guitarras,
> entre relinches y coces
> y turbias bofaratadas,
> un triste cuadro flamenco
> ... toda la gran pandereta
> de esa estropajosa España. (p.6)
>
> (Amongst wines and guitars,
> amongst neighing and kicking
> and unfortunate slaps,
> we'll see appear
> a sad flamenco troupe
> ... all the great tambourine-banging
> of that despicable Spain.)

As they step aside the curtains open to reveal the façade of a 'gran caja de cerillas de la época monárquica' (large matchbox of the monarchist era) (p.6) which in turn opens slowly to reveal the interior of Queipo de Llano's headquarters.[14] Adorning the walls are the trappings of picture-postcard Spain – bullfight posters, a cardboard bull's head and the darts and daggers of the bullfight. In the middle of the stage, adopting absurdly exaggerated flamenco postures are Queipo and his mistress, Clavelona, surrounded by Falangists. In the farcical scene which ensues, Queipo and his associates, unaware that the microphone is switched on, caper buffoonishly about the stage on hands and knees imitating animal noises in a mock bullfight. The props mentioned by Alberti are used in a bullfight parody which is interrupted by a cruel, sneering Nazi officer who enters unexpectedly and dismisses the absurd spectacle as 'la España romántica' (romantic Spain) (p.7). At the end of the play, as the 'matchbox' closes, Queipo's head is trapped and then beaten by the *pueblo* as the curtains close.

Even this brief summary of the play suggests the farcically good-humoured spirit of the piece as well as hinting why it was apparently so popular in its puppet version.[15] Alberti achieves much through scene painting and simple props. The matchbox effect, for example, was probably achieved by painted screens positioned behind the curtains, while at the back of the stage a second screen could have held the bullfight instruments and the animal mask. The matchbox screen was itself perhaps only a painted canvas which could be removed to provide further, different screens for other plays in the same programme.

Arising from a ministerial initiative, the Guerrillas del Teatro seem to have worked with a relatively high level of resources and can be deemed to have offered the most sophisticated of the playing areas used by mobile groups during the war. Although operating on identical principles other companies seem to have performed in similar but less favourably endowed circumstances. Dieste's memory of a performance seen in a public place in Valencia recalls, for example, 'acaso un telón de fondo, pero sin trastos ni decoraciones' (perhaps a curtain backdrop, but without props or décor).[16] This stage probably belonged to the Altavoz del Frente group which, under the name Retablo Rojo, was touring in the region at this time. Of particular interest, however, is the playing area described by Mussot in his role as writer and director of *teatro de urgencia* for the

Commissariat. In overall charge of six groups, Mussot did not have portable staging to equip the groups, and it was necessary instead to present the plays upon the ground. Mussot recalled, for example, that the performers would use a rock as a table.[17] Troupes must have been accustomed to such improvisation since tours themselves were, Mussot recalled, hastily improvised as and when lorries and fuel became available. Reporting to the commanding officer, the actors awaited a suitable moment to present their programme and then used the environment to describe the scene. The opening of Mussot's *La evasión* offers an indication of this in practice when it advises the actors to enter 'por uno de los lados del lugar en que han de presentarse' (from one of the sides of the place in which the performance has to be given).[18]

Whatever the precise details of the staging facilities available to particular groups, the resulting playing area was the focus of a performance intended both as political meeting and *fiesta*. *Teatro de urgencia* was presented as part of a wider programme of material considered appropriate not only for the education but also the entertainment of soldiers and civilians. The ministerial decree which established the Guerrillas del Teatro, for example, arose from the perceived need to 'poner a las masas populares en contacto con las realidades del momento' (put the popular masses in contact with current realities)[19] and the resulting *teatro de urgencia* presented throughout Barcelona displays an appropriately hard-edged, uncompromising and overt political message. By contrast, the prologue to *La evasión* explains to its audience that the propaganda section of the Commissariat has told the actors:

> Id a los frentes, distraed y deleitad con vuestras coplas y con vuestros bailes y decirles [*sic*], que son como la esencia del alma popular, a esos compañeros, a esos hermanos vuestros que dan su sangre en las trincheras para que construyemos una España grande, culta y buena. (p.1)
>
> (Go to the front lines, entertain and delight with your verses and your dances and tell those comrades, those your brothers who are giving their blood in the trenches so that we may build a great, educated, good Spain, that they are the essence of the popular soul.)

Such popular entertainments brought music, variety and a festive air to performance and were presumably intended to complement more overt or serious propaganda. León, for example, recalls the Guerrillas del Teatro presenting regional dances,[20] presumably accompanied by the portable piano which was part of the group's equipment, and the photographic evidence mentioned earlier shows that traditional Spanish dancing formed part of the repertoire of the Guerrillas del Teatro of the Army of the East. The appropriation of other traditional folk arts by *teatro de urgencia* was also an element of performance. Alberti urged the *romance* as a means of contemporary celebration when he praised 'los miles de romances y poemas que en hojillas, revistas y recitales recorren las trincheras' (the thousands of ballads and poems that in flysheets, magazines and recitations spread through the trenches)[21] and, in similar vein, Los Faraones Antifascistas (The Anti-Fascist Gypsies) in *La evasión* utilized popular verse forms as the basis of Republican propaganda which was set to simple tunes:

> Han invitao al extranjero
> a una guerra de invasión.
> Dispondrán de su dinero,
> pero no del corazón
> del patriota sinsero
> que defiende su nasión. (p.2)

> (They've invited the foreigner
> to a war of invasion.
> They'll dispose of his money,
> but not of the heart
> of the true patriot
> who defends his nation.)

Since the audience was arranged in more or less random fashion around the playing area, and because performances were often given in the open air, *teatro de urgencia* writers lent to their work a commanding start which signalled the opening of the play. In *Despedida de reclutas* (*Farewell to the Recruits*), for example, while one of the company erects a large banner on the stage, the actors sing, solo and in chorus, verses, clearly traditional in form and tone, which encapsulate the problem which the ensuing short drama will test:

> Ya se van los quintos, madre.
> Ya se va mi corazón.

> Ya se va quien me tiraba
> piedrecitas al balcón.²²
>
> (Now the conscripts are leaving, mother.
> Now my heart is leaving.
> Now the one is leaving who threw
> little stones to the balcony.)

The sense of absence and loss felt in the verse contrasts with the banner's call for the audience to overcome such feelings and commit all to the common struggle: 'el esfuerzo de la retaguardia dará a nuestros soldados lo que necesitan para vencer' (the effort of the rearguard will give our soldiers what they need for victory) (p.17). In similar fashion, *Barco de traidores* (*Ship of Traitors*), a play which celebrates a rare Republican naval victory, opens with the jubilant enthusiasm of a group of sailors who command the stage in 'actitudes de camaradería alegre' (comradely postures) to sing:

> No hay quién pueda, no hay quién pueda
> con la gente marinera,
> marinera, luchadora,
> que defiende su bandera.²³
>
> (Nobody can try it on, nobody can try it on
> with the sea-going folk,
> sea-going, struggling,
> who defend their flag.)

A marked characteristic of Mussot's surviving plays is an arresting prologue which is intended not only to focus the audience's attention but also the spectators' minds on the events they are invited to consider. Thus, before watching 'A la orden de la República' (At the Orders of the Republic), an actor alerted the audience to the performers' desire to

> daros a conocer esta producción por varias razones, siendo las esenciales: exaltar la figura noble, leal y prestigiosa . . . del protagonista, para estímulo y como ejemplo . . .²⁴
>
> (make known this production to you for various reasons, the essential

ones being: to exalt the noble, loyal and distinguished figure ... of the protagonist, as a stimulus and example ...)

Unambiguous and with an air of declamation, much *teatro de urgencia* opens in a manner which is, as the above examples suggest, didactic to a greater or lesser degree. The opening moments of *¡Hacia la victoria!* likewise demonstrate this idea, seeking to pose the wider issue of the drama in an easily digested form through the principal character who, consciously tending to address the audience rather than his fellow performers, proclaims:

> Camaradas, os he llamado para ver si resolvemos un problema del que depende nuestra dignidad como soldados del Ejército del pueblo y como defensores de la independencia de España.[25]

> (Comrades, I've called you together to see if we can resolve a problem on which depends our dignity as soldiers of the People's Army and as defenders of the independence of Spain.)

The precise duration of the performances which followed upon such emphatic introductions is largely a matter of conjecture since the preserved material comprises individual scripts rather than the structured sequence of an entire programme. Given the differing circumstances of numerous locations and events it is quite probable that performances varied considerably in length. The Guerrillas del Teatro working in urban areas were, at least in the case of those operating in Barcelona during the spring of 1938, often seeking to capture and hold the attention of passers-by, the audience least likely to remain for an entire programme if it was unduly long or presented without the power to sustain interest. The less haphazard atmosphere of a recreational *fiesta* amongst a military audience might, on the other hand, be expected to encourage a more substantial programme, particularly of *teatro de urgencia*. The street performances in Barcelona are characterized by short, intense plays dramatizing an unambiguous idea which is to be sharply etched on the mind of the spectator. By contrast, a play such as Ontañón's *El saboteador*, which lasts about twenty-five minutes, is frequently referred to as a successful element of more structured festivals and benefit performances which were often presented indoors and, presumably, in circumstances more amenable to an extensive, even leisurely, programme intended to raise consciousness and celebrate perceived strengths and achievements.[26]

More certain than the length of performance, however, is the manner in which at least some performances proceeded since, under the general title of *En las trincheras*, four plays were published which were intended to be played as a sequence.[27] The edition offers a valuable insight into the performance style by including the lines to be spoken between the plays, and so it is possible to gain a sense of how, in an apparently informal and natural manner, the spectators were addressed directly while the stage was prepared and the next play introduced. The final moments of the first play, for example, descend towards a moving silence as a peasant who has escaped from the Nationalist zone bemoans the ruined desperation of his village:

> Tristeza, melancolía,
> indignación, odio y lágrimas,
> ésto es un pueblo fascista
> perdido en tierras de España.[28]
>
> (Sadness, melancholy,
> indignation, hatred and tears,
> this is a Fascist village
> lost in the land of Spain.)

As he concludes, the *miliciano* actors embrace the peasant in silence and, as the play ends, one of the actors turns to the audience and moves the performance forward with the words 'ahora, camaradas, conoceréis un boceto dramático titulado "La muerte y la vida". Un momento, sólo un momento' (now, comrades, you're going to get to know a dramatic sketch entitled 'Death and Life'. One moment, just one moment) (p.5). Subsequent references also seem concerned to reassure the audience that the next play is imminent, requiring only 'un instante de espera, tan sólo un instante' (a moment's wait, only a moment) (p.8). There is perhaps a hint here of nervousness on the part of the actors that any interruption to the authoritative flow of action will cause the audience, possibly one in poor circumstances for seeing and hearing well, to lose the focus of attention.[29]

En las trincheras suggests an air of structured informality in the presentation of much *teatro de urgencia*, moving from the rehearsed drama itself to an apparently more spontaneous direct contact with the spectators. It would often undoubtedly have been important that the performers explained their presence, and indeed their own role in the conflict, to audiences who might perhaps take a cynical view of non-combatants urging commitment and sacrifice which it appeared they themselves did not have to make. Mussot's Los Faraones Antifascistas seem sensitive to this when they tell their audience that, although their task has been assigned by the Commissariat,

> si llegara un momento en que hubiera que cambiar la copla por el grito de guerra y la guitarra por el fusil, no dudéis que nosotros cumpliríamos también. (p.1)
>
> (if the moment arrived when it became necessary to exchange the ballad for the battle-cry and the guitar for the rifle, don't doubt that we ourselves would also do our duty.)

The evidence of *En las trincheras* is also important because of the light it sheds on the acting style of performance, not just of the four plays included in the volume but, since these are not untypical, of *teatro de urgencia* in general. There is a strong sense of the actors adopting a powerful, marked attitude, physically and vocally, which contrasts sharply with the lines spoken between plays. The opening of *El pueblo fascista* (*The Fascist Town*), for example, calls for the actor to initiate the performance with 'grandes ademanes de pánico y muestras de terror y ansiedad' (broad gestures of panic and indications of terror and anxiety) (p.2), and the lines have an equally heightened emotionalism: 'compañeros, no disparéis, que vengo huido de los fascistas. He corrido toda la noche. ¡Qué angustia!' (comrades, don't fire, I come fleeing from the Fascists. I've run all night. What pain!) (p.2). Such a style is not infrequent, especially in plays which adopt an exhortational style such as *España no es Austria*, a work which was written and performed within days of the German annexation of Austria.[30] The enormous performance energy of the piece derives from a female Agitator whose harangue of the audience and the characters of the play is relentless in its conviction that Fascism will not triumph in Spain. The anger and the violence of the play's language, and the dragging from the spectators of a performer representing an Italian prisoner of war, calls to mind a lynch mob, the Agitator exploiting the foreign soldier as a figure of hatred for the audience:

¡Sí, camaradas, éste es el invasor, el asesino! ¡El que obedece a un amo criminal, el que no habla nuestra lengua, el brazo ciego de asesinato de Mussolini! ¡Clavaos bien ese nombre en vuestro odio, compañeros! ¡El que no ha tenido ni una vacilación en dejar caer las bombas del crimen sobre Barcelona, porque él viene a eso, a destruir, a matar, a sembrar la ruina, el terror, para que su amo se apodere de nuestra libertad! (pp.45–6)

(Yes, comrades, this is the invader, the murderer! One who obeys a criminal master, one who doesn't speak our language. Mussolini's blind arm of murder! Fasten that name well in your hatred, comrades! One who hasn't had any hesitation in committing the crime of dropping bombs on Barcelona, because he comes for that, to destroy, to kill, to sow ruin, terror, so that his master can take possession of our liberty!)

More predominant, however, would seem to have been an acting style which, although markedly externalized and vocally strong, sought a less forthright tone. The dominant moods are rational, explanatory, especially when *teatro de urgencia* is seeking to offer training perspectives such as in Mussot's *Mi puesto* or to clarify unhelpful perceptions of the war as in *Juan ríe, Juan llora* (*John Laughs, John Cries*). In this latter play, Doña Realidad (Mrs Reality) seeks to balance the equally unhelpful attitudes of defeatism and misplaced optimism with a sober realism designed to offer calming guidance:

Si no toleré amos en 1808 cuando nos lo quería imponer Napoleón, genio de otra especie que Hitler y Mussolini, ¿cómo podéis suponer que hoy los aguantaré? Nos costáis sudores, sangre, dolor hondísimo y un esfuerzo terrible, pero saldremos adelante: ni tan fácilmente como tú dices, Juan Optimista, ni tan difícilmente como supones, Juan Pesimista.[31]

(If I didn't tolerate masters in 1808 when Napoleon, a genius of another kind than Hitler or Mussolini, wanted to impose them on us, how can you suppose that I'll tolerate them today? You cost us sweat, blood, the deepest pain and terrible struggle, but we'll come out ahead: not as easily as you say, John Optimist, nor with such difficulty as you suppose, John Pessimist.)

The simplicity to which so inherently complex a period of history is reduced is intended to reassure and enable daily struggle to be placed in a clarified, purposeful context and, in this respect, the play becomes a paradigm of all *teatro de urgencia*.

Perhaps an important contrast to such a persuasive tone occurred when a characteristic *teatro de urgencia* performance was drawing to a close. Although obviously important that the play should end in a manner as striking as that in which much *teatro de urgencia* begins, the often rather stylized conclusions of many of the plays arise from the emphasis on celebration which is a common feature of the final moments. Generally, the knowledge of insight gained, wrongdoing cast out or victory won returns the play to the mood of *fiesta* which characterizes the wider performance. A *romance* or a song having been used to initiate a play, the ending tends to reiterate it, since the drama has often been structured around demonstrating the meaning or perceived wisdom of the verse.[32] Particularly frequent is the chanting of slogans which presumably brought performers and spectators together in an important act of solidarity. In *Pueblos de vanguardia* (*Vanguard Towns*), for example, the inhabitants of the front-line communities come to realize the role they must play in evacuating injured military personnel, and set about preparing their town to a chorus of 'Todo el pueblo los ayudará ¡Viva el Ejército Popular!' (The whole town will help them. Long live the Popular Army!).[33] *Defendemos la tierra* is even more explicit about the exultant mood which the conclusion of the play is to foster when the actors, shouting the slogan which is the play's title, leave the stage as if, according to the stage directions, they felt upon their faces the beating wings of heroism, and as if carrying aloft the sharp, shining light of their bayonets.

The jubilation and feeling of certain success which characterize this play's conclusion recall the similar mood evoked at the end of *El cuartel* and raise the question of the ways in which *teatro de urgencia* might have progressed in its attempts to construct an active, more effective relationship with its audiences than that which is inherent in proscenium theatres. Balbontín's play was clearly a 'closed' spectacle in which the audience's function is to remain apart from the drama, a passivity which is emphasized by all the other scenic elements which are incorporated into the making of the performance. Yet, a similar assertion might be made with regard to *Defendemos la tierra* and, indeed, other *teatro de urgencia* if we were to consider the spectator as a bystander with all that this implies in terms of detached uninvolvement. As the actors leave the stage, inspired and with bayonets aloft, one wonders whether a viewer's reaction would differ substantially from the spectator of Balbontín's play when, waving flags and chanting Republican slogans, the actors made their exit and the curtain fell. The use of an improvised stage and close physical proximity between actor and spectators cannot, it seems, be deemed the defining characteristics of an active, purposeful relationship between stage and audience.

An illuminating parallel might be found, however, through consideration of a previous Republican attempt to widen the accessibility of theatre, that of the Teatro del Pueblo of Misiones Pedagógicas which toured Spain with a largely Golden Age repertoire during the early years of the Republic.[34] Although this group, like Lorca's La Barraca, utilized similarly portable equipment to that of the Guerrillas del Teatro and played before audiences gathered outdoors in a loose grouping around the stage, a difference occurs when we consider the purpose of the task undertaken by the two groups.[35] For Misiones Pedagógicas the performance was the *goal* of their efforts, whereas for much *teatro de urgencia* the performance was the *means* to achieve highly particular ends. This is a crucial distinction enabling us to see *teatro de urgencia* as a task-orientated drama in which each spectator, representing Republican Spain in microcosm, was to be guided in the direction demanded by the task in question. Balbontín's work is not dissimilar to that of Misiones Pedagógicas in that it sees the audience as, in effect, a crowd. Most *teatro de urgencia*, by contrast, saw in the crowd the possibility of the co-ordinated collective through which victory might be won. Although the spectator of *El cuartel* and *Defendemos la tierra* might seem to share a passive role, in the latter play the spectator's role is only apparently passive, since the drama seeks to mould the spectator, preparing him to act in the sphere of practical reality beyond the drama. In this sense, the 'closed' structure of Balbontín's play has been challenged and with it the traditional function of the spectator.

The new relationship between stage and audience which *teatro de urgencia* encouraged was, therefore, more than a matter of the external technical apparatus of staging. Important though this was in fostering a bond between actors and audience based on physical proximity, a more substantial achievement arose from the different role in the drama which was imposed upon the spectator. Indeed, the conventional notion of action might be said to be absent from *teatro de urgencia* because this aspect of the drama is often handed over to the spectator who is urged to fulfil the task explored by the play after the performance has ended. In essence, *teatro de urgencia* opposed the concept of the spectator and believed, rather, in the participant. The consequences of this for performance dynamics are profound, and it is here that we can most accurately test the extent to which *teatro de urgencia* achieved the kind of audience relationship which Sender had identified as particularly important in challenging what the Left perceived as the inadequacies of the mainstream theatre.

The actively involved model citizen participating not in fictions but in action beyond the confines of the theatre event was the goal of *teatro de urgencia*. The objective was to transform the audience into actors in the widest sense of the word, something which implied the elimination of the boundary between performer and spectator. Paradoxically, however, some of *teatro de urgencia*'s most radical manifestations of actor–audience dynamics are seen to be caught between a desire to facilitate participation and an unwillingness to do so since to surrender control of the performance threatens to undermine the propaganda clarity of the work.

The blurring of the boundary between stage and audience, if not its elimination, is a prominent feature of many *teatro de urgencia* works. In *Cuatro batallones*, for example, the performers on the back of the lorry which served as a stage, are interrupted by the Enlisted Worker in a manner which seems at first to disrupt the rehearsed flow of the dialogue.[36] Similarly, in *Barco de traidores*, a performer in military uniform comes from the audience and, ascending the stage, declares nervously:

> Yo no he subido nunca a más altura que el segundo piso del tranvía ese que va al Tibidabo, y no he *navegao* más que un día en una lancha, y eché la comida de seis meses; pero yo os felicito a los camaradas del Mar y del Aire. (p.29)

> (I've never been higher than the top deck of the tram which goes to Tibidabo, and I've never 'navigated' more than one day on a launch, and I threw up six months' food; but I congratulate the comrades of the Sea and the Air.)

Such a technique diminishes theatricality and enhances the sense of reality so that the spectator's function in the performance undergoes a further change in keeping with that mentioned earlier of encouraging certain behaviour and action in the reality beyond the drama. The metaphorical basis upon which a theatrical event is built is being deliberately undermined and the spectator regards the fiction in a new way, less capable of distinguishing between the real and the feigned. This is particularly prominent in *Lección y escarmiento*, in which a soldier and a worker take issue with a friend over the progress of the war.[37] The friend's lukewarm support for continued resistance is challenged by the other characters' reasoned persuasion but this does not satisfy 'uno del público' (one of the public) who barracks from the audience, persistently shouting slogans in support of the Popular Army and demanding that the friend be incarcerated. At the close of the play 'del público sube un guardia de Asalto al tabladillo' (from the public an Assault Guard mounts the stage) (p.38) and, forcibly dragging the friend from the stage, escorts him away to some presumably unpleasant fate.

In adopting such techniques *teatro de urgencia* wished to enhance the mood of popular feeling appearing to erupt and overwhelm the stage. What had appeared to be a play seemed to have been transformed into a boisterous political meeting in which all present were able to contribute. This attempt to fuse spectator and action is so heavily marked in Aub's *¿Qué has hecho hoy para ganar la guerra? (What Have You Done Today to Win the War?)* that the audience cannot be certain that it is in fact watching a drama.[38] The play begins in an abrupt fashion with the Woman, a figure dressed in black, asking the assembled crowd what practical meaning the slogan 'hay que ganar la guerra' (we must win the war) holds for them and what they have done that day to contribute to victory. The other performers are amongst the spectators, indistinguishable from them, and the dialogue which ensues between them and the Woman is consciously structured so as to create the impression that a spontaneous, real exchange is occurring. Initially, the script capitalizes on the hesitant response to the question which has been posed and, in teacher-like fashion, the Woman wonders whether the spectators are asleep or whether perhaps shame has stuck their lips together while they bite their tongues. Focusing her attention, in apparently random fashion, on a girl in the crowd, the Woman addresses the question directly to the figure of the Young Woman and a frosty exchange occurs which reinforces the spectators' perception that, although the external trappings of theatre seem to be present, the actual drama has not yet begun:

MUJER   Tú, mocita, ¿dónde trabajas?
MOZA   ¿Y a usted qué le importa?

MUJER	A mí, Juana Herrero Martín, nada; a mí, española, mucho.
MOZA	¡Vamos, anda! (p.287).

(WOMAN	You, young lady, where do you work?
YOUNG WOMAN	And what does it matter to you?
WOMAN	To me, Juana Herrero Martín, not at all; to me, Spaniard, a great deal.
YOUNG WOMAN	Come off it!)

The spirited defence which the Young Woman makes of her contribution to the war effort produces apparently spontaneous reaction from the audience in the form of a performer, designated as 'El del olé' (The one who shouts *olé*), whose vociferous support of the Young Woman leads to his being summoned to the stage to answer the same question as has been put to her. Again, his reluctance to ascend the stage increases the sense of an outdoor meeting, an atmosphere which is sustained throughout the rest of the play as further characters come forward with increasing confidence to discuss their own daily commitment to the war effort. The figure of the Young Lad, for example, shouts from amongst the crowd that his desire to contribute to the war as a pilot is frustrated by his family's wish that he continue at school. Unsurprisingly, through the Woman's admiring approval, this elicits the characteristically fervent Republican response to education:

Tus padres tienen razón. Debes estudiar: ésa es tu arma; en ese ejército estás alistado: ahí debes continuar; en ningún otro sitio cumplirás mejor con tu obligación. (p.290)

(Your parents are right. You must study: that's your weapon; you're enlisted in that army: you should continue there; nowhere else will you better comply with your duty.)

The attempt which Aub's play makes to destroy the boundary between actor and audience is, however much it may appear otherwise, a complete failure. Since the spectator is deprived of the possibility of viewing the play as a play no relationship can exist between audience and actors as conscious elements of a theatrical event. The cul-de-sac which the play represents as an attempt to erase the line between stage and audience can be perceived through noting the highly interrogative nature of the play. Questioning, not only in the title of the work, is a persistent feature as the Woman attempts to initiate a discussion with the 'audience'. These questions, however, are not asked without certainty as to the desired response being given since this might damage reception of the propaganda message which is intended. A contradiction is inherent in the play between the desire to invite the spectator to become a participant and fear that he will participate 'wrongly'. Such temerity leads Aub to construct the play as the *appearance* of spontaneity, excluding the genuine spectator from taking part in real debate through questions which will be answered as part of the drama's unpredictable exploration.

Aub's refusal to surrender the play to the spectators, thereby enabling them to fuse with the actors and become participants, makers of the drama, is in striking contrast to *Mi puesto,* in which, unlike much *teatro de urgencia,* the spectators speak with their own voices rather than have this function delegated to a character who speaks apparently on their behalf.[39] Unlike Aub's play, too, *Mi puesto* draws very clear attention to itself as drama, particularly through the prologue delivered without 'afectación, de la manera más sencilla, más natural' (affectation, in the simplest, most natural manner) (p.1). Mussot's instructions on how to speak the prologue indicate a desire to avoid an over-declamatory, perhaps histrionic style, seeking to break down conventional expectations on the part of the audience of what kind of play they are about to see:

> La comedia que vais a presenciar no se parece en nada a las comedias que hasta hoy habéis visto: la niña cursi que sufre porque su papá la tiene destinada a un hombre rico mientras ella se muere de amor por otro macho que no tiene un real. ¡Qué comedia! ¡Qué argumento! (p.1)
>
> (The play you're going to observe isn't anything like the plays you've seen before today: the pretentious girl who suffers because her daddy has her destined for a rich man while she's dying of love for another man who hasn't a penny. What a play! What a plot!)

The conscious recall of the kind of theatre which had so frustrated many writers on the Left before and during the war is made in order to establish a contrast with what the Guerrillas troupe is seeking to attempt. The aim, the spectators are informed, is that in the ensuing drama the audience will see itself represented, and that its problems, felt and lived daily, will be posed for consideration. Significantly, the theatre is described as belonging to its audience, of being 'carne, sangre y nervios' (flesh, blood and nerves) (p.3) of the spectators, a statement which throws into sharp relief the situation in ¿*Qué has hecho?* where 'ownership' of the drama remains firmly in the hands of the author and the performers. Whereas Aub's work had also very consciously reduced the spectators' sense that they were witnessing a play, Mussot's prologue emphasizes quite the opposite when, at its close, the actor turns to the other actors gathered in the playing area and, remarking '¿No empezáis, compañeros?' (Won't you begin, comrades?) (p.3), signals the start of the action.

In keeping with the notion that the spectators should see themselves represented in the drama, the play begins with a dialogue between two soldiers in which the First Soldier is asked to write a letter dictated by an illiterate comrade who wants to send news home that he is safe and well. He agrees unwillingly, chastising the Second Soldier for not taking advantage of the opportunity presented by army life to learn to write. The letter, however, becomes the cause of a dispute between the two when the Second Soldier declares: 'lo único que me tiene disgustao es que no dan permiso ni a Dios y eso no creo que esté ni medio bien' (the only thing that's got me annoyed is that they don't give out leave passes, not even to God, and that I don't believe is even half OK) (p.5), and his comrade cautions against writing this down in case 'tu madre lee eso y cree que los Jefes obran caprichosamente' (your mother reads that and believes that the leaders operate capriciously) (p.5). In the ensuing discussion emotional bonds are pitted against sense of duty as each seeks to explain why his viewpoint is correct. For the Second Soldier five months without leave is an unreasonable strain both on himself and his family, but his comrade recalls the Moroccan war in which his brother 'dos veces sufrió el paludismo, un balazo recibió y ni un día le concedieron de permiso para abrazar a sus padres' (twice suffered from malaria, he was shot and they didn't grant him a single day's leave to embrace his parents) (p.6). Countering that such deprivation was a feature of earlier army life and ought not to characterize the Popular Army, the Second Soldier is unmoved, and this provokes a passionate call from the other soldier who urges him to see that 'no debíamos tener otro pensamiento que ganar la guerra cuanto antes ni otro deber que dar cuanto esté en nosotros' (we mustn't have any other thought than winning the war as soon as possible, nor any other duty than giving everything which is within us) (p.7). For him the Second Soldier fails to sense the honour of belonging to what he describes as the 'Ejército de la Libertad' (Army of Liberty) (p.8) and their discussion reaches an impasse.

The prologue's emphasis on 'ownership' of the performance is now tested since the First Soldier consults the audience by asking, unlike Aub's Woman figure, questions to which there is no scripted answer. The spectator is invited to cross the boundary of the playing area and contribute to the course of the drama when the First Soldier, remaining in role but breaking the action, addresses the spectators and asks them if they agree with his viewpoint. At this point in the script Mussot inserts advice to the actors that, although it is to be hoped that the audience will agree with the First Soldier, means must be adopted to ensure it happens. The prospect of a debate has arisen in which viewpoints can be multiplied, perspectives extended or anecdotes offered. A list of further questions is included in the script, some, all or none of which were probably used depending on the precise reaction of different audiences. There is, however, perhaps a tentative edge to some of these questions which suggests a nervousness on the writer's part that, as Aub similarly feared, the spectators might participate 'wrongly'. It is difficult, for example, to regard Mussot's fourth suggested question as anything but a leading one:

> ¿Verdad, compañeros, que si el Fascismo triunfara en nuestro país, nos convertiría en esclavos, destrozaría nuestros hogares, deshonraría a nuestras mujeres, mataría a nuestros hijos? (p.9)

> (Isn't it true, comrades, that if Fascism were to triumph in our country, it would turn us into slaves, destroy our homes, dishonour our women, kill our children?)

Up to this point the play has not sought to remove the distinction between the theatrical and the real; rather, it has brought each into fruitful conflict with the other. The real world of the soldier audience has been invited into the fictional world of the stage soldiers. Now, however, the relationship begins to blur as an actor, dressed as a soldier and, therefore, purposely indistinguishable from the other spectators, emerges from the audience and asks whether he may attempt to make the Second Soldier understand his comrade's viewpoint. Prior to this the audience has been invited to cross the boundary between it and the actors only by making verbal contributions. The actor who has so far watched the play now brings spectators with him into the performance area by selecting various soldiers from among the audience: 'ven tú, y tú, y tú y vosotros dos, y tú también y aquél, y ese otro y tú . . .' (come along you, and you, and you and you two, and you as well and that one, and that other one and you . . .) (p.10). The aim of the assembled group is, asserts the actor, to teach the Second Soldier by making him repeat the words spoken by the spectators in answer to the actor's questions. Mussot is at pains to stress in the script's instructions to the actor that his questioning must elicit the fullest possible response but, as before, the fear of inappropriate participation is felt and the actor is forewarned of the need, if necessary, to make the soldier 'comprender el error explicándole el alcance de la pregunta' (understand the mistake, explaining to him the scope of the question) (p.12). The resulting next stage of the play is in sharp contrast to all other *teatro de urgencia* as the spectators/participants offer the lines which the actor is to speak. The image is a powerful one, even despite what could be seen as Mussot's reluctance to risk questions which might lead the play in directions not desired by the writer. To the genuinely speculative question of whether liberty is more important than life must, therefore, be added the simplistic: '¿tú qué eres, fascista o antifascista?' (you, what are you, Fascist or anti-Fascist?) (p.12). As the questioning proceeds the spectators occupying the performance area become teachers of the actor, providing script which is created anew with each performance. To this already radical alteration of traditional theatrical relationships is added that of those spectators who remain outside the playing area for whom the impression created is that the audience and the actors have entirely reversed roles.

As the real seems to have superseded the theatrical in the play, in turn this is reversed when, at the end of the Second Soldier's lesson, two women enter hastily and in distress. Having endured the violent destruction of their village by the Nationalists they have fled and finally come to find refuge in the Republican encampment. As they are comforted the Second Soldier recognizes one of the women as his sister and learns of the horrific experience to which she and the rest of his family have been subjected. Left alone together, the Second

Soldier confronts the meaning of the lesson he has been taught and articulates his understanding of the need to work ceaselessly to defeat the forces which have raped his sister and forced her to watch the murder of her husband. Summoning his fellow soldiers, both performers and spectators, he declares that 'mi puesto está en las trincheras' (my place is in the trenches) and makes a solemn promise:

> Mi deber es combatir sin descanso, mi obligación es la de vengar a las madres, a los niños asesinados, a las mujeres violadas, a nuestros muertos, a todos, a todos los antifascistas. (p.24)

> (My duty is to fight without rest, my obligation is that of avenging the mothers, the murdered children, the raped women, our dead, all, all the anti-Fascists.)

Following upon this conclusion to the performance might have been that intended sense of common purpose and collective achievement which had been to a large extent enacted in the drama itself. The final moments of the play see audience and actors united onstage as participants in an enterprise in which all have actively shared, the play's resolution having been, to an extent, shaped by the spectators themselves. In most theatrical performance the foremost element in determining the course of the action or the content of the play is the actors and, controlling them, the author. Authority, as it were, lies with the text. To a degree, however, Mussot relinquishes this authority and attempts, as the play's prologue suggests, to offer a kind of drama which is new to both performers and audiences alike. Nor is this innovation, he suggests, confined solely to the theatre, since the war must be viewed as the opportunity to overturn all previously accepted notions and uses of social and cultural life 'desde la raíz a la cúspide' (from the root to the cusp) (p.1). Such thinking, and the resulting drama, enable *Mi puesto* to be viewed as an aspect of that interest in proletarian literature which had been prominent in the pre-war period and which wished to encourage cultural forms emerging from the proletarian class itself rather than those created on their behalf by members of other social classes.[40]

As we have earlier noted, since the early years of the century the Spanish Left had perceived social transformation in terms of individual empowerment not only through the alteration of economic relationships, crucial though this was, but through the acquisition of education and culture. Ownership of the means of economic production was an essential aspect of the socialists' view of their task, but allied to this was ownership of other means of production, including that of culture. The socialization of the Madrid theatres in the late summer of 1936 illustrates such an attempt at ownership, which was intended to deliver into the hands of the *pueblo* the means by which the working class could express itself through art seized from bourgeois control. That this process of take-over largely failed ensured that the drama presented in the capital during the war did not effect any radical alteration of the relationships involved in theatrical performance. By contrast, much *teatro de urgencia*, as an element of the Left's efforts to achieve profound social and cultural transformation, sought to transform such relationships, and in *Mi puesto* what Mussot most significantly achieves through the surrender of the actors' and author's control is the transfer to the spectator of the means of theatrical production.

Mussot's achievement in this respect is considerable and indicates the extent to which, during the three years of the Civil War, *teatro de urgencia* engaged with the political and aesthetic issues involved in developing a role for the spectator which would be active and participative, one which would be consistent with that sought for the working class in the socialist view of the ideal society. On the other hand, despite being the surviving script which extends furthest in its exploration of the fusion of performer and spectator, *Mi puesto* also exhibits important limitations which reveal inherent contradictions between propaganda and participation. Examination of the varying performance features of plays such as *El cuartel* and more radical manifestations of *teatro de urgencia* clearly illustrates the extent to which the genre achieved a significantly different relationship with its audience. The different circumstances of the proscenium and the *tablado* or improvised stages, allied to the varying perceptions of the propaganda task under consideration, engineered changed roles for the audiences. The particularly significant role which Mussot allots to the audience of *Mi puesto*, however, is predicated upon the notion announced in the prologue that the performance is 'vuestro teatro' (your theatre) (p.3), that it forms part of the root-and-branch social and cultural transformation to which the prologue also refers. The various mechanisms built into the script which are designed to rectify the spectators' 'errors' indicate, however, the extent to which ownership of the performance, although undoubtedly surrendered, can easily be regained by the performers through Mussot's interpolation within the text of controlling devices.

Significantly, therefore, at the same time as Mussot achieves his declared goal as a socialist dramatist, namely, to transform the theatre into a forum in which reality would be shaped and perhaps altered by the spectator, he falters. The radical dramatic form he creates cannot be allowed to achieve the ends which it logically seeks to pursue because the needs of propaganda remain paramount and the script's controlling devices will be called into play to ensure that the spectators' theatre is used, ultimately, in line with Republican orthodoxy. A useful parallel can be found by comparing *teatro de urgencia* with Brecht's early *Lehrstücke* experiments. Brecht, too, had rejected traditional audience relationships in the search for a new role for the spectator and, in the 'learning plays' of the early 1930s such as, for example, *He Who Says Yes*, had developed a dramatic form which views the spectator's function in a manner not unlike that of Mussot.[41] Both desired to liberate the spectator as viewer but, whereas Brecht liberates the audience so that it can exercise critical judgements, Mussot is, ultimately, only prepared to liberate it if the performance can still guarantee adherence. It is interesting to speculate how very different *Mi puesto* might have been had its structure been available to groups such as Nosotros since, in an agitational context, its radicalism of form would have been unhindered and the notion of ownership been capable of more sustained exploration.

Despite its limitations, however, I would suggest that *Mi puesto* is a particularly significant example of revolutionary drama, one which, although almost unknown, should be considered alongside the well-researched Russian and German innovations of the earlier part of the century by virtue of its shared concern with questions of audience reception and its attempt to find strikingly effective solutions to the problem of how to create utilitarian dramatic forms. The play demonstrates the great extent to which *teatro de urgencia* provides evidence of an important level of experiment with regard to the nature of performance and does so to a degree which contradicts the widespread view of the wartime years as theatrically insignificant. Diffuse and scarcely recorded as it was, the propaganda drama displayed, in some of its manifestations, the emergence of a new theatricality. The stage was reassessed, its purpose and potential being tested in directions which were, by virtue of the circumstances of war, often uncertain or unclear but which might, had the conflict resolved itself differently, have yielded important theoretical lessons applicable in the development of a post-war theatre. As we saw earlier, Marrast observed that, by and large, the wartime period was a failure in terms of radical theatre initiatives. The basis of his judgement was that the repertoire of the commercial theatres did not really change in keeping with the ambitious political and cultural aspirations of many on the Left. His view ignores, however, the degree of experimentation represented by the *teatro de urgencia* which occurred outside the mainstream theatre context. If Marrast could have enjoyed access to some of the texts of this *teatro de urgencia* he would surely have revised his assessment and recognized the significant success it achieved in terms of the experimental nature of performance. Mussot's *Mi puesto*, in particular, represents, I believe, an aesthetic breakthrough for agitprop in its Spanish context, an achievement which can only be evaluated since the reappearance of the text itself. Marrast's research has been fundamental and scrupulous in reconstituting much of the theatrical history of the Civil War. His work lacked, however, a textual orientation which might have deepened his judgement. This crucial dimension can now be addressed through a consideration of the plays themselves, so that a detailed picture can be furnished of the nature of the propaganda to which citizens were exposed through drama.

~ 4 ~
Attacking the Enemy

Wartime propaganda tends to conjure images of a highly co-ordinated state bureaucracy utilizing its power to mould numerous aspects of a population's likely responses to conflict. Recent studies of the subject in relation to the First and Second World Wars provide ample reason for such images, demonstrating, for example, how, while the Civil War was in progress in Spain, the British authorities undertook a review of the propaganda strategies it would be necessary to adopt with regard to civilian morale in the increasingly likely event of a new European war.[1] Such centralized control of propaganda was not, however, a predominant feature of the Civil War. Different social, economic and cultural circumstances applied and the military histories of the two countries ensured that differing attitudes emerged towards wartime propaganda.[2] For *teatro de urgencia*, like a number of other Republican propaganda initiatives, this occasioned that sense of improvisation and uncertainty which we have noted earlier. No single authority was established to control propaganda output, a reflection of the strengths of the various political elements which constituted the Republican military and political machine. This is not to imply that propaganda did not play a prominent role in the Civil War, but to suggest that its role was a diffuse one, characterized by the independent adoption of numerous strategies by a plethora of organizations.[3] If the Second World War was marked by the radio as a principal means of propaganda, perhaps the Civil War was distinguished by what Abella describes as 'la batalla de la tinta' (the battle in print), the many newspapers, battalion flysheets, posters and wall newspapers which transmitted news and opinion along the various fronts and throughout the rearguard.[4] The propaganda drama formed a part of this broad effort, contributing with considerable variety of style and content as demanded by the specific task with which it was confronted.

In tracing how *teatro de urgencia* emerged as a genre capable of achieving such a task, a prominent feature underpinning the discussion thus far has been the commitment shown by the Left in the decades prior to the Civil War to the notion of individual empowerment through educational progress. Characteristic socialist undertakings such as the creation of workers' schools, the cultural programmes of the *casas del pueblo* (socialist community centres) and the campaigns against illiteracy were made in the belief that such measures would encourage rational, critically conscious citizens who would display commitment to ideals of justice, equality and progress. Abella demonstrates how such activities were strikingly echoed during the conflict in the numerous initiatives of government, trade union and political groups to satisfy what he describes as the 'anhelo salido de la masa' (the desire coming from the masses) (p.285) for access to educational and cultural opportunities long the preserve of a privileged minority. Cultura Popular, for example, an organization which, amongst other tasks, initiated literacy campaigns amongst Republican troops, encouraged the notion of the independent, aware individual through the use of posters bearing slogans such as 'el soldado del Ejército del pueblo debe estar cada día más capacitado – pide un libro en la biblioteca' (the soldier of the People's Army must every day be more able – request a book from the library) (p.289). In similar fashion, the CCT stressed the importance of encouraging workers to seek opportunities through which they might independently construct 'el edificio de su cultura' (the edifice of their culture).[5]

In theatrical terms, however, we have also analysed the contradiction which arises between ideals such as those outlined above and the view of the audience as 'material' to be led towards the affirmation of particular values or the endorsement of certain viewpoints. Mussot's ambivalent attitude towards the spectator-participant of *Mi puesto* clearly demonstrates such a clash, the notion of 'vuestro teatro' (your theatre) being true, ultimately, only insofar as the audience responds to the play in a manner approved by Republican orthodoxy. Monleón, basing his views on a very limited number of scripts, tends to suggest that, rather than propaganda, *teatro de urgencia* should be viewed as a teaching theatre and that it arose from the commitment of writers such as those in the Alliance to educate an entire people.[6] There is undoubtedly some truth in this view but it is also true, none the less, that, as the example of Mussot demonstrates, the exigencies of propaganda would always be paramount and the idea of the individual being impartially taught and invited to formulate independently made critical judgements, must be treated with caution. It is true that Aparicio's assessment of the lost play *Fortificación* does indicate a degree of problem-solving and critical judgement on the spectator's part,[7] as does ¡Hacia la victoria! with its analysis of the appropriate reaction when, in the heat of battle, retreat seems the only possible course of action. Yet these are exceptions to the rule that *teatro de urgencia* was a propaganda theatre which, while it did encourage the spectator to make genuine, rational decisions about issues raised through drama, was characterized to a much greater extent by its appeal to the spectators' emotions. In this it was consistent with any political propaganda, combining language and image in ways designed to communicate an emotionally appealing message whose veracity is less important than its impact upon the viewer or reader.

Such an approach was energetically adopted in *teatro de urgencia*, concerned as it was to present to its audience a view of the enemy against whom it was exhorted to struggle. This fundamental task of wartime propaganda was achieved through the creation of a compelling emotional image of Spain as a maternal figure threatened by a range of powerful and ruthless enemies. In Herrera Petere's *La voz de España* (*The Voice of Spain*), for example, the figure of Spain implores the help of her sons, reminding them of her role in their lives as beneficient, loving provider:

> soy vuestra madre española
> entraña de vuestro llanto,
> la leal, la liberada
> de opresores y malvados,
> la que a sus hijos reserva
> fábricas, cosechas, campos,
> cultura e independencia,
> alto y seguro salario.[8]

> (I am your Spanish mother,
> heart of your weeping,
> loyal, free
> from oppressors and the wicked,
> the one who stores up for her children
> factories, harvests, fields,
> culture and independence,
> a high and secure wage.)

Seeking to destroy the motherland was a coalition of reactionary interests whose composition reflected the uncompromising ideological divide which had given rise to war. Sheltering behind an arrogant military caste was to be found a conspiracy of clerical, capitalist and Falangist forces which sought to ingratiate itself with the German and Italian military for whom theatrical propaganda reserved its most bitter scorn.

The images of the enemy which are presented in *teatro de urgencia* are largely consistent with those found in other forms of Republican propaganda. One has the impression that, in the absence of a central controlling organization, certain views filtered through channels such as ballads, posters, newspapers and popular imagination and gradually deposited pictures of the enemy which, with considerable propaganda effectiveness, became the 'truth' – rather than highly selective versions of it.[9] This was particularly true of the Republic's desire to portray the war not as civil strife but as a foreign invasion. German and Italian Fascism persistently recur as the explanation of the conflict. In Bleiberg's *Sombras de héroes*, for example, a Nazi officer confides to his Italian counterpart that access to Basque steel and the opportunity to test the efficacy of military hardware motivate his country's 'acción colonizadora' (colonizing action).[10] It was perhaps inevitable that *teatro de urgencia* should attempt to offer such a gloss on the conflict since it not only appealed to patriotic emotion, but also avoided inappropriate emphasis on a conflict which had divided families physically and politically and urged citizens to take up arms against their compatriots.

As a consequence of this desire to explain hostilities as the ruthless cynicism of outsiders manipulating a discredited Spanish officer class, *teatro de urgencia* sought to portray the ordinary enemy soldier as a confused, often unwilling victim of the uprising who had been, by and large, coerced into service. Lacking the crusading optimism generally so characteristic of the Republican soldier, the Nationalist equivalent is afflicted by uncertainty. Even combatants traditionally as committed as the Carlist *requetés* are seen in *Amanecer* (*Dawn*) as weary and uninterested. Standing guard while another cold dawn breaks over the trenches, the First Requeté's spirit is, in effect, broken and, longing only 'que termine esto como sea' (that this ends however it will), his mind dwells on the security of home.[11] The notion of the reluctant conscript, caught up in hostilities in which he does not feel involved, is given great prominence in *Defendemos la tierra* through the figure of García, a soldier who has passed over to Republican lines and is being escorted to brigade headquarters by two *milicianos*, Juan and Pedro.[12] The anonymous author of the play is at pains to contrast the military correctness of the Loyalist soldiers' uniforms, their 'casco, correaje y bayonetas agudas' (helmet, belt and sharp bayonets) (p.79), with the Nationalist García's 'ropas sucias y a jirones' (dirty, tattered clothes) (p.79) and his unshaven, unwashed appearance. Invited to tell the story of his treatment behind enemy lines, García paints a picture of the ordinary Spaniard's brutal exploitation by a largely foreign military hierarchy imposing its rule through whip and pistol. Failing to answer his captain, Comeloni, in Italian, García has been subjected to 'fustazos hasta que pronuncié unas palabras a su gusto' (lashes until I pronounced some words to his liking) (p.81). His image of army life is that of soldiers treated as a herd of swine, driven at the whim of 'oficialillos fascistas' (jumped-up Fascist officers) (p.80) for whom any error or suspicious behaviour merits the firing squad.

García's emotive description of his and his fellow conscripts' daily life as 'aquel infierno' (that hell) (p.80) encapsulates the view of the Nationalist zone which *teatro de urgencia* sought to foster. The rebel soldier is seen as a soul in hell, deprived of the spiritual and physical comfort of the Republican paradise. Aub pursues such an idea through another character given the commonplace surname of García when, in *Pedro López García*, a work significantly subtitled 'auto' (allegorical religious play), he presents the Nationalist soldier as a kind of Everyman figure journeying towards the recognition, presented in strikingly Christian terms, that the true Spain is a kind of Eden which lies behind the trenches which confront him and to which he ultimately crosses.[13] As in *La voz de España*, the image of Spain as a maternal figure is keenly felt, here mingled with a sense of divine power, as the figure of the Land appears, Madonna-like, before Pedro as he stands guard and, urging him to abandon 'el fusil que te han dado para asesinarme' (the rifle that they have given you to murder me) (p.98), presents herself not only as his mother but as all that exists, 'el Principio y el Fin' (the Beginning and the End) (p.97). First performed in front of a church altar, the play's sense of the soldier ultimately moving towards fusion with a god is powerful, a feeling which is enhanced by Pedro, having left behind the Nationalist trenches, calling through a loudspeaker to urge similar action from his comrades. It is as though a Republican deity, a trinity comprising land, mother and nation, speaks as a disembodied voice imploring those souls in limbo to abandon their hopeless state:

¿Me escuchas Juan Chamorro, y vosotros Rafael González, Luis Hernández Prieto, Vicente Marco, y tú Antonio Zabalbide? ¿Me oís, españoles? La tierra de España es nuestra y su aire también. (p.100)

(Can you hear me, Juan Chamorro, and you, Rafael González, Luis Hernández Prieto, Vicente Marco and you, Antonio Zabalbide? Can you hear me, Spaniards? Spain's land is ours and its air too.)

In making this call Pedro seeks to draw attention to himself as a representative figure, indistinguishable from the individuals he names except insofar as his suffering in the Nationalist trenches has led him to move beyond considerations of strategic survival. Overcoming his earlier fear that in attempting escape he will be shot by other conscripts, Pedro slips over the parapet and crosses to what the Land has convinced him is his true brothers' trench. His belief that he will be killed by 'ese que vigila allí para que yo no pase, igual que yo le vigilo para que él no lo haga' (the one who stands guard there so that I cannot pass, just as I watch him so that he may not do it) (p.97), is shown to be misplaced as his fellow guard, relieved that he too no longer has to conceal his true allegiance, follows Pedro's example and, declaring, 'ya podía haberlo dicho antes. Con el miedo que yo tenía de que fuese fascista de verdad' (he could have said so before. The fear I had that he was really a Fascist) (p.99), crosses to join him behind Republican lines.

The image of the Nationalist soldier as a soul deprived of the sight of heaven is richly explored in Alberti's *Cantata de los héroes y la fraternidad de los pueblos* (*Cantata of the Heroes and the Fraternity of Peoples*),[14] in which Spain is again presented as an Eden, this time corrupted by 'la traición y la desgracia' (treason and disgrace) (p.185) of the military rebellion. Like García in *Defendemos la tierra* who tended horses before the outbreak of war, and the shepherd Pedro López García, the rebel soldier of the *Cantata* recalls the peacetime years of the Republic as a secure and perhaps idyllic time before:

> . . . Me arrancaron,
> a empujones y al alba, de mi aldea.
> Aquí está mi fusil. Mejor andaba
> con mi cayado tras de mis ovejas. (p.187)

> (... They uprooted me,
> at daybreak, pushing me from my village.
> Here is my rifle. It was better when I walked
> with my crook behind my sheep.)

For Spain, again presented on-stage as a Madonna-like figure eliciting worship and homage from the other characters, this son has been cast into a barren landscape of waste and disease:

> ... los tíficos pantanos,
> los pálidos, febriles lodazales,
> las pestíferas charcas macilentas,
> los vengativos, despiadados mares. (p.189)

> (... the diseased swamps,
> the pale, feverish quagmires,
> the stinking, putrid pools,
> the vengeful, savage seas.)

The sense of a tortured soul suffering in some Dantesque region of hell is powerful, as is Alberti's ritual unification of it with the Republican deity through the gradual insight of the rebel soldier. Standing before Spain, in whose throat he has caused 'un llorar de cadenas' (a lament of chains) (p.187), the soldier initially expresses only confusion and frustrated anger as Spain rejects his desire to serve her through serving 'esos que junto a ti me pisotean' (those who, together with you, trample me) (p.189). The entrance of International Brigade soldiers to place their banners at the feet of Spain, and the subsequent ritual handing of these to soldiers of the Popular Army by the Spanish Women, cause the rebel soldier to be stricken with remorse, and give him the revelatory insight which enables him to glimpse the means by which he may be reunited with Spain. Kneeling for absolution, he is able, like the returned prodigal son, to recognize the error of his ways:

> ¡Qué crimen! ¡Qué dolor! ¡Ay, qué engañosas
> tinieblas en mis ojos me pusieron!
> Tú eres la sola España verdadera,
> la de los españoles verdaderos. (p.197)

> (What a crime! What pain! Oh, what deceiving
> darkness they put in my eyes!
> You alone are the true Spain,
> the land of true Spaniards.)

Tearing from his uniform the insignia of the enemy, the 'tristes cadenas que me han puesto' (sad chains into which they have put me) (p.197), he reaches towards Spain, seeking reincorporation into the lines of *milicianos* and, on being reintegrated, is able to declare joyfully, '¡soy campesino!' (I am a peasant!) (p.198).

Such a portrayal of the rebel soldier emphasizes the notion of a composite character representing various aspects of the same fundamental experience, and thus offers an image of the soldier as an allegorical figure undertaking the journey of the erring soul towards the path of righteousness represented by escape to the Republican zone. Aub draws further attention to this idea when the Nationalist Sergeant who conscripts Pedro López García reveals that he too is called Pedro. In a subsequent parallel to Pedro's awakening of faith in the Republic, the Sergeant is seen to struggle with his conscience's guilt, troubled persistently, for example, by the bombardments of Madrid in which he has participated, and the gruesome memory of 'aquellas hileras de niños destrozados' (those lines of annihilated children) (p.96). Initially, however, the Sergeant is portrayed in terms which associate him with the devil as, in the angry whirlwind of his arrival to demand food and recruits, his jaws seem, in the words of one character, to emit flames. Ignoring the angry pleas of Pedro's mother, he orders Pedro from the hut to join his new comrades and, in a fast-moving, violent scene, he responds to the Mother's anger at the loss of her son by ordering her execution. As she is dragged from the hut and shot, Aub suggests two means by which the actor can portray the crisis of conscience which now besets the Sergeant. Either the figure of the Masked Man is to enter the scene dressed in the *mono* uniform of the militias, or the Sergeant actor is to speak the lines as a monologue. Both means serve to emphasize further the idea of a single unified figure at war with itself as the soldier struggles to repress the moral repugnance felt by his 'true' nature as a Spaniard:

> Dicen que tus abuelos mataban infieles en nombre de una majestad católica, eso tenía cierta grandeza. Hoy son los infieles los que matan españoles por defender unos privilegios y la posesión de las tierras. (p.90)

(They say that your grandparents killed unbelievers in the name of a Catholic majesty, that had a certain grandeur. Today it's the unbelievers who kill Spaniards to defend some privileges and the possession of land.)

The depth of the Sergeant's confusion is such that, in an image consciously reminiscent of the entrenched divisions of the war, he seeks to shrug off the masked figure's solemn insistence on facing the meaning of one's actions, by asserting, 'Levanto una pared entre tú y yo' (I'm raising a wall between you and me) (p.91). Yet the futility of this attempted dichotomy of the self is sharply felt as his mind fails to suppress the memory of his most recent violence:

> ... de aquellas niñas del otro día y de aquel panadero más blanco que la harina desparramada a su alrededor ... y de aquella retahíla interminable de la plaza de Badajoz. (p.91)

> (... of those children the other day and of that baker, whiter than the flour spilt all around him ... and of that endless stream in the square at Badajoz.)

The soldier is again reminded that he is a lost soul since 'aquello era el infierno' (that was hell) (p.91), a judgement which captures the religious struggle between good and evil contained in the enemy soldier's character, and rendered poignant by the masked figure's enquiry whether the Sergeant is a Catholic. Affirming this serves further to aggravate his conscience as his *alter ego* ponders whether the rats will gnaw the fingers of Pedro's murdered mother in the name of God. In frustration and fury, he seeks to break free of his conscience by firing his pistol at the Masked Man who, unflinching, pities the Sergeant as a 'pobre tonto' (poor fool) (p.91).

In the second scene of the play the moral and spiritual anguish of the Sergeant, now promoted to *alférez* (Second Lieutenant), is unabated. His mind broods on the 'mil bajezas' (thousand despicable acts) (p.95) of which he fears he is capable and, haunting him, is the guilt-laden question of how he has so easily murdered children in the name of war and yet would shrink from any such action with regard to his own family. He senses no way out of his dilemma but, as he watches his namesake abandon his post and cross to the Republican lines, he fails to use his pistol to prevent him. Shrugging his shoulders, he remains with his head between his hands. In the final moments of the play, however, as two officers with marked foreign accents order an artillery attack, the Sergeant seems to go further in endorsing the soldiers' reluctance to comply and, as the play ends with him reaching for his pistol, it is deliberately unclear on whom he intends to use it. Aub's purpose is to utilize the experience of the Sergeant to create in the *auto* the sense of a soul so deeply sinful that restoration to a state of grace is a more troubled and painful process than is encountered in other portrayals of enemy soldiers. The Sergeant is thus seen as more culpable in his actions, more of a willing participant, and is therefore required to suffer greater anguish before the prospect of absolution. The end of the play emphasizes this by failing to resolve the dilemma for the character; indeed it is possible that, in drawing his pistol, suicide is intended rather than some redeeming act of rebellion. The prospect of this ultimate act, which would certainly prevent unification of the soul with God, demonstrates how the enemy soldier may condemn himself through a despair which arises from the absence of self-worth consequent upon his lack of integration with the Republic.

By contrast, the unification of the enemy soldier with what is described in the *Cantata* as 'la sola España verdadera' (the only true Spain) (p.197) delivers him to paradise through a peaceful death at the end of a life which has seen him as master of his own destiny. This idea is stressed by Aub in the interlude which divides the scenes of *Pedro López García*, through the figure of the fast-talking, chirpily confident Merchant who, directly addressing the audience, attempts to auction to the highest bidder what remains of Spain after the Germans and Italians have taken all that they desire. A Nationalist soldier interrupts, enquiring whether his home town of Rivadesella has yet been sold and, despite the satirical humour which Aub predominantly intends, the soldier's reasons for wishing to buy it reveal with great poignancy the deep bond which *teatro de urgencia* emphasized between the misguided enemy soldier and the homeland it presented him as seeking to destroy:

> Quiero comprarme a mí mismo para ser libre e independiente y acabar mi vida tranquilo, tumbado frente al mar, en mi tierra, bajo mi cielo envuelto en mi viento, dueño de mis destinos. (p.93)
>
> (I want to buy it for myself, to be free and independent and to end my life peacefully, lying down facing the sea, on my land, beneath my sky, shrouded in my wind, master of my destiny.)

Death is presented almost as an idyll, an immersion into the earth, not just physical but as a union with spiritual forces which have shaped and nourished the soldier's life. The persistent image of hell which characterizes the rebel soldiers' experience is abandoned, replaced by a sense of satisfied release and self-worth, and recalls the frustrated desire of Bleiberg's dispirited *requeté* in *Amanecer* to 'volverme a casa y olvidarme de frentes, de parapetos y de guerra' (return home and forget about fronts, parapets and war) (p.31).

The predominant impression created of the rebel soldier is, indeed, perhaps best expressed by the Merchant who seeks to exploit him. Describing him as 'simpático e inocente' (nice and innocent) (p.93), he draws attention to the manner in which *teatro de urgencia* sought to elicit sympathy from its audience for a figure which, by and large, was seen as an ordinary peasant or worker unwillingly caught up in oppressive circumstances. This was in sharp contrast to the portrayal of the Nationalist hierarchy which, consistent with the view of the rebel zone as a region of hell, was diabolized through the exaggeration of dehumanized figures or as grotesque satirical parodies. Propaganda posters of the period offer an impression of such an approach in the threatening hooded figures who loom darkly over terrified refugees or stalk ravaged urban landscapes. The artist Toledo, for example, portrayed the enemy as a helmeted skeleton riding an emaciated horse and holding aloft the Roman *fasces*,[15] while the cover of the first edition of *El Mono Azul* was illustrated with *milicianos* in the characteristic *mono* uniform vanquishing 'los chimpanceses facciosos' (the rebel chimpanzees). In the anonymous play, *La muerte y la vida* (*Death and Life*),[16] death and Fascism are seen to be inextricably linked, the figure of Death appearing 'lo más grotescamente posible' (as grotesquely as possible) (p.5) and described as 'la querida de Franco, la Generalísima' (the darling of Franco, the Generalissimess) (p.6). Dieste seeks a similar effect in *Nuevo retablo de las maravillas* (*New Tableau of Wonders*), painting a picture of the Nationalist officers as sacrilegious and cruel monsters: 'ni en las pesadillas pudo ver nadie tales horrores. Primero humillan, después matan, después afrentan a los muertos' (not even in nightmares could anyone see such horrors. First they humiliate, after that they kill, after that they insult the dead).[17]

This method of 'inventing' the enemy, the shaping of his image in the collective mind, is a contradictory process which involves implanting both the notion of rampant evil, aggressive and strong, and its simultaneous weakness in the face of determined resistance. The enemy is thus given many faces, as required by distinct propaganda tasks. In *teatro de urgencia* the Nationalist military hierarchy is, for the Woman in *Amanecer*, 'aquel gusano horrible' (that hideous worm) (p.27), while in *¡Unidad!* (*Unity!*) they are 'las furias destructoras' (the destructive furies).[18] Such language, promoting a view of the enemy as bestial, threatening and vengeful, also makes him seem invincible. As a worm he undermines, burrows and gnaws relentlessly, while as destructive fury he soars overhead and tears down upon his helpless victim. Yet, when such figures appeared on-stage, their grotesque caricatures were often presented in a burlesque fashion, lending another face to the enemy, one which exploited farce to present him as an arrogant bully who is no match for the *pueblo*.

Despite its predominantly naturalistic tone, *El cuartel* illustrates something of this humorous technique when the character of the General, who throughout the play has been a ruthless, sinister figure, is suddenly reversed as the play momentarily undergoes a disconcerting change of style. As a Republican bomber attacks the barracks in anticipation of the imminent revolt, the General fears he is wounded and, in a manner reminiscent of knockabout comedy, his martial posturing is instantly deflated:

(*llevándose la mano a la cabeza*) ¡Ay! ¡Me han matado esos canallas! Míreme usted la herida, coronel. Dígame si es de muerte.[19]

((*lifting his hand to his head*) Oh! Those swine have killed me! Look at my wound for me, Colonel. Tell me if it's fatal.)

This light-hearted image is pursued as, with the *pueblo* now storming the gates of the barracks, the General demands '¡Calma! ¡Valor!' and '¡Serenidad!' (Don't panic! Bravery! Calm!) (p.17) while racing fruitlessly about the stage, powerless as his authority evaporates and his true cowardice comes to the fore. Finally, comically trembling and huddled in a corner, arms raised in surrender, he declares both himself and his fellow officers to be 'simplemente unos equivocados' (just mistaken wrongdoers) (p.20).

Dieste is also concerned to puncture the pretentiousness of the rebel officers, exposing treachery through a technique of ironic deflation. In *Al amanecer* this is achieved through the ridiculing of a Nationalist lieutenant, Medina, who forms part of a conspiracy to ambush a Republican column by luring it to a town square in which it will be massacred.[20] Medina's fellow plotters, the Italian-sounding bishop, Capellini, the industrialist, Echave, and the rebel captain, Agüero, await Medina's arrival, bringing important news of the militia column's strategy, in the decaying palace of the Marquis of Piedraquemada. Having crossed Republican lines, Medina enters, to the confusion of other characters, disguised as a heavily pregnant peasant woman and declares with swaggering pride, '¡todo esto hay que hacer por la patria!' (all this one has to do for the fatherland!) (p.105). Satirically undermining the military figures' sense of honour as they seek to prove to the bishop that as officers they have always served the ideals of 'paz, orden, familia, nada de huelgas' (peace, order, family, no strikes) (p.108), Dieste deflates Medina's pompous lauding of the prestige of military dress as he arrogantly gestures towards his uniform only to hit himself 'con el puño en el bulto de la preñez fingida' (with his fist in the lump of his feigned pregnancy) (p.108). Declaring that even obedience to military orders must surely have its limits, he tears off his disguise with a proud shout of '¡Arriba el uniforme militar!' (Long live the military uniform!) (p.108).

Perhaps the most sustainedly effective example of the manner in which an enemy figure is satirically humiliated is, however, Alberti's lampooning of the Nationalist general, Queipo de Llano, in *Radio Sevilla*.[21] The targeting of a real-life figure whose nightly broadcasts from Seville were deemed by the Republic to be a major and irritating source of comfort for fifth-columnists, draws attention to the clash between Queipo's own successful propaganda presentation of himself as vengeful, aggressive and merciless and the Republic's consequent desire to counter this through his portrayal as a buffoon. Surrounded by ingratiating 'señoritos falangistas' (Falangist rich kids) and a 'prostituta monárquica' (monarchist prostitute) who persistently and slavishly flatter him, Queipo is shown as the scene opens to be preparing for his nightly broadcast but, as events unfold, his increasingly drunken antics lead to a farcical confusion which is inadvertently broadcast. Lauded by his entourage as 'nuestro salvador', 'Sultán de Persia' and 'Majestad' (our saviour, Shah of Persia and Majesty) (p.6), Queipo is made to present himself rather differently by the author when, promising his listeners that he will soon be galloping into Madrid, he describes himself in language which reduces him to a dull, bestial level:

> Ya se me atiranta el lomo,
> ya se me empinan las ancas,
> ya las orejas me crecen,
> y los dientes se me alargan,
> la cincha no viene corta,
> las riendas se me desmandan,
> galopo, galopo ... al paso. (p.7)

> (Now my back is tightening,
> now I'm getting up on to my hind legs,
> now my ears are growing,
> and my teeth are getting longer,
> my girth isn't very small,
> the reins are out of control,
> I'm galloping, I'm galloping ... I'm off.)

His boast that he will capture Madrid, closing the colleges and opening the taverns, occasions a chorus of '¡vivas!' and applause from his Falangist supporters and from the prostitute, Clavelona, who is unable to contain her admiration for:

> Queipo Requeipo,
> Queipo Quepillo,
> me tiene muerta
> tu bigotillo. (p.6)

> (Queipo Requeipo,
> Queipo little Queipo,
> your little moustache
> slays me!)

Overwhelmed by his own performance at the microphone, Queipo invites his followers to address the listeners and, following the example of their 'Generalísimo', a chorus of animal noises erupts in which Queipo eagerly joins:

QUEIPO   El gallo, ¡a mí, déjemelo a mí! ¡Kikirikii, kikirikii! ¿Qué tal?
CATITE   Como siempre, ¡un talentazo! (p.7)

(QUEIPO   The rooster for me, leave it to me! Cock-a-doodle-do! Cock-a-doodle-do! How was I?

CATITE: As always, an incomparable talent!)

Queipo's image as a donkey metamorphoses into that of a bull as, drunken, degraded and on all fours, he crawls around the stage engaged in a mock *corrida* with his supporters. Into this 'triste cuadro flamenco' (sad flamenco scene) (p.6) steps a Nazi officer who, sneeringly dominant, 'promotes' Queipo to the rank of 'limpiabotas del Ejército del Sur' (bootblack of the Army of the South) (p.7) and forces him, on hands and knees, to polish the officer's jackboots. Aghast, his entourage looks to Queipo for signs of resistance, but the threat of losing German and Italian military support instantly convinces Queipo of his course:

> ... señoritas y caballeros, mostrad en todo instante a estos buenísimos señores el hondo agradecimiento que tenéis, el respeto profundo que les guarda mi España. (p.8)
>
> (... ladies and gentlemen, display at every moment to these exceptionally good men the deep gratitude you have, the deep respect which my Spain shows for them.)

Humiliated, not only before his own supporters but before the imagined radio audience, Queipo's final image is that of his punishment by the *pueblo* as, to the accompaniment of singing and dancing, he is beaten with sticks and brooms while the curtain falls.

This brief summary of the central elements of Alberti's play gives an impression of its fast-moving, rather zany style in which agile physical action, vocal resourcefulness and elaborate, witty word-play combine in a manner which recalls popular theatre traditions such as puppetry and the *commedia dell'arte*. Indeed there would seem to be a clear line of descent from the *commedia* to *teatro de urgencia* in its portrayal of the rebel general. The 'fanfarronería y audacia' (bragging and audacity)[22] which Monleón attributes to Alberti's Queipo is, like the similar preening arrogance of Balbontín's and Dieste's Nationalist officers, reminiscent of the *commedia* mask of the Spanish Captain who, under its various manifestations as, for example, Rogantino, Spavento della Valle Inferno or Giangurgolo, could never brag or strut too outrageously to please an audience. Duchartre's observation that, in the Captain's ultimate downfall, his cowardice and punishment were never 'too contemptible, nor the blows he received ever too numerous or hard',[23] also offers an illuminating view of the conclusion of Alberti's play in that it recalls the characteristic violence of the puppet theatre. The trapping of Queipo's head in the screens which close as the scene ends, presages a beating which seems a direct echo of Punch's ferocious use of his stick to expel the devil.[24] Dieste concludes *Nuevo retablo* in a similar fashion when the overbearing General, who has been made by the Harlequin-like character, Fantasio, to ride a cardboard hobby-horse in a mock entry into Madrid, is overwhelmed by the newly confident peasants who beat him soundly despite his protests that '¡éste es un desacato evidente!' (this is clear disobedience!) (p.79).

The strong sense of *ser* and *parecer* (appearance and reality) which can be felt with regard to the manner in which the apparently invincible power of the rebel general is revealed as a mere posture masking cowardice, is reflected in the loss of dignity visited upon military uniform. The riding boots which are painstakingly polished by the soldiers at the opening of *El cuartel* symbolize not just oppressive power, but hint at a characteristic Nationalist bestiality:

> SOLDADO 1   ¡Vaya pies que gasta el general! No parecen de persona . . . más que pies son pezuñas. (p.1)
>
> (1ST SOLDIER What feet the general's got! They don't seem to be a person's . . . they're more than feet, they're hooves.)

In the final moments of the play, however, the General and his Colonel rapidly strip themselves of their uniform in an attempt to escape apprehension by the *pueblo* and are farcically revealed 'quedándose en camisa' (standing there in their shirts) (p.18), their earlier military swagger in pathetic contrast to their trembling comic fear. As with the beatings which conclude *Radio Sevilla* and *Nuevo retablo*, the loss or desecration of the uniform is an essential element of the comic deflation of Nationalist officers, offering the spectator an important visual symbol of the enemy's merely superficial strength. Mussot pursues a similar effect in *¡No pasarán!* when the General, a threatening bully, is finally vanquished by collective action and his uniform stripped of its medals and decorative crosses.[25]

There is perhaps a hint in these two examples of the traditional pantomime devices of the 'bottomless trunk' from which a seemingly endless variety of objects can be seized, and the comic removal of objects from within a character's costume, leaving him deflated and ridiculed.[26] Aub and Alberti employ such devices more consciously in their pre-war agitprop pieces, *Farsa* and *El agua*, through the reduction of the Priest and the Boss to their underwear, and, in Aub's play, when the Banker, the Priest and the Commander are stripped of objects associated with their power which are plucked from within their costumes until, literally and metaphorically, they have been shrunk and stand before the audience 'tristísimos' (very, very unhappy).[27]

In the desire to drive apart the audience from the enemy and encourage the alienation upon which farce depends, Alberti emphasizes the notion of two distinct worlds. The Soldier and the Girl are of the *pueblo* and are described in the stage directions as 'personas' (people), while Queipo and his followers, as caricatures, are described as 'personajes' (characters) (p.6). The separate nature of these worlds is central to Alberti's desire to present the enemy as the forces of reaction, and, thus, he encloses its action within the painted screens which, in their decoration, consciously recall the ornamented design of the matchboxes of the earlier monarchist period. The enemy's world is seen as a time warp in which representatives of an outmoded ultra-traditional Spain are held up to the ridicule not only of the wider audience in the theatre, but also to the *pueblo*'s representatives in the performance, the Soldier and the Girl. These two characters are seen as belonging to a dynamic present of Republican zeal and military success. Dieste achieves a similar effect in *Nuevo retablo* when the General and the buffoonish collection of aristocratic, clerical and bourgeois figures who surround him come to inhabit the fantasy world into which they are tricked by Fantasio. By claiming to see what is not there, they seek to prove they are free from the stain of Marxism. With characteristic bluster the General presents arms before 3,500 approaching German troops:

> ¡Ante vosotros, nietos de Carlos V, primos de la Imperial España que hoy renace, ante vosotros, digo, presento armas y beso rendidamente los atributos de vuestros mariscales! (p.75)

> (Before you, grandsons of Charles V, cousins of that Imperial Spain which is today being reborn, before you, I say, I present arms and I submissively kiss the insignia of your marshals!)

Absence of illusion, the ability to perceive the world as it really is, rests with the *campesinos* (rural workers) who, having witnessed the amazed naïvety and absurd posturing of the enemy whose power they had imagined as natural and inevitable, drive it out to initiate the 'verdaderas maravillas . . . que se ven cuando los ojos están claros y libres' (true wonders . . . that are seen when the eyes are clear and free) (p.79).

Such a satirical portrait of the Nationalists as a coalition of 'old' Spain enlarged the focus on the enemy to include the non-military figures who were seen as the rebellion's spiritual and political backers. In *El cuartel*, for example, the First Fascist, who boasts of having 'doscientos falangistas armados hasta los dientes que están deseando hacer sangre' (200 Falangists armed to the teeth who are looking forward to drawing blood) (p.5), is discovered to be a duke, while the General, revealing the powerful vested interests which he suggests underpin the army's action, revels in its having 'todo el dinero de don Juan March, de los grandes terratentientes, de la gran plutocracia, del alto clero, de los jesuitas' (all the money of Don Juan March, of the big landowners, of the grand plutocracy of the high clergy, of the Jesuits) (p.9). These latter figures, the higher echelons of the Catholic Church and its most zealous religious order, are mercilessly satirized by Alberti in *Los salvadores* through striking images such as the opening stage direction's call for machine-guns to be placed in the church towers which dominate the play's setting.[28] The military rebellion is seen in this play to be sanctioned by the Church through the literal blessing it receives from the ludicrous figure of the Bishop who holds the pyx above the rebel General, mumbling an absurd Latin-sounding nonsensical homily which reveal Alberti's comic skill in evoking the uprising as a mock-heroic new *reconquista*:

> Nos, unibusquibusque fascio Deo.
> Hispania nunquam regnum judeorum
> Socialismus, marxismus, anarquismus.
> Salve, Francus et Quepus Llaneorum! (p.15)

The Church's perceived role in initiating the conflict is derided in similarly humorous terms by Dieste in *Al amanecer* through the figure of Capellini, for whom the rebels are the Paladins of Christ eager to destroy the Satan of the Republic. The rather pompous and inflated language with which these clerical figures speak enhances the mood sought by Alberti in *Radio Sevilla*, which portrays the enemy as anachronistic, trapped by past dogma and alienated from the life of the *pueblo*. In a manner similar to the portrayal of the rebel soldier as misguided rather than anti-patriotic, *teatro de urgencia* did, however, seek to distinguish between the levels of clerical hierarchy, perhaps suggesting an awareness of that perception which saw the local priest as often a principal and influential defender of ordinary people. In Bleiberg's *Amanecer*, the Wife remembers her wedding day and marriage to her now murdered husband. Recalling the priest's belief that she and her husband would never be separated, she bitterly regrets the death of the old priest and his replacement by one who fails to see the Church as belonging to the people. Whereas the former had given sustenance and hope to the 'labradores agonizantes' (dying farmhands) (p.30), the latter is seen as hating the poor, as sanctioning the murder of peasants and, gruesomely, as overseeing the graveyard rather than the church.

The view of the spiritual backing offered to the rebellion by the Church was complemented by theatrical propaganda which stressed the support emanating from the nexus of political forces which had been hostile to the Republic from its inception. Prominent amongst these were the Falangist 'señoritos' who were presented as a kind of death squad, doing the rebel army's bidding by terrorizing the population of the Nationalist zone. In *El pueblo fascista*[29] the Falangists are seen as stalking the streets and squares of villages while the ordinary people close their windows and doors in fear, hearing in their hearts 'el sonar de las descargas' (the sound of gunshots) (p.3). Portrayed by Alberti as a parasitic, leisured class in both *Radio Sevilla* and *Los salvadores*, drunkenness is amongst its chief attributes and, in Bleiberg's *Amanecer*, the military might of German and Italian Fascism underwrites the Falange's reign of terror in which the walls of the village houses have become like glass, open to scrutiny, inviting suspicion and encouraging the brutal elimination of opponents.

The role of Falangists was not, however, confined solely to the Nationalist zone since, finding themselves trapped in Loyalist areas, such figures became an obvious concern of *teatro de urgencia* seeking to counter the likelihood of sabotage or rumourmongering. In de la Fuente's *El café . . .*[30] and in *¡Aplastar a Franco!* (*Crush Franco!*)[31] individuals who are noticeably bourgeois in appearance or manner, or who fail to embrace whole-heartedly the deprivations and shortages occasioned by the conflict, become objects of suspicion and denunciation by Republicans of unimpeachable loyalty. In the former work, the earnest Juan García, on leave from the battle front, summons the Assault Guard and denounces the two individuals who have questioned him closely about his war work and, in his view, undermined belief in ultimate victory: 'No sé si estarán bien o mal documentados. Pero yo los denuncio como derrotistas y "demasiado curiosos"' (I don't know if their papers are in order. But I denounce them as defeatists and 'too inquisitive') (p.148). A similar fate is met by the two well-dressed café customers of *¡Aplastar a Franco!* who, in their impeccable suits, with hats and ties, are challenged by the Young Woman for their defeatist opinions and talk of concessions to achieve a negotiated end to the war.

The dangers of fifth-columnism, particularly prevalent in the circumstances of the Civil War, received its most effective and sustained treatment in Ontañón's *El bulo*, which was presented by the TAP on 12 November 1937.[32] Satirizing the rebellion's sympathizers who found themselves stranded in Madrid after the uprising's failure, the play, preserved only in a rare edition, is on a par with *Radio Sevilla* for the farcical ingenuity of its rapid action and its memorably ridiculous caricatures of numerous targets of Republican propaganda. Set in the comfortable salon of a bourgeois household, the action takes place between 7 November 1936, eve of the insurrectionists' attempt to capture the capital, and the same day one year later. Gathered in the salon, surrounded by reproductions of religious art and portraits of the ex-royal family, a group of pretentiously affected Nationalist sympathizers play a game of lotto while they await the nightly broadcast of Radio Requeté Salamanca for news of the rebellion's progress.

With a comic gusto typical of the play's style, the numbers are called briskly until thirteen brings the assembled company to its feet in a display of loyal respect for '¡Alfonso! Nuestro señor!' (Alfonso, our Master!) (p.18). As they sigh nostalgically, recalling the ex-king, the clamour of Radio Requeté's excited broadcast is heard, confusedly uncertain of its precise loyalties: 'al servicio de generalísimo von Faupel . . . del generalísimo von Franco, del generalísimo Franco . . .' (at the service of Generalissimo von Faupel . . . of Generalissimo von Franco, of Generalissimo Franco . . .) (p.19). Promising the imminent entry into Madrid of victorious

Nationalist columns, the radio announcer's patriotic fervour erupts in a chorus of adulatory praise for the rebellion's 'amados y heroicos jefes' (beloved and heroic leaders) (p.19) who, latter day versions of the Catholic kings, are declared to be guarantors of 'España única, España fuerte' (the one, strong Spain) (p.20). As the listeners cluster around the radio in eager anticipation of further news, four pious old maids burst in, clad in mourning and laden down with rosaries, but singing in gleeful rhyme their sense of joy at the prospect of liberation. Racing about the stage 'como ratas de alcantarilla' (like sewer rats) (p.20), they are joined in celebration by the radio listeners, hysterically embracing and kissing each other. While some of the assembly seek to ready themselves for the Nationalists' arrival, opening their hidden arms cache or preparing elegant dresses for the much-missed fashionable *paseo* (stroll), the devout old ladies gather on their knees, hands worshipfully clasped, to listen to the radio's thinly disguised parody of a typical broadcast by Radio Seville:

> Señores. Buenas noches. Me van a perdonar que esta noche les beba, digo, les hable poco, porque como nuestro ejército está entrando en Madrid tengo que marcharme para oír la misa de campaña que vamos a celebrar en el paseo de la Castellana. (p.27)

> (Gentlemen. Good evening. You will pardon me if tonight I drink, I mean, I talk to you only a little while, because as our army is entering Madrid I have to leave in order to hear the campaign mass which we're going to celebrate in Castellana Avenue.)

Boasting of the capture of all the government ministries 'menos el de Guerra, Gobernación, Hacienda, Fomento, Marina, Justicia, Comunicaciones y Agricultura' (except those of War, the Home Office, Finance, Public Works, the Navy, Justice, Communications and Agriculture) (p.27), the radio also proudly announces the capture of a million and a half Russians along with 'dos peones camineros que estaban haciendo cunetas en la calle de Alcalá' (two road workers who were mending the kerbs in Alcalá Street) (p.27). As the radio frequency fades, distorted signals are emitted to which reverent attention is paid by the old maids, awestruck by the speaker's eloquence.

Explosions in the street below send the company scurrying to the window in expectation of seeing the first columns of liberating

Moorish soldiers, but in fact to witness the dreaded '¡Quemaconventos!' (Conventburners!) (p.29), the Republican militiamen engaged in resisting the Nationalist attack. They flee the room, and only Bredes, a Falangist 'señorito', remains, pleading hysterically with the voice of the radio to make 'un esfuercito más y Madrid será nuestro' (one more little effort and Madrid will be ours) (p.32). Nostalgically recalling his leisured life before the war, he yearns for the return of:

> tardes con té en el Palace, poker en casa de los Maldonado y en la de Spínola, viernes en Jesús y estrenos a diez pesetas en el Callao. (p.32)

> (afternoon tea at the Palace, poker at the Maldonado's house and at Spínola's, Fridays at Jesús and premières for ten pesetas at the Callao.)

Overwhelmed by the pleasurable memory of earlier pastimes he breaks into a waltz, embracing the radio set as if it were a dance partner while a 'romanza cursi' (twee romance) strikes up and he sings:

> Yo te espero, general amado,
> con el alma llena de ilusión,
> a que vengas de laurel cargado
> y en el casco un pompón bicolor.
> Aquí estaré pidiendo a Dios
> el ser tu esclavo con fervor.
> Italia, sí; Germania, sí;
> pero los rojos, no, no, no. (p.32)

> (I'm waiting for you, beloved General,
> with my heart full of hope,
> that you'll come covered in laurel
> with a two-coloured pompon in your helmet.
> Here I'll be praying to God
> that I'll become your abject slave.
> Italy, yes; Germany, yes;
> but the reds, no, no, no.)

As if in answer to his prayers, the radio accompanies his song, declaring itself to be the triumphant voice of Franco who will soon occupy the capital:

Tengo un millón de marroquís,
otro de Roma y de Berlín,
dos requetés,
flechas dos mil,
que van a entrar hoy en Madrid. (p.33)

(I've got a million Moroccans,
another million from Rome and from Berlin,
two requetés,
two thousand cadets,
who are going to enter Madrid today.)

In unison, Bredes and the radio sing and dance their vision of an ideal future in which military law will have full jurisdiction, all teachers will be priests and Spain will find itself garlanded again with imperial glory. Finally, sinking contentedly into an armchair, Bredes proceeds to drift into sleep, dreaming of the return of the king.

In a farcical restoration of the monarchy, this now occurs as, a spotlight focusing on a round table, Alfonso XIII crawls out from under, dressed as a knight of the Order of Calatrava. Gazing around in wonder at being in Spain again, and noting that it is somewhat changed, he is disturbed by a noise and turns to find his son, the Prince of Asturias, emerging from behind the curtains. Since Franco has promised him the throne, he has returned, and as the two begin to quarrel over who is its rightful occupant, the ghost of the royal pretender, Don Carlos, appears, further to complicate matters by claiming the throne for himself. As each advances his claim in terms more farcically angry, Don Carlos declares his qualifications to include having been educated abroad and, displaying his command of German with an authoritative 'Achtung', seems to summon Hitler, who appears, to the amazement of all, from behind another curtain. As each continues to lay claim to Spain, Hitler is consumed with hysterical laughter and, from behind yet another curtain, brings out Mussolini to share the joke that Spain might belong to Spaniards. Demanding, as the price of the throne, payment for machine-guns, 'barcos fantasmas' and 'submarinos desconocidos' (phantom boats and unknown submarines) (p.40), the would-be monarchs can only find a ten-*céntimo* piece between them and are instead promised work in the mines or in the fields. Producing the cut skin of a bull, unfolded to show the outline of Spain, Hitler and Mussolini break into song as they set about dividing their territory amongst themselves:

> HITLER Me place mucho Galicia,
> que tiene ricos pescados;
> y bajando por Zamora
> hasta Sevilla he llegado.
> MUSSOLINI Aragón me gusta horrores,
> la Mancha y alrededores. (p.43)

> (HITLER Galicia pleases me a lot,
> because it's rich in fishing;
> and going down through Zamora
> I've arrived in Seville.
> MUSSOLINI I love Aragon terribly,
> La Mancha and its surroundings.)

As all join in, laying claim on the skin and tearing it to pieces, exclamations and insults abound until, in the flash of a sudden explosion, all disappear and Bredes, with a long beard, hollow eyes and pallid skin, is again discovered in his armchair. A year has passed and 'el hambre ya no es hambre, es hambro . . . y ésos, ¡sin entrar!' (hunger in't hunger now, it's *staaarving* . . . and still they haven't entered!) (p.47). Bemoaning the insulting deprivations of his life-style – having to seek a work permit, his mother having to eat donkey meat when she is such a refined lady that 'ni montar ha hecho sobre ese animal vulgar' (she hasn't even ridden on that vulgar animal) (p.47) and his sisters having to queue for food – Bredes ignores the untuned radio's distorted sounds and puts his faith in the half-million Italians who he claims have arrived in a single plane-landing. The re-entry of the old maids, excitedly bringing news of a bombing raid which will be 'de los gordos' (a terrible one) (p.50), one not even seen at the cinema, brings all to their knees and their rosaries, praying fervently 'que sean eficaces las bombitas' (that the little bombs are effective) (p.51). As they wait and quietly pray in the eager silence, the distant sound of artillery is heard. With a jubilant cry of '¡la salva!' (the salute!) (p.52) from the fifth-columnists in support of their saviours, a blinding explosion follows upon the shell which bursts through the window and, as all lie dead upon the floor, the curtain falls.

The violence which concludes the play is an important indicator of its performance style, one which echoes popular theatrical traditions such as puppetry and clowning. The frequent beatings and blows which accompany such forms are meted out to caricatures of such starkness that an audience's ethical concern for the violence does not emerge as significant. Like Alberti in *Radio Sevilla*, Ontañón succeeds in dehumanizing the enemy, portraying affected, absurd stereotypes which perhaps reflected popular prejudices. The exaggeration of a few essential features enabled the audience to perceive, rather than a human being, an idea which could be firmly rejected through ridicule. This technique is particularly evident when dealing with the play's royal characters, but it can also be felt in the less knockabout comic style of characters such as Lolín who lauds, with wide-eyed wonder, a rumoured new Nationalist weapon which consists of 'unos polvos invisibles . . . y sólo matan a los que están en pecado mortal' (some invisible dust . . . and it only kills those who are in mortal sin) (p.48).

Ontañón sustains this light-hearted tone with ease, confidently inventive both in the increasingly absurd situations and in the humorous language of the various characters. Nor must the role of music be underestimated in lending an air of *fiesta* to a celebratory piece intended as a morale-booster for citizens of a city under siege. A comparison with *Radio Sevilla* is compelling not only in the light of much of the above, but also in the wide range of enemy figures which both plays target so effectively. While Alberti undoubtedly displays greater poetic skill, particularly in the creation of the ludicrous figure of Queipo himself, Ontañón skilfully weaves together reactionary figures from past and present aspects of the conflict and offers a view of the enemy which is highly original both in the breadth of its perspective and in the treatment of its propaganda targets. A humorous and telling detail in this respect is the portrayal of Portugal, a figure seen to accompany Germany and Italy in desiring to profit from the political upheaval of the Republic. In contrast to the appearance of specific dictators in the case of Hitler and Mussolini, Portugal's appearance is as a 'niño vestido de portugués' (a little boy dressed up like a Portuguese) (p.41) who, as he is humiliated and mistreated by Hitler and Mussolini, is seen to be out of his depth as one of the parties eager to carve up Spain for its own ambitions. As he bounds on to the stage, 'pedante y engolado' (pedantic and pompous) (p.41) and proudly offering a Fascist salute, he is momentarily ignored before Mussolini greets him without interest or enthusiasm. Portugal's enquiry about what it can expect to receive from its Fascist allies is answered with similar brusqueness as, again echoing popular dramatic traditions, he is given the first of four fierce slaps which, throughout the middle section of the play, throw him to the floor in a comic display intended to suggest Portugal's role as a political stooge for the Axis powers.[33]

Portugal's naïvety, besides suggesting an illuminating contemporary viewpoint on perceptions of strategic interest, offers a striking insight into the distinctions which *teatro de urgencia* made between the various foreign elements felt to be conspiring against the Republic. The series of pratfalls which is, in essence, Ontañón's slapstick technique to satirize Portugal's doomed attempts to establish an influential, powerful role for itself in the conflict, contrasts markedly with the portrayal of German and Italian officers whose actual or suggested ruthlessness imposes upon them the role of bestial, alien force. It was in the Republic's interest to present the war as a foreign invasion, the exploitation of Spain by an aggressive, expansionist Fascism and, in *teatro de urgencia*, this often translated itself into a technique, characteristic of much wartime propaganda, of presenting the enemy as diabolical in the wickedness of their actions and intentions. Although the puppet theatre, La Tarumba, is known to have presented Hitler in the comic grotesque manner frequently found in British propaganda in the Second World War, this was not characteristic of the portrayal of the German military in general.[34] As the Woman attempts to flee the rebel zone in *Amanecer*, for example, it is to escape from a world 'que agoniza bajo la risa sucia y criminal de los alemanes' (which is dying under the dirty, criminal laughter of the Germans) (p.31) in which the foreigners plunder houses, demand food and humiliate the native population with cruel, arbitrary punishment:

> ¿Te acuerdas de Isabel? Un día le cortaron el pelo, aquel pelo negro como cipreses, y con la cabeza calva la obligaron a estar dos días y dos noches en la plaza, de pie, entre dos guardias civiles. (p.28)
>
> (Do you remember Isabel? One day they cut her hair, that hair as black as cypresses, and with her shaved head they forced her to be two days and nights in the square, standing, between two Civil Guards.)

Similar barbarism features prominently in Bleiberg's *Sombras de héroes*, the third scene of which is set in the ruins of Guernica where, amongst the corpses of civilians, a German commander laughingly admires the 'magnífico y hermoso bombardeo' (magnificent, splendid bombardment) (p.113). Bleiberg's play, which shared first prize in a competition for new works,[35] is a bitterly angry work and probably the most savage denunciation of German involvement in the Civil War. Stationed some five miles from Guernica during the spring of 1937, Bleiberg recalled how he sought to unite in the play some of his enduring impressions of the time, particularly the outrage felt at the destruction of the ancient symbol of Basque nationhood.[36] His deepest impression is that of the refugees who, ironically, head towards Guernica to escape the fighting in the surrounding countryside and whose spirits, after death, appear before the *miliciano*, Leonardo, urging him to fight even until his own death to avenge them.

The German commander in the play is a brutal figure, keen to boast of the technological efficacy of German weaponry in wiping out the civilian population, and repeatedly kicking the corpses which lie scattered about the stage. Callously desecrating the bodies of his victims, he is seen to receive 'unos miserables gramos de oro procedentes de estos ilustres muertos' (some miserable grams of gold from these illustrious dead) (p.116), in the gold rings cut from the corpses' fingers. For him these are the 'buenas frutas' (rich fruits) (p.116) of Spain, easily plucked through colonizing aggression while, ineffectually, 'se excitan los franceses y protesta el Reino Unido' (the French get worked up and the United Kingdom protests) (p.115). To such cruelty is added a sexual perversity in the sniggering enjoyment with which he taunts Leonardo's *novia*, Isabel. She, having survived the bombing, is seeking the body of her mother, but is handed over with sneering laughter to be raped by Moorish soldiers.

As the figure of Portugal was seen to be weak and dominated by the Axis powers, a similar sense of hierarchy was discernible in relations between Germany and Italy. In *Sombras de héroes*, the Italian officer is presented as the fawning admirer of German military efficiency who, although equal in cruelty to the German commander, accompanies rather than directs events. Similarly, in *Radio Sevilla* and *El bulo*, Mussolini and Italian officers are portrayed less as tending to initiate action than as invited to participate, something which they do with the swaggering relish suggested by the Italian officer's enjoyment of Isabel's imminent violation:

> No te molestes por la carne de las rojas. Esa carne es apta para trilita más que para besos. (*Señalando a los moros*) Y además, los señoritos se entenderán mejor con esa criatura. (p.118)

(Don't worry about the flesh of Red women. That flesh is best for blowing up rather than for blowing kisses. (*Indicating the Moors*) And besides, these gentlemen will get along better with that creature.)

The physical grossness of his sentiments links him to the Moors who, seizing Isabel, drag her violently from the stage and might suggest a racist perception on the part of *teatro de urgencia* in which the Aryan is seen as detached and cynically cold, whereas the Latin temperament of the Italian is presented as lascivious and little different from the animalistic status awarded to the Moroccans. While it is possible to view the above example in such a light, this is not always true of *teatro de urgencia* as a genre. The references to the Germans and the Italians as beasts, executioners, hyenas, monsters or assassins are numerous but, as a fundamentally socialist drama, it sought too to consider the foreign enemy from a class perspective. In *En las trincheras*, for example, the Militiawoman calls upon the divided combatants, 'nacidos del mismo suelo' (born from the same soil),[37] to explain what has brought them to Spain to fight. For the German Anti-Fascist it is to avenge the comrades who died at his side in the concentration camp from which he has fled as if from 'un infierno' (a hell) (p.9). The Italian Anti-Fascist, too, is seen as a victim, having escaped his homeland after Fascists had murdered his wife:

> y a mí en el alma me hirieron.
> Logré escapar, aquí estoy,
> vine a luchar, porque quiero
> volver a ver mi país,
> sus campos, su alegre cielo. (p.9)

> (and in the soul they injured me.
> I managed to escape, here I am,
> I came to fight, because I want
> to return to see my country,
> its fields, its happy sky.)

For both men a chief source of regret is to face, in the opposing trenches, their compatriots but, when the Militiawoman demands an explanation of their presence in Spain, it becomes clear that they too, like the conscript Nationalist soldier, suffer in a kind of hell, afraid to speak out for fear of the firing squad:

> No debo hablar, si me oyeran
> comenzaría mi tormento.
> Los soldados del fascismo
> deben de guardar silencio. (p.10)
>
> (I mustn't speak, if they hear me
> my torment would begin.
> Fascism's soldiers
> must keep silent.)

Recounting his unwilling conscription, the German Fascist laments, knowing nothing of his family nor being able to write to them and, like Pedro López García, is reluctant to confide his unhappiness to others for fear of denunciation. As he regrets his lack of idealism, a quality which Hitler, he suggests, has destroyed, a shot rings out and, as if executed, he falls to the ground dead. With a similar desire to escape from what he declares to be mere slavery, the Italian Fascist then pleads for a place in the Republican trenches, certain that the triumph of Fascism in Spain can only mean its victory throughout the world. Yet, as the German Fascist has died, so too must the Italian Fascist suffer, and the Militiawoman calls for a verdict which condemns the Fascists as criminals, however unwilling, who must bear responsibility for the violence:

> Muere también criminal,
> muere ya verdugo a sueldo,
> que la sangre de ese hermano
> que a tus plantas yace muerto
> vengada quede contigo,
> cobarde sayón siniestro. (p.12)
>
> (Die, too, criminal,
> die, paid executioner.
> The blood of that brother
> who lies dead at your feet
> is avenged with you,
> vicious, cowardly executioner.)

The delicate question of racist perceptions of the enemy is also explored by Dieste in *El moro leal* (*The Loyal Moor*), a short play written to stimulate a repertoire of 'marionetas en batalla' (puppets in battle) in accordance with a plan established by the propaganda section of the Commissariat.[38] Contrary to the widespread view of the Moor as a fearful anti-Christian figure, a brutal pagan intent on rape, Dieste's Moor is a sympathetic but naïve figure whose sadness at the start of the play derives from unhappiness that his wife is no longer the beautiful young woman she once was. The brusque entry of the crude Nationalist Sergeant who promises him money and beautiful women if, in exchange, he agrees to kill communists, tempts the Moor until he realizes that the Sergeant's description of the communists as child-eating monsters will end in throat-cutting: '¡Moro no querer ir! Con pescuezo cortado no poder entrar en el cielo de Alah' (Moor no want go! With throat cut no be able enter Heaven of Allah) (p.99). Like so many rebel soldiers in *teatro de urgencia*, however, the Sergeant makes it clear that, voluntarily or otherwise, the Moor will be conscripted in any case:

> Sí, ser voluntario venir o no venir, pero si tú no vienes te quemaremos jaima, te comeremos niño y mujera y después te cortaremos pescuezo y otra cosa. Moro puede venir o no venir, pero la suerte cambia. (p.99)

> (Be volunteer come or no come, but if you no come we'll burn home, we'll eat child and wifey and afterwards we'll cut throat and something else. Moor can come or no come, but luck changes.)

As a sop, the Sergeant offers the Moor a banknote but, as he scrutinizes it closely, the Banker enters hurriedly, denouncing the money as worthless since it is German currency from the First World War which the Banker had foolishly been tricked into buying in great quantities and which has left him ruined. Furious, the Sergeant orders the Moor to leave and then, in league with the Banker, hatches a plot to buy three million marks for ten pesetas, thereby tricking the Moor into believing immeasurable wealth will be his reward for joining the rebel forces. Since the Moor proves not to be sufficiently gullible, the Sergeant offers independence to the Moroccan tribes and the blandishments of jewels, silks, good wine and the beautiful women of Spain. As the Moor begins to falter, the Voice of Allah is heard, warning him that those who fight for the Nationalists will be broken 'como el mar contra las peñas' (like the sea against the rocks) (p.103), and, pointing the moral of the tale, declares the Moor to be a noble figure 'mientras no estar vendida [*sic*]' (while no be sold) (p.104). Unable to hear the voice or understand why the Moor trembles with fear, the Sergeant denounces him as a savage, but, as Allah appears, masked and carrying a silver cudgel, the Moor declares himself to be in heaven since '¡yo estar viendo la cara de Alah, grande como el sol!' (I be seeing the face of Allah, great like the sun!) (p.104). Eager to obey his God, he asks what he should do with 'el sargento de Franco' (Franco's sergeant) (p.104) and, in a thunderous voice as he hands the cudgel to the Moor, Allah orders '¡duro con él!' (don't spare him!) (p.104) and the Moor unleashes a furious beating upon the Sergeant. As the Banker returns, demanding his money from the Sergeant, a similar beating is ordered for the Banker until both reactionary figures lie dead. While the Moor is taken up into the clouds, his Wife enters in a hurry not to be left behind, but, exhilarated by his good fortune, the Moor looks forward only to the houris he will meet in heaven. Weeping and wondering where she can go to hide her lack of youth, Allah lifts her too in his hands, transforming her into a beautiful houri and declaring: 'toda mujer es hurí, aunque esté disfrazada con vejez' (every woman is a houri even if she is disguised by old age) (p.105). As both ascend into heaven, Allah's thunder dies away and is replaced by the music of clarinets as the curtain falls.

With brevity and good humour, Dieste presents the Moor, not as the bloodthirsty mercenary, which was a predominant stereotype, but as a figure whose essential goodness did not differ from that of other human beings and contained a similar number of shortcomings. Such a view acts as a balance to the image of the Moor presented in *Sombras de héroes*, apparently the only other *teatro de urgencia* play in which Moors appear as part of the action. Whereas Bleiberg presents them as lustful savages eager to violate the already despairing Isabel, Dieste manages to use the puppet tradition, despite its tendency towards broad caricature, to communicate a more subtle and perceptive view of the Moor, one which displays great cultural understanding and concerned tolerance. That this is so is the more unusual given, as Thomas reports, the traditional role of the Moor as the villain of numerous Spanish fairy stories and, during the Civil War, as the focus of terror allegations in each region which fell to the advancing Nationalist army.[39]

Dieste's sympathetic view of the Moor is indicative of the breadth of enemy images which *teatro de urgencia* sought to present to its audiences. A comprehensive portrait of the enemy emerged which, although it could not accurately be described as centrally directed, did reflect commonly shared perceptions of political, military and government organizations which were felt to be important for communication to the wider population. The body of surviving scripts reveals a panorama of civilian, military and religious perspectives on the conflict which represented the Republic's view of the enemy against whom it exhorted the *pueblo* to struggle. The enemy's world was variously a nightmarish hell of torture and humiliation in which the human dignity of decent, ordinary Spaniards had been denied, or a somewhat surreal fantasy world in which buffoonish figures from the leisured classes, the Church or the army indulged in nostalgia for imperial grandeur and plotted the return of traditional privilege. Combining, in the words of a contemporary observer, 'la risa y el llanto' (laughter and weeping),[40] two broad responses were sought from the spectator, each fundamentally emotional, which aimed to fuse the audience with the orthodoxy of the Republican perspective. The broad humour of writers such as Ontañón and Alberti, with its deep roots in popular dramatic traditions, was intended to fortify the audience's spirit to resist despite increasingly frequent military reversals. At the same time, emotional images of Spain as the suffering motherland betrayed by her own sons, stressed the bond which explained the war's meaning and demanded total absorption in the struggle.

Such moods were evoked through dramatic forms and styles which are striking in their variety and indicate yet again *teatro de urgencia*'s concern always to tailor its work to the location and requirements of particular audiences. The 'romance dialogado' (dramatized ballad) approach, for example, which underpins works such as *El pueblo fascista* and *La muerte y la vida*, seeks to use verse rhythms and poetic imagery to summon a vision of rural Spain rendered desolate by Fascism. Intended for performance before troops, the plays' emphasis lies on a sequence of memorable and powerfully emotional images, their easy recall and a vision of the life-style and villages which many of the spectators had, presumably, left behind and for whose liberation they were urged to fight. By contrast, Ontañón in *El bulo* seems to be consciously drawing upon the tradition of the *sainete* (one-act farce) which formed such a popular element of the Madrid theatrical repertoire during the early years of the century.[41] Here, music, satire and humorous word-play combine to offer a sophisticated knockabout comedy with a distinctly urban flavour typical of Madrid. Similar variety can be felt in Dieste's adaptation of the *entremés* in *Nuevo retablo* and his parody of late nineteenth-century romantic drama in *Al amanecer*. With the not infrequent influence of puppetry making its presence felt, a strong impression can be gauged of the extent to which, in its portrayal of the enemy, *teatro de urgencia* mined the rich vein of tradition found in Spanish popular theatre. It is fitting that this should be so, since both sides of the conflict claimed that they were fighting for Spain itself, and the solidarity which the Republic sought was fostered through images and forms which emphasized nationhood, tradition, shared language and the proud cultivation of the land, all threatened by external forces conspiring with a treacherous caste which had proved itself unworthy as Spaniards.

~ 5 ~
Forming the Soldier

The considerable number of hostile forces against which the Republic perceived itself to be ranged occasioned the adoption by *teatro de urgencia* of a striking variety of approaches to the portrayal of the opposing forces. The enemy was not single but many, a phenomenon which arose from the need to emphasize the conflict as a mixture of foreign aggression and Spanish military treachery rather than a more fundamental breakdown of social cohesion within the larger community. By contrast, resistance to this enemy focused to an enormous degree solely on the figure of the Republican soldier. Given the deep ideological schisms within the Republican camp it is remarkable how, in its propaganda, it was able, by and large, to construct an image of a collective hero in whom were often fused the discipline, forceful vision and ideological clarity felt necessary to victory. To a certain extent it was, of course, obvious that, having constructed images of a well-financed, reactionary and cruel enemy, Republican propaganda should counter this with a portrait of its own soldiers as steadfastly determined, loyal combatants whose limits of endurance were boundless and whose commitment to victory was unflinching.

Such traditionally heroic qualities recall the characteristic presentation of Republican soldiers in propaganda posters produced during the conflict. The artist Parrilla, for example, gave a prominent emphasis to alert, muscular figures of soldiers launching an attack or marching in strict unison. Massive and solid of feature, they fix their eyes on a distant goal, unseen by the viewer but perceived by the soldier with resolute clarity. It is an approach clearly redolent of Socialist Realism. In *¡Con disciplina se defiende la República!* (*With Discipline One Defends The Republic!*), for example, Parrilla seems to sculpt the soldiers against a background of heavy industry and enhances the mood of heat, strength and steel in the metallic blue and glowing red of their uniforms.[1] The intensity of battle and the ferocious energy brought to it by the Republican combatant is also felt in Parrilla's *Primero: ganar la guerra. ¡Menos palabras vanas!* (*First: Win the War. Less of Idle Words!*) in which the soldier launches forward while simultaneously turning his face to the rear, urging onward those who are following his lead.[2] The deep crimson of his greatcoat, the dominant focus of the poster, is thrown into relief by the two accompanying soldiers whose portrayal suggests the increasing heat of combat. The figure in the foreground, with the cold, hard blue of its battle helmet and attacking bayonet, blends with the crimson and, subsequently, with the gold of a background figure who seems molten, incandescent as he carries the battle to the enemy.

The idealized portrayal of the Republican soldier suggested by Parrilla's work can also be found in much *teatro de urgencia*. Yet whereas poster art, despite its often brilliant and subtle manipulation of the propaganda medium, is essentially static, drama's distinctive dynamics often permit, even in a theatre of essential simplicity, a more wide-ranging exploration of issues. The portrait of the Loyalist soldier fostered by *teatro de urgencia* was, therefore, comparatively complex. Many of its most significant features derived from the numerous difficulties which the Republic faced in creating a military force capable of defeating the rebel army, while simultaneously sustaining a commitment to perceived cultural, social and educational needs of the *milicianos*. An anonymous article in the brigade newspaper *Pasaremos* offers an indication of such difficulties when it describes a visit to the barracks at Hortaleza to interview new recruits from the provinces of Toledo and Ciudad Real.[3] Despite the newspaper's motto, 'más vale una trinchera tomada al enemigo que cincuenta palabras de revolución pronunciadas en la retaguardia' (a trench taken from the enemy is worth more than fifty revolutionary words delivered in the rearguard), the article's emphasis lies almost exclusively on the non-military obligations of recruits. A young soldier from Molinillo, for example, is warmly encouraged to ponder '¡qué alegría se llevaría su madre si volviese al pueblo sabiendo leer!' (how happy his mother would be if he were to return to the village knowing how to read!), while another recruit, from the south of Toledo, is lauded for his desire to spend 'todo el día leyendo periódicos' (all day reading newspapers). By contrast, Alpert reveals the frustration felt by the chief of staff, Rojo, who complained bitterly of widespread insistence on outdated battle tactics, disobedience, frequent abandonment of terrritorial gains and a widespread lack of confidence.[4]

Rojo's rather despondent conclusion, as late as 1938, that the Republic had created an army in name only, suggests the considerable and persistent challenge involved in fulfilling propaganda's task to provide political orientation, exhortation and training in a variety of military spheres. Loyalist organizations, however, approached the task with zeal. Their literacy and educational programmes were presented as not only intrinsically worthy but perhaps on a par with military training as a basis for victory. Such programmes find a reflection in *teatro de urgencia*'s concern with the *miliciano*'s cultural formation and illustrate how, unlike poster art, drama explored a rather more complex portrait of the soldier. In *Mi puesto*, for example, the Second Soldier has failed to learn to read despite the available opportunity, and it is this shortcoming which, it is implied, hinders his understanding and acceptance of the scarce availability of home leave. The structure of the play is largely the journey which he makes from a kind of naïve innocence about the war's meaning to a more mature experience derived from the news of his own family's suffering at the hands of the rebel army. Persuaded of the justice of the Republic's cause, he vows not to seek leave 'mientras el fascismo no sea por nosotros exterminado' (while Fascism remains to be wiped out by us).[5] The sense of transformation as the individual comes to a fuller understanding of his duty as a soldier is portrayed as a deeply personal experience in Mussot's play and reflects that belief in the ideal citizen which had so marked socialist cultural thinking during the years prior to the Civil War. By contrast, however, *teatro de urgencia* also emphasized obedience rather than the persuasion which so characterized Mussot's play and many other Republican efforts at education and training. The exhortation of soldiers to accept military hierarchy, their grounding in the nature of tactical deployment and in the need for more forceful defence of military positions, stimulated theatrical propaganda which insisted upon a more conventional notion of army life. Narezo's *¡Hacia la victoria!*, for example, reflects to an extent Rojo's desire to oversee a traditionally disciplined body of men responding obediently to an officer's blunt analysis: 'hemos retrocedido, y eso ha de terminarse de una vez' (we have withdrawn, and that has to stop once and for all).[6]

Alpert's observation that the Republican army was forged from militia units which were untrained but heroic and inspired by a social ideal, can be tangibly felt in Narezo's and Mussot's plays. Both plays share a common vision but, stressing different aspects of it, offer insights into *teatro de urgencia*'s presentation of the *miliciano* as one which extended the technique of poster art into a more searching examination of slogans, perceptions or tactics. Strongly suggested by Mussot and Narezo are two notions which underpin the presentation of the *miliciano* in *teatro de urgencia*: the portrayal of the combatant as an individual who expresses the essence of the *pueblo* in the ideological clarity he brings to the struggle, and, on the other hand, the uncertain and sometimes unwilling member of the collective force who must be trained, made conscious of the meaning of army life and the duties and obligations consequent upon it. In attempting a comprehensive analysis of the portrayal of the ordinary soldier, a central concept is, therefore, that of transition. The model combatant was, as Rojo attests, more likely to be an ideal than a reality, and theatrical propaganda's task with regard to the Republican soldier was, therefore, to assist in the formation of a revolutionary fighter, politically inspired and displaying military prowess.

Such an undertaking was a task of great magnitude. While, at the end of the late 1938 play, *Defendemos la tierra*, the *milicianos* leave the stage as if 'sintieran en la cara aletazos de heroísmo' (they felt on their faces the beating wings of heroism),[7] sentiments of such inspiration can be sharply contrasted with the less resolute, uncertain moods of *teatro de urgencia* produced in the initial weeks of the war. In Mussot's ¡*No pasarán!*, for example, a confused squad of conscripts, fearful of its own survival, dares not disobey its superiors' orders. Written in September 1936, the play takes place during the early hours of the military rebellion and deals with events which occur when the soldiers are ordered to participate in the uprising. The emphasis of the play is, significantly, upon the regular army and the presentation of the soldier, not as the Republican *miliciano*, but as the raw material from which the ideal revolutionary soldier must be forged.

The play's initial action, receiving drill instruction, establishes the soldiers as mere automata. Chanting the drill in unison while marching, they are threatened by the Sergeant with physical violence for failure to maintain a disciplined rhythm: 'sigan dando media vueltas sin perder el compás . . . al que le pierda le daré un pez . . . co . . . zón' (keep doing the drill march without losing rhythm . . . whoever loses it I'll *wring . . . your . . . neck*).[8] The image of brutality sought by Mussot, a veteran of the Moroccan War, is emphasized as the soldiers come to a rest and, standing at attention, one of the squad is beaten for failing to place his rifle on the correct side.

Demanding that they remain 'derechos como una vela' (straight as a candle) (p.1) until his return, the Sergeant leaves and, as the soldiers remain at attention, their customary collective response to orders alters and they articulate a deeper perception of themselves, principally as puppets whose strings are controlled by officers:

> SOLDADO 1 Cuando nos tocan el resorte decimos 'sí' y 'no'... andamos para atrás, para adelante...
> SOLDADOS ¡Autómatas! ¡Autómatas! (p.2)
>
> (1ST SOLDIER When they pull our strings we say 'yes' or 'no'... we walk backwards, forwards...
> SOLDIERS Automata! Automata!)

The presentation of the soldiers as robotic has a dramatic as well as thematic purpose in that it provides Mussot with a non-naturalistic performance style which enables an inclusive political analysis to be presented to the spectators within the short playing time of the work. The First Soldier thus acts as a kind of chorus leader, offering ideas which the other members of the troop, in unison, subsequently endorse or amplify. The soldiers' sense of themselves as puppets is explained, therefore, in broad class terms as arising from fear of imprisonment or execution by a powerful, exploitative clique:

> SOLDADO 1 Defendemos a los ricos; guardamos el dinero de los ricos, y en nuestra casa falta el pan.
> SOLDADOS ¡Hambre! ¡Hambre! (p.2)
>
> (1ST SOLDIER We defend the rich; we protect the money of the rich, and in our house there's no bread.
> SOLDIERS Hunger! Hunger!)

The image offered is of a cruelly oppressive life-style where the only difference between civilian and military life is that, as soldiers, 'nos dan más latigazos' (they give us more lashes) (p.2). Whereas, earlier, the trade union had saved 'nuestro pellejo y nuestro estómago' (our skins and our stomach) (p.2), the soldiers now see themselves as helpless, 'muñequitos de bazar' (little bazaar puppets) (p.3), who have been removed, not only from their families but, in an image which unites the industrial and rural working class, from mines, workshops, factories and countryside. Concluding that they have unwillingly become murderers who would, if ordered to shoot, decorate their families with 'rojas condecoraciones' (red medals) (p.3), the First Soldier urges his comrades to break the strings by which they are controlled, freeing themselves in order to behave independently and in their own interests.

It is at this point that the unanimity with which the soldiers have explained their situation breaks down. The clarity of analysis displayed by the First Soldier leads to his resolute determination for action, but such a course unsettles the troop who fail to share his certainty that their liberation can be achieved by his apparently simple advice to act with unity. How such unity might be achieved is now, however, tested in practice since the arrival of the General signals the commencement of the military rebellion. Describing the soldiers as 'columnas y sostén de la patria' (columns and support of the fatherland) (p.4), the General declares that society and sacred rights of ownership are in danger. He orders the soldiers to be ruthless with the agitators by imposing order in the streets and giving 'su merecido a la plebe imbécil' (their just deserts to the imbecile masses) (p.4). The First Soldier's blunt refusal to participate arouses the General's fury and the soldiers' fear of reprisals. For them, disobedience threatens to bring the firing squad and, as though paralysed, they are unable to respond to the First Soldier's plea not to kill their own comrades. Denounced by the General as a traitor and a bandit, the First Soldier avoids blows from the General's baton, violence which immobilizes the soldiers until they too are threatened: '¡Pronto! ¿Qué esperáis, estúpidos? ¿Queréis perder vuestras cabezas?' (Quick! What are you waiting for, fools? Do you want to lose your heads?) (p.5).

The failure of individual action to inspire collective revolt seems inevitable, the First Soldier crying out, '¿Me dejáis solo camaradas?' (Are you leaving me on my own, comrades?) (p.5), as some of the troop accept their orders and prepare to exit. Fearful that they will be shot for disobedience the soldiers repeat their desperate refrain, '¿Qué hacemos? ¿Qué hacemos?' (What are we to do?) (p.5), confused as to their best course of action. Their question is answered as the First Soldier's plea for unity is taken up by off-stage voices calling '¡Uníos! ¡Uníos!' (Unite!) (p.5). The soldiers, aware that the barracks are under attack by the *pueblo*, begin again to form a united squad despite the General's rabid warning that they will face the harshest punishment. Gaining confidence from the soldiers, the Sergeant, too, denounces the military rebellion, declaring that he too is one of the *pueblo* and placing himself at the squad's orders. Demanding 'un camino seguro' (the right path) (p.6), the soldiers are uncertain of their next step and can only answer the First Soldier's demand as to why they do not answer the *pueblo*'s call by staring at the General whose power they still fear. With a shout of 'Pues fuera obstáculos' (No more obstacles) (p.6) the First Soldier shoots dead the General with his own pistol and all subsequently strip the uniform of its crosses and medals, encouraged by the First Soldier's angry denunciation of each medal as signifying a murder and each cross the death of one of their comrades. Liberated by their defeat of the General, the soldiers heed the call of the *pueblo* and, in a final tableau in which all spiritedly chant the play's title, the newly united soldiers set out determinedly for the combat front.

Mussot's play offers important insights into the crisis within the army during the early days of the war. Written on the cusp of the fragmentation of the old army and the creation of the new, *¡No pasarán!* records, as it were, the birth of the *miliciano* as the soldiers exit, united with the *pueblo*, to shouts of '¡Vivan las milicias populares!' (Long live the Popular Militias!) (p.7). The plundering of the General's uniform serves as a ritual purging of the old regime and, increasingly confident, the soldiers participate in a spontaneous celebration of collective strength which displaces their earlier machine-like repetition of marching orders. A central consequence of this sense of liberation on the part of the soldiers is that they cease to be conscripts and become volunteers, members of the apparently spontaneous, newly formed Popular Militias. In political terms an onset of purposeful confidence has proved possible as soldiers and masses unite, volunteers in the face of the common enemy. In military terms, however, a more complex scenario was inevitably going to present itself when it became evident that, to conscripts lacking in adequate military skills were now to be added civilians whose anti-Fascist enthusiasm would never prove sufficient in the face of a considerably more experienced army which was also better organized and more prepared for combat. While describing achievements to date as a triumph, the Commissariat itself drew attention to the situation, suggesting that its army's military experience 'no podía ser más tenue' (could not be more tenuous),[9] given the circumstances of its creation. In this context, the soldiers' line 'necesitamos un camino seguro' (we need the right path)[10] acquires a significance beyond a desire for immediate guidance and becomes an index of the trajectory of *teatro de urgencia* with regard to the emerging figure of the *miliciano*.

As we have seen earlier, the notion of seeking guidance, of finding the correct path, was a prominent feature of *teatro de urgencia*'s portrayal of the ordinary soldier from the opposing army. Confused and coerced into unenthusiastic service by the rebels, he attempts to cross to Republican lines and reintegrate himself with what is presented as the authentic *pueblo*. Aub's Pedro López García, for example, responds to the Land's call for him to abandon his post and join his Republican comrades in terms which suggest the embracing of faith or the insight of spiritual revelation: 'no acabo de entender lo que me dices. Pero creo que debo de pasarme' (I haven't quite understood what you are telling me. But I believe that I ought to cross over).[11] Aub's play concludes with the incorporation of Pedro López García into the Republican forces and his appeal, through loudspeakers aimed at the enemy trenches, for others to take the same path and cross to the opposing lines. Aub's play, like *¡No pasarán!*, was an early *teatro de urgencia* work and both plays perhaps reflect the euphoric atmosphere of the initial stages of the war when, given the rebellion's limited success, the prospect of an extensive civil war was less apparent. While both plays end, therefore, with an overwhelming sense of conviction about victory, it is a belief which is untested by the drawn-out trial of battle. It is as though the soldier, having discovered the right path, knows little as yet of the demands of the journey ahead. A character such as Pedro López García illustrates the deepening portrait of the soldier, demonstrating how the task of *teatro de urgencia* was to indicate to him this right path and, in so doing, build an effective army from the Popular Militias.

The Commissariat's recognition of the tenuous military experience of the army was based on the wide range of civilian backgrounds which characterized the Popular Militias. A disciplined fighting machine had to be rapidly formed from what were described as valiant *campesinos*, members of the liberal professions and modest clerks, individuals who had been uprooted from an atmosphere of peace and work and who had never handled 'otras armas que las del trabajo y el estudio' (other arms than those of work and study).[12] The contribution of *teatro de urgencia* to the task of forging the ideal combatant from individuals of such disparate and militarily limited experience is illustrated with great clarity in *¡Hacia la victoria!*, a play written by a commissar which seeks to offer a kind of basic training in battle tactics to soldiers whose sense of their own inadequacy in combat is both honest and poignant. The play, an extended debate structured to explore the reaction of soldiers under enemy fire, centres on two *milicianos* whose uncertainty in battle derives from inexperience and fear. Observing that in two months the brigade has retreated several kilometres, the Captain notes that, as a result, positions have been lost which should have been defended 'a sangre y fuego' (with blood and fire) (p.4). For the *milicianos* the explanation of the failure lies in their own shortcomings, particularly the absence of a disciplined response to enemy fire. As one of them remarks of his comrades: 'dicen . . . "¡Bah, unos cuantos metros hacia atrás qué importa!". Y retroceden' (they say 'Bah, a few metres backwards – what does it matter'. And they retreat) (p.4). Lack of understanding of the enemy, suggests the Captain, breeds fear of him, a view which is heartily endorsed by the soldiers. For them, their inadequacy and that of their comrades is found in the insular nature of their previous lives and their perception of themselves as ignorant peasants: 'soy campesino y . . . no tengo muchas luces. Antes de la guerra casi no había salido de mi pueblo' (I'm a peasant and . . . I'm pretty dim. Before the war I'd hardly ever left my village) (p.6).

It is surely significant that the play is the work of a political commissar since to the character of the Commissar now falls the central task of the drama, that of convincing the *milicianos* that the enemy is not 'gente del otro mundo' (people from another world) (p.6) but men who are 'un poco menos hombres que nosotros' (lesser men than we are) (p.6) and far from invincible. Illustrating this through an explanation of the Falangists, offered in *romance* form, he undermines the enemy in the soldiers' eyes through the characteristic technique of scornful ridicule:

> Escuchad: El falangista
> se levanta muy temprano
> (las doce de la mañana).
> Se peina, se hace las uñas,
> se pone el traje y se calza.
> Sale contento a la calle
> y al bar de moda se marcha. (p.6)

(Listen: the Falangist
gets up very early
(midday).
He combs his hair, does his nails,
dons his suit and shoes.
He goes happily out into the street
and takes off to a fashionable bar.)

A picture is painted of a leisured, decadent life-style and a hatred of the *pueblo* which manifests itself through insurrection and a treacherous alliance with the foreign invaders. Denounced as cowards who flee like rabbits, the Falangists recall, for the First Soldier, the 'señoritos' of his own village who, having as a gang attacked one of the villagers, locked themselves away inside their houses for a fortnight to avoid the collective anger of the rest of the *pueblo*. This moment of insight and recognition is seized upon by the Commissar as he urges the soldiers to see the connection which the First Soldier has made, that the enemy in wartime is no different from the traditional enemies of the *pueblo*, and that if each soldier behaves like 'un hombre de verdad' (a true man) (p.8) the Falangist soon loses his 'talones' (claws) (p.8).

Bestial imagery such as this is, as we have previously noted, frequently associated with the enemy, particularly the Moors who, described as 'perros rabiosos' (rabid dogs) (p.8), now become the focus of the Commissar's conviction that the *milicianos* possess the ability to overcome an apparently insuperable enemy. For the soldiers the Moors are 'fieras' and 'salvajes' (wild animals, savages) (p.8) whose seeming fearlessness, observes the Second Soldier, causes panic amongst the *milicianos* and accounts for recent retreats. Whereas the Commissar's tactic with regard to the Falangists had been one of scornful derision, more strategically practical advice is offered with regard to the Moors, troops whose reputation in battle was fearsome. The Commissar notes a significant cultural difference between the *milicianos* and the Moroccan troops in that the Moors fear knives much more than they fear bullets and that, when under attack, fixed bayonets will quickly drive the enemy out of sight. This practical advice is enthusiastically acknowledged by the soldiers. Declaring 'Camarada Comisario, poco a poco vamos sabiendo más' (Comrade Commissar, little by little we're getting to know more and more) (p.10), the First Soldier requests further insight into the nature of the foreign enemy since, as *campesinos*, he and his comrades know little of 'estos europeos que han invadido nuestra patria' (these Europeans who've invaded our homeland) (p.10). *Teatro de urgencia*'s portait of the German and Italian military as barbaric and cruel was, as we have seen, generally confined to officers. The ordinary soldier, by contrast, was often presented as a misguided recruit or an unwilling conscript. To some extent the notion of class solidarity might account for the phenomenon, but it also made good sense in military terms to cultivate an image of the *miliciano*'s immediate opponent on the battlefield as discontented or lacking in commitment. It is precisely such a picture which the Commissar paints in response to the soldier's question, graphically describing the Fascist states as militarist regimes which absorb and stain all. Through hunger and oppression, ordinary workers are driven into military adventures which promise the chance to earn 'el pan para los suyos' (bread for their own) (p.10). The foreign soldiers are, thus, deceived, lacking in spirit and, crucially, therefore, 'no son tan fieras como los pintan' (they're not as fierce as they're painted) (p.11).

As a vivid example of the Commissar's explanation, a commotion off-stage heralds the entry, between two *milicianos*, of an Italian soldier who has passed to the Republican lines. His clothes in tatters, and shocked from having narrowly avoided machine-gun fire from his own lines as his escape was detected, the Italian recounts his experiences in an Italianized Spanish, events which confirm the Commissar's portrait of cowed and abused men: '¿qué podíamos hacere? En Italia fusilare presto a no fascistas' (what could we to do? In Italy shoot not Fascists quick) (p.13). A similar picture of exploitation is drawn with regard to the Italian's time in Spain, a period of hunger, cold and exposure to front-line danger while 'falangistas ... sempre atrás, noi italiano, avanti sempre' (Falangists ... alway back, us Italian, alway forward) (p.13). As the new arrival is offered food, with the promise that there is plenty for him to eat his fill, the First Soldier thanks the Commissar: 'cúantas cosas hemos aprendido en unos momentos' (how much we've learnt in a few moments) (p.14). The play's conclusion emphasizes the notion of realization, suggesting that the Commissar has provided a demonstration of the true nature of the enemy, that he can be 'known' rather than darkly feared. The emphasis is upon knowledge which must be transmitted to other *milicianos* 'que sepan lo que vosotros sabéis' (so that they know what you know) (p.14). Practical military advice is seen to replace confusion, ill-discipline and ignorance of the world. As a result, the soldiers' view of themselves alters. From the self-deprecating, naïve peasants of the play's opening, they prepare to fuse with 'el bloque de acero de nuestros cuerpos' (the steel block of our bodies) (p.15), an image which recalls idealized poster images such as those of Parrilla and suggests the movement, so discernible in the presentation of the *miliciano*, by which the ideal seeks to forge itself from the real.

Narezo's play is a significant example of the manner in which theatrical propaganda contributed to the training of the soldier, seeking to form consciousness through imparted knowledge, inculcation of skills and the demonstration of appropriate military behaviour. That professional military competence was essential to victory was an attitude which *teatro de urgencia* persistently sought to engender in the presentation of the *miliciano*. As we have already seen, for example, the lost play *Fortificación* was lauded by Aparicio for its effectiveness as a training device through which soldiers could explore the importance of fortification and the varying effectiveness of different approaches to it.[13] For Aparicio the usefulness of *teatro de urgencia* such as this lay in its ability to draw together in common purpose the 'sencillos campesinos, obreros [y] empleados' (simple peasants, workers and clerks)[14] and thereby encourage the skills, discipline and unity of an effective combat unit. The anonymous play *Pueblos de vanguardia* similarly highlights the professionalism demanded of the *miliciano* by offering its audiences a model relationship between the soldiers and the Company Commissar.[15] Efficiency, mutual respect, acceptance of military hierarchy and a sense of strategic purpose characterize their exchanges as they prepare to fall back and concentrate their forces in a small, front-line town. Having saluted the Commissar, an exemplary *miliciano*, for example, reports his captain's order that their forces garrison the town and requests the Commissar's authority to proceed: 'ya están emplazadas las baterías. ¿Cómo nos distribuimos por el pueblo? ¿Requisamos víveres y casas?' (the batteries are in place. How shall we distribute ourselves about the town? Shall we requisition supplies and homes?) (p.76). The mood of professionalism is strong, but the sense of automata which characterized the 'old' army as perceived by Mussot in *¡No pasarán!* is absent, since all are presented as willingly engaged in a collective endeavour. Military priorities are dominant, but so too are human priorities, and the soldiers are reminded by the

Commissar that access to the town's foodstuffs and accommodation must be achieved, not through imposition or plunder, but by a request for assistance which respects the inhabitants: 'este pueblo tiene sus autoridades. Primero, voy a hablar con ellos, con los campesinos, que nos ayudarán en todo lo que necesitamos' (this town has its authorities. First, I'm going to speak to them, with the peasants, who will help us with everything we need) (p.76).

The emphasis which *teatro de urgencia* laid upon forming and enhancing the combatants' military capability was complemented by its desire to inculcate a vision of the war's meaning which would unambiguously suggest collective struggle against reactionary forces and foreign aggression. Practical knowledge of *how* to fight was thus combined with images designed to provoke amongst *milicianos* political awareness, even inspiration, as to *why* the fight was worth waging. Particularly eloquent in its efforts to evoke revolutionary fervour was Garfias's ¡*Que nos quitan nuestra tierra!*,[16] a play, cast in the form of a dramatized *romance*, which sought to offer the *miliciano* a view of his situation which linked the necessity of building military effectiveness with the need to end for ever the social exploitation which, it is suggested, has led to the conflict. Like Narezo's play, Garfias's work opens by addressing an issue of military prowess as the Commissar asks one of the soldiers why during recent combat he has been frightened, even to the point of cowardice. The question is essentially rhetorical and is answered, not by the soldier, but by the Commissar's enquiry whether the soldier understands *why* he fights. Again, the question is not answered, and this enables the Commissar to illustrate in powerful language the experiences which should underpin and offer meaning to the conflict.

Central to these experiences is the nature of the soldier's earlier life as a rural labourer. Since childhood, observes the Commissar,

> Tus espaldas conocen bien
> la lluvia, el viento y el sol.
> Tienes las sienes horadadas
> por las agujas del sudor. (p.7)

> (Your back well knows
> the rain, wind and sun.
> Your temple, pierced
> by needles of sweat.)

This vivid evocation of the seasons' constant harshness and the physical punishment it metes out is intensified by the Commissar's suggestion of landless poverty and rural exodus in the 'vientos de aventura' (winds of chance) (p.7) which carry the labourer to the city. Having left behind the harsh land, the *campesino* is now seen as an urban worker, alienated in the metropolis, suffering cold, hunger and 'la terrible soledad' (the terrible isolation) (p.7) of the displaced. For the Commissar it amounts to a lifetime of labour with little guarantee of security or even sustenance. In this opening section of the play, the Commissar encapsulates a great deal of the social experience of many Spaniards during the peacetime years of the Republic, 'comiendo tarde, mal y nunca' (eating late, badly or never) (p.8), and, in so doing, his image of the soldier's life becomes representative and is addressed to most of the audience. It is, in effect, to the soldiers present *en masse* that the Commissar now speaks when his picture of civilian life merges with the current military struggle:

> Y ahora la guerra . . . Camarada
> soldado, ¿sabes por qué luchas? (p.8)
>
> (And now war . . . Comrade
> soldier, do you know why you're fighting?)

Again, the question is rhetorical, and in his answer the Commissar recalls the images of pre-war life, asserting that the soldier is fighting:

> Por la tierra que tú labraste
> y la fábrica en que trabajaste;
> por el pan que te regatearon
> y la instrucción que te negaron. (p.8)
>
> (For the land which you tilled
> and the factory in which you worked;
> for the bread which they begrudged you
> and the education they denied you.)

This is seen as a struggle for all that there is and all that has been denied, since, declares the Commissar, like the bird, the star and the worm, men must own the world as their birthright. In the second section of the play, social deprivation is again seen as an affliction of all the *pueblo* but, on this occasion, it triggers a powerful call for military and political unity to win the war. The ideological fracture within the Republic is implicit in the call issued to Anarchists and socialists to recognize that, whether Republicans follow Marx or Bakunin, the sweat of their labour runs into the same Spanish soil. Evoking the generations' daily fight for survival, the Commissar regrets how naïve he and his fellow activists have previously been in failing to see their common purpose, namely, to ameliorate the suffering of

> . . . tu compañera descalza y hambrienta,
> y mi niño enfermo,
> y nuestros ancianos
> que todo lo dieron,
> sobre la cuneta
> buscando una capa de sol a sus huesos. (p.8)
>
> (. . . your barefoot and hungry partner,
> and my sick child,
> and our old folk
> who gave their all,
> on the street
> seeking for their bones the warmth of the sun.)

The war is seen as having resolved indulgent political differences, denounced by those comrades whose deaths 'gritan el delito de nuestras disputas' (cry out against the crime of our quarrels) (p.9) and, in the final section of the play, the soldiers are urged to seal a fraternal pact by expelling the invaders from the land:

> Los hombres, firme la planta,
> dura la mirada ciega,
> embisten como los toros
> contra la gente de fuera. (p.10)
>
> (The men, standing firm,
> gazing with a hard blind stare,
> charge like bulls
> against the outsiders.)

However idealized its portrait of Republican unity, Garfias's play offers the *miliciano* a broad and articulate political vision of why the war is being fought. An idealism born of deprivation and suffering is urged upon the soldier so that the conflict, while often presented as a foreign invasion, is also seen as a social transformation whose purpose is to usher in a progressive new era of economic well-being, justice and cultural enlightenment. Such a view permeates *teatro de urgencia*, the soldier being persistently invited to connect the war with his own life prior to its outbreak and recognize that he serves in what Mussot describes as 'el Ejército de la Libertad' (the Army of Liberty).[17] The *miliciano* is seen to be fighting to forge a new world in which there will be 'unas leyes que favorezcan al trabajador' (laws which favour the workers),[18] a goal whose attainment is seen in Hernández's *Los sentados* (*The Seated Ones*), for example, to be possible only through force of arms to defy 'la tiranía y [el] hambre' (tyranny and hunger).[19]

The achievement of this task depended upon *milicianos* following the 'camino seguro' (right path) for which the soldiers of *¡No pasarán!* had called in order to free themselves from an oppressive social and military caste. In response, *teatro de urgencia* forged a route which sought to engender skills of combat and the ability to articulate the necessity of combat. The purpose was to unite the elements which together would constitute the ideal fighter. The conclusion of Garfias's play hints at such a combatant in the image of the troops who, he suggests, are like bulls in their preparedness to attack 'la gente de fuera' (the outsiders) (p.10). *¡Hacia la victoria!* concludes with images of similar ferocity when the soldiers' bodies are lauded as a block of steel against which all opposition will be smashed. The essential purpose of such plays was to contribute to the fundamental military and political education of the *miliciano*, and their conclusions suggest an idealized figure who has absorbed the lesson of the drama and emerges from it unflinchingly confident of the route to victory. In keeping with the notion of transition, therefore, *teatro de urgencia* can be seen to move beyond a concern with the basic formation of the soldier, offering its audiences a model combatant, one for whom no sacrifice is impossible and whose exemplary dedication arises from revolutionary clarity about the war's meaning, and a stoical determination to endure its deprivations.

Such a heroic figure is prominently explored in Bleiberg's *Sombras de héroes* through the character of Leonardo, a *miliciano* who is the lone survivor of a Nationalist attack but who refuses to abandon his post, defending it until fatally wounded by an explosion.[20] In this play the notion of training the soldier is absent since not only Leonardo but the other *milicianos* who appear are so conscious of their responsibilities that they seem almost members of a cult, bonded together by duty, struggle, fraternal respect and love of their homeland. At the play's opening, for example, the soldiers are seen paying their respects to the last to abandon his post, their now dead comrade, Javier. Earth, blood, sacrifice and the swearing of oaths are the elements which characterize a funeral ritual which is a display of exemplary comradeship. As earth is scattered over the grave it is lauded as Basque earth 'para los que han sabido morir por Euzkadi' (for those who have known how to die for the Basque country) (p.97), earth which covers Javier in glory since it is the earth from which he sprang and to which he has returned with the name of Spain on his lips and with its pain in his blood. His sacrifice is declared the standard by which his surviving comrades swear to live, promising to avenge his death and to remain true to 'esta tierra que te envuelve' (this earth which shrouds you) (p.98).

As the *milicianos* continue to shovel earth into the grave, refugees enter, exhausted survivors of a bombing raid which has destroyed their village and left their lives' work 'como polvo por los caminos' (like dust by the roadsides) (p.99). Despondent and close to despair, the Old Man and the Mother bemoan all that they have lost and the Mother worries for the safety of her son, 'lejos y frente al enemigo' (far away and facing the enemy) (p.99). To her daughter, Isabel, however, material possessions matter little in comparison with the enormity of the struggle which is being waged, and she assures her mother that she, at least, feels no fears for her brother's well-being since 'tiene un puesto en el frente y un fusil para la defensa de Euzkadi' (he has a place at the front and a rifle for the defence of the Basque country) (p.99). As she recalls her brother, the Old Man is reminded of the *milicianos* who used to visit their hamlet to rest from the strain of duty. For Isabel this invites memories of Leonardo and less violent times before their village was drawn into the front line: '¡en qué tardes tan distintas hablé yo con él!' (on what very different afternoons I spoke to him!) (p.100). From the other side of the stage, having completed the burial of their comrade, the *milicianos* begin to make their exit and, maintaining the play's ritual, stylized quality, Leonardo and Isabel come to face one another in a reunion whose joy is muted by the loss of Javier. Placed at the centre of the stage while the others form a group to one side, Isabel and Leonardo exchange what they recognize might be the last words they speak to each other. Aware of the dangers which lie ahead and the sacred duty to defend Euzkadi, Leonardo confides his desire to die telling her 'lo último que debes saber de mí: que te quiero' (the last thing that you must know about me: that I love you) (p.102), a sentiment which he had shared only with the now dead Javier. Reciprocating his love, Isabel finds in his words the strength to continue the journey and, as the refugees head towards their destination of Guernica, she reveals her certainty that Leonardo and she will meet again.

In the play's second scene, which takes place at dawn, the Voice of the People appears, delivering a passionate call to arms by urging Basque men to emulate the example of the *milicianos* who, in an image which recalls the funeral oration of the opening scene,

> ... antes en tierra convierten
> su cuerpo de miliciano
> que, vivos, la tierra entreguen. (p.107)
>
> (... turn their soldiers' body into earth
> rather than, living, surrender the land.)

As the call is answered, men fill the stage and, in rapid and forceful dialogue, demand rifles to avenge their dead women and children and to defend the motherland against German and Italian domination. Their departure for the front, singing, is paralleled by the arrival of further refugees who, it is implied, are also heading for the apparent safety of Guernica. However, in the third scene, which takes place at dusk in the now ruined town, their corpses litter the stage, kicked and abused by German and Italian officers admiring the results of the 'magnífico y hermoso bombardeo' (magnificent and splendid bombardment) (p.113). Searching amongst the corpses for that of her mother, Isabel enters, weeping in exhausted despair. Surprised at discovering a survivor who has escaped violation and death, the German officer cynically declares that the Moorish troops must have 'perdido el olfato' (lost the scent) (p.117); he offers her to them once more, and Isabel is brutally dragged from the stage to the laughter of the foreign officers. Her fate becomes explicit in the final scene when her spirit appears before Leonardo defending his post alone at night after the deaths of those comrades who had sworn to avenge the death of Javier. In an ironic fulfilment of her certainty that she will see him again, she returns as 'un recuerdo' (a memory) (p.124) to reveal that her remains are amongst the ruins of Guernica and that 'un moro me violó y tres me asesinaron después' (a Moor raped me and afterwards three murdered me) (p.125). As she vanishes, an explosion mortally wounds him and, as day dawns, the Voice of the People enters and, through the funeral oration offered over the body, Leonardo's death is linked to that of Javier as one of noble sacrifice.

Relatively speaking, Bleiberg's play is extensive and detailed, features which are reflected in the character of Leonardo. The *miliciano* emerges as a figure who, while exhibiting many of the characteristics of poster art, also moves beyond them as the central figure of a play which, in Bilbatúa's view, displays both 'amplitud y profundidad' (breadth and depth).[21] His distinctiveness as the ideal soldier is persistently felt, not only in his understanding of, and active commitment to the military struggle, but also in more personal qualities such as the depth of feeling and loyalty shown to Isabel. Indeed, his commitment to the war and his love for her are indistinguishable and he urges her, for example, to feel certain of his love, not only because he is a man who has exchanged vows with her, but because he fights to defend 'la tierra que te dio la vida' (the land that gave you life) (p.103).

It is his disciplined bravery in defence of this land which offers the most striking illustration of his role as a model combatant by integrating, in a Trinity-like fashion, the concepts of faith, duty and sacrifice. His last moments see the culmination of these qualities in a final battle of endurance for which the *miliciano* seeks strength in all that has given meaning to his life. Alone at night, aware of impending death, one is reminded of Gethsemane, and the symbolism of Christ's agony is felt in his fear that he will fail this last test of faith. The impression is reinforced as he recalls his parents, finding that, despite his solitude: '¡ . . . qué cerca os siento hoy, en esta noche fría y muerta!' (. . . how close I feel you today, on this cold, dead night!) (p.123). In his fear, it is as though he considers denying the faith and duty he has so passionately espoused, by seeking to avoid the fate which awaits him. Since he is alone, under cover of darkness and knows 'todos los caminos de Euzkadi' (every road in the Basque country) (p.123), he feels the temptation to abandon his rifle and flee to Bilbao. It is in response to this wavering that the spirits of the Basque dead appear, reminding him of their own spilt blood, suffering and the fear that they will be forgotten amongst the ruins.

Unable to resolve his crisis of conscience, the *miliciano* struggles to drive them from his sight and his mind, but the appearance of the spirit of Isabel to warn him that he has sought to forget his 'deber frente al enemigo' (duty in the face of the enemy) (p.125) confronts him with the recognition of his sworn duty. Her call for him to fight until he conquers is taken up by the appearance of the spirit of the Old Man who, in a manner which recalls God the Father, urges Leonardo to fight until death rather than betray his people by deserting his post. As a blinding explosion wounds the *miliciano*, what has been a dark night of the soul ends and, in dying, Leonardo realizes that, given the blood which has been spilt, his own matters little. His defence of Euzkadi has been until death and his sacrifice is seen as one which, Christ-like, will redeem the land, since, in his final words, the *miliciano* asserts his belief that 'los hombres de España sabrán vengar este crimen' (the men of Spain will know how to avenge this crime) (p.126).

The profound relationship with the Spanish earth which predominantly characterizes Leonardo connects him with the *campesino* of ¡*Hacia la victoria!* who so eagerly sought to acquire basic military knowledge and discipline. Although the latter figure declared, 'no tengo muchas luces' (I'm pretty dim) (p.6), his determination to become a paragon of Republican virtues parallels Leonardo's own achievement of such a status. A useful perspective upon the figure of the *miliciano*, therefore, is to consider the notion of a collective character, one whose nuances of personality reflect *teatro de urgencia*'s desire to illustrate for its audiences the variety of experiences which might hinder or encourage the formation of the model soldier. The *miliciano* was thus seen at various stages of a journey towards an almost mystical incorporation into the body of noble warriors suggested by the soldiers who gather to bury Javier at the opening of *Sombras de héroes*. The commitment of theatrical propaganda to forging such a combatant from the reality of the militias is undoubtedly seen at its most idealized in Bleiberg's work. In *Amanecer*,[22] for example, the *milicianos* arrive to take over their duty watch accompanied by their customary singing and, when a woman is shot attempting to flee to the Republican lines, they care for her young son. As he gazes at his mother's corpse, the child is warned by the soldiers that 'de niño empiezas a sentir el sacrificio que a todos nos ha impuesto España' (from childhood you begin to feel the sacrifice which Spain has imposed on us all) (p.33), but they comfort him with the knowledge that, in the trenches, he has found true brothers who will always care for him. As dawn breaks over the trenches the *milicianos* shrug off the biting cold, aware that '. . . si España lo exige, cosas más duras habremos de soportar' (if Spain demands it, we'll have to endure harder things) (p.34), and that no sacrifice is too much.

It is perhaps a feature of propaganda that desired ends are distinct from current realities. What credibility with spectators could such an idealized image of the *miliciano* possess, given that the perceived need to cultivate and celebrate the image might indicate its absence in reality? The answer perhaps lies in propaganda's uncertain relationship between the real and the ideal. Clearly, Leonardo exists, for example, as a complex mediation of the author's beliefs and hopes, as well as images from his own experience of active service as a *miliciano* in the Basque country and at Teruel.[23] The emotional force of the image can, in drama and circumstances of this kind, acquire a truthful reality, and it is to this emotional world that *teatro de urgencia* frequently made its appeal. The nurturing of an idealized image of the *miliciano* such as that of Bleiberg raises a drama of example to a poetic level, seeking to elicit an emotional response from the spectator which it is hoped will inform his or her more rational, daily behaviour. It is surely significant, however, that in *teatro de urgencia* which is known to have been presented before troop audiences, and whose principal focus is the *miliciano*, idealized images of combatants are eschewed in favour of a more broadly realistic exploration of military life and its obligations. By contrast, in *teatro de urgencia* presented in the rearguard, the idealized *miliciano* is prominent to the extent that a cult status attaches to the figure, both through his own actions and through the responses to him of other characters. *Sombras de héroes* is itself an example of such a work, having been presented, as part of the repertoire of the TAP, at the Teatro de la Zarzuela in December 1937. The absence of any recorded performance of the play as part of a guerrilla troupe's repertoire is perplexing, given the quality of the play's language and the fact that it was well known during the war. Not only did it win first prize in a competition for *teatro de urgencia* organized by the JSU, but the play was also published in an anthology of propaganda dramas. An identical question arises concerning Bleiberg's other play, *Amanecer*, which remained unperformed despite having been entrusted to Alberti.[24] One might imagine that technical demands or the scale of the works might have deterred guerrilla troupes such as those of Mussot from presenting the plays, but adaptation was simple and *Radio Sevilla* and *Los salvadores* were popular examples of the effectiveness of such an approach.

The feeling of poster art in the image of the warrior hero was, therefore, an aspect of *teatro de urgencia*'s portrayal of the *miliciano* which seems to have been aimed much more at civilian audiences. Such spectators were repeatedly offered images of supremely dedicated individuals as a means of urging similar effort by the rearguard population. In *Lección y escarmiento*,[25] which was performed in the streets of Barcelona, for example, the soldier has been given a few days' leave but declares that he wishes only to return to the front line since 'ya tiene uno ganas de volver' (already one has the urge to get back) (p.34). The play's setting, the corner of a busy bar, becomes the scene of a frank encounter between the soldier and the character of the Friend, the defeatist of the play. The Friend's pessimistic view of the war's progress is challenged by the soldier in terms which emphasize for the spectators his experience of the fury of battle and his hardened resistance to it. His catalogue of suffering, which has caused his hand to 'crispar de rabia . . . el cerrojo del fusil' (grip his rifle bolt with anger) (p.36), leads him to have more faith than ever in victory. Unshakeable commitment such as this also figures prominently in *Barco de traidores*, a play which presented urban audiences with a joyful celebration of the Republic's armed forces following the sinking of the Nationalist warship, the Baleares, in March 1938.[26] The mood of battle is graphically evoked for the spectators as Mariano, the hero of the play, recalls that 'la orden de ataque fue para nosotros la emoción que deseábamos con ansia' (for us, the order to attack was the excitement which we eagerly longed for) (p.26), and that his blood boiled in his veins as 'la negrura del mar y de la noche se rompió con una rabia de luces de nuestra artillería' (the blackness of the sea and the night was broken by the raging lights of our artillery) (p.27). Unusually for *teatro de urgencia*, soldiers, sailors and air force personnel appear in this play and, in a burst of collective triumph, the audience is invited to share the pride felt by Mariano's *novia* (girl-friend) at his bravery, and to admire the mutual respect which characterizes all the elements of the Republic's armed forces. The pilot, for example, embraces the *miliciano*, recognizing that all the weapons and aeroplanes of modern technology are worthless 'sin una infantería heroica como esta que tenemos nosotros' (without a heroic infantry like the one which we have) (p.29), and lauds him as a brave comrade who has to resist and attack along every inch of the trenches.

A principal aim of exposing civilian audiences to images of the *milicianos*' selfless devotion to combat was to encourage like effort on the part of spectators. The soldiers' struggle and sacrifice was presented as an undertaking on behalf of the rearguard, one to guarantee its freedom. As the soldier of *Lección y escarmiento* remarks: 'de las cárceles de Franco no se regresa jamás' (from Franco's jails none ever return) (p.35). The civilian population was seen as the means by which the military would be supplied with the equipment, clothing, food and supplies necessary to victory. Clarifying the rearguard's importance, and the individual's contribution to it, involved, therefore, the poster-art image of a heroic warrior as an example both to admire and to follow. In *Despedida de reclutas*,[27] for example, workers bid farewell to Alfredo, a young recruit, with the assurance that they will continue to demonstrate by example that 'el frente de la producción tiene que ser igual que el otro donde tú vas ahora' (the production front has to be the same as the other one to which you're now going) (p.20) and that, like Alfredo in the front line, they will forfeit rest days and *fiestas*. Alfredo's mother is exemplary in this respect since, with three sons already in the front line, her regret is that she does not have more to give to the cause.

Clearly discernible in *teatro de urgencia* offered to military audiences, however, is a picture of the *miliciano* which qualifies the flawless perfection of his image as presented to civilians. Indeed, the emphasis upon various aspects of training suggests that the portrait of the soldier would be drawn from more fundamentally realistic materials. It must be borne in mind that, whereas civilian audiences were largely offered an *image* of the *miliciano*, military audiences were, by contrast, largely offered a *self-image* and that a much greater degree of objectivity was required in this aspect of theatrical propaganda. Undesirable images of soldiers were thus offered as a means of contributing to the military education of the audience. The very title of Ontañón's *El saboteador*, for example, perhaps suggests the far from idealized view of the soldier which it was also necessary to present.[28] The Republican military authorities regarded with suspicion many regular officers who had remained loyal, fearing that their true sympathies lay elsewhere and so, along with the defeatist, the saboteur was a prominent target of *teatro de urgencia*. Ontañón, for example, dealt with the issue again in his other propaganda work, *El bulo*, satirizing the fifth-columnists who were an ever-present danger in the capital throughout the war. *El saboteador*, with its front-line setting, is intended not only to entertain the *milicianos* through the dramatic unmasking of a saboteur, but also to contribute to their training by demonstrating behaviour which is likely to appear to sabotage the war effort.

The action of *El saboteador* takes place in the military operations headquarters established in a country house close to the front line. The increasing ferocity of the Nationalist attack, particularly the threat that the enemy will succeed in cutting road communications, makes it imperative that Serrano and ten other *milicianos* secure a warrant which will allow them to travel immediately to Coriza. The necessary document must be authorized by Montes, but his prevarication delays the departure of the convoy by half an hour, minutes which prove tragically crucial. The enemy's advance is gathering momentum and a vital bridge is destroyed by explosives as the soldiers' truck passes over. All the *milicianos* are killed, including Enrique, the brother of Nati, a young girl from Madrid, who has arrived at the headquarters to pay a visit and whose good-humoured, flirtatious banter with Montes turns to horrified despair as she realizes the nature of her brother's death. Salas, a quietly efficient and dedicated soldier, has observed events shrewdly, increasingly certain that Montes's intention is sabotage by delaying the *milicianos'* efforts to counter the Nationalist offensive. As Nati is helped from the room in distress, denouncing the murderers of her brother, Salas declares the murderer to be Montes, a traitor 'más vil que los que disparan desde enfrente' (more vile than those opposite who are firing) (p.87). Demanding the justice of military law to be swift, Salas orders Montes's arrest, and the play closes with the remaining soldiers advancing upon him, the truth of his sabotage dawning upon them.

Despite Ontañón's stage direction that soldiers enter to hear 'la verdad que está aclarando Salas' (the truth which Salas is making clear) (pp.86–7), the action itself leaves unresolved the question of how deliberate is Montes's sabotage. This offers an open-ended quality to the play and was perhaps designed to encourage post-performance discussion amongst the spectators of what might be deemed to constitute sabotage. Montes's undermining of the Republican cause thus offered the audience an object lesson in inappropriate military behaviour. At the opening of the play, for example, his lack-lustre commitment is suggested in his persistent drinking and in the wine which he repeatedly offers to other *milicianos* despite Salas's warning that such conviviality is inopportune given the closeness of the enemy. To Montes, Salas's objections are puritanical and he accuses Salas of failing to see that what he describes as a good dose of wine will add vigour to the *milicianos'* attack. Montes's apparently frivolous, lackadaisical manner is characteristic of his attitude to military affairs. When a telephone request is made to speak to him, he excuses himself from having to answer on the grounds that, since it is six o'clock in the evening, the matter can only concern 'las idioteces que se le ocurre a la gente' (the rubbish that people get into their heads) (p.78).

The threat which Montes represents to the soldiers' common purpose is principally manifested in his failure to provide Serrano with the documentation enabling him to proceed to the front line. At first, his idle chatter with other soldiers prevents him reading the document, while later, to Serrano's frustration, he declares that he has only skimmed the matter. While he reads with evident slowness, he requests a soldier to hurry his work at the typewriter in order to expedite Serrano's demand, but when the soldier suggests that he might interrupt his current work, Montes declines the offer and delays Serrano yet further. When, finally, the necessary permit is typed, the official stamp cannot be found and Montes berates his comrades for their inefficiency:

Pero ¿cómo no lo encuentras? Tiene que estar ahí. (*Busca*). Algún imbécil lo habrá cogido. ¿Lo habéis cogido alguno de vosotros? (p.66)

(But why can't you find it? It has to be here. (*He searches*). Some idiot will have taken it. Have one of you taken it?)

His apparently surprised discovery of the stamp in his pocket brings an apology from Montes and invites the suspicion on Serrano's part that Montes's ineffectiveness is due to excess alcohol. As he finally leaves for the front line, Serrano's purposeful manner is scorned by Montes, who declares him to be a mere boy who, given a simple task, imagines himself head of a division. As the noise of combat is increased by the arrival of fighter planes overhead, Serrano returns, angered to have discovered that although Montes has supplied the order, he has failed to specify the relevant quantity. Blaming Serrano for failing to check the document, Montes sets about rectifying the error, but the arrival of Nati distracts him yet again and, as he flirts with her, Serrano is unable to contain himself. Accusing Montes of negating his duty, he demands that he behave with military correctness. Sarcastically, Montes rises to the challenge by sending Serrano's documentation to the commandant so that, with maximum correctness, it can receive appropriate scrutiny. While all wait, Montes, rather contemptuously, lights a cigarette and pours more wine. His confidence is checked, however, when the document is returned with the commandant's response that his signature is unnecessary. Finally able to depart, Serrano expresses the ironic hope that next time greater efficiency will be possible and leaves to meet what now turns out to be his death and that of his comrades.

The undesirable characteristics shown by Montes are reiterated by Salas once the news of the *milicianos*' fate has reached the headquarters. In a long speech of denunciation he lists the shortcomings displayed by Montes, flaws which he declares to equal those of the 'miserable fascista que puso la mano en el contacto de la mina' (miserable Fascist who put his hand on the contact of the mine) (p.87). There is a keen sense of the presentation of evidence before the spectators so that they may judge Montes guilty, or clarify in their own minds the reasons why sabotage can fairly be assumed from his behaviour. Ontañón's intention is to place the final emphasis on the *miliciano* in the audience, who is invited by example to measure his own behaviour against that of Montes, or perhaps to watch the action with a discerning eye for inappropriate actions, expressions or values. In achieving this, the play combines, as it were, both *deleite* and *doctrina* (entertainment and instruction) in that its almost melodramatic unmasking of the villain is accompanied by the illustration of qualities deemed to undermine the military struggle. It is a technique which offers a morality-play spirit to the drama, the correct path being marked out through the display and defeat of the vices represented by Montes. This spirit is reiterated in *Tres soldados*, another play to offer a negative image of the *miliciano* in order to lay before its audience the problems which may encourage desertion and the means by which they must be overcome.[29] Performed during spring 1938 on the eastern front, the action portrays the breakdown of a *miliciano* who is unable to withstand the ferocity of combat and the deprivations of trench life. Terrified, he deserts but, as he flees, he hears the cries of a wounded comrade. Uncertain whether to assist the injured man or continue to run away, the deserter vacillates and, in despair, confesses to the wounded *miliciano* that:

> . . . no puedo con este cansancio. ¡No puedo soportar esto! ¡No puedo! Mira. Desde el amanecer nos están tirando con artillería. Todo el campo es un infierno. Y los italianos avanzan . . . avanzan . . . ¡No es posible contenerlos! Yo me voy. ¡No resisto esto! ¡No lo resisto! (p.89)

(. . . I can't carry on with this tiredness. I can't stand this! I can't! Look. Since dawn they've been shelling. The whole countryside is an inferno. And the Italians advance and advance . . . It's impossible to hold them back. I'm leaving. I can't take it!)

In shame, he confesses that 'no me aguantan los nervios' (my nerves can't stand it) (p.90), but it is this sense of dishonour, of shameful failure, which enables the wounded soldier to recapture, as it were, the deserter's soul and rekindle his faith in the success of continued resistance. Speaking in a fraternal tone, he contrasts the current battle situation with that of Madrid, Guadalajara and the Jarama, urging the deserter to see that from the very worst military circumstances victory is possible because 'hay pocos como tú' (there are few like you) (p.91). Falling silent, the deserter is uncertain and exhausted when, from the other trenches, another deserter arrives. Avoiding the rifle fire of his own side, the Nationalist soldier has swum across a river by taking hold of a floating tree trunk. His account of life in the other zone is one of the brutal murder and exploitation of peasants: 'todas las noches a filas y filas de presos . . . como a perros' (every night, to line after line of prisoners . . . as if to dogs) (p.93). Yet, in spite of such terror, he proudly recalls, nobody doubts that the Republic will liberate them through 'vuestra heroica resistencia' (your heroic resistance) (p.92). Declaring 'le das a uno fe' (you give faith to one) (p.93), the Republican deserter begins to rediscover his commitment and, as the noise of a counter-attack is heard, he declares that he too will rejoin the struggle for 'el bienestar de mañana' (the well-being of tomorrow) (p.94). There is a touching simplicity about the play, in both its style and its conclusion, which recalls the medieval dramatic tradition. The 'camino seguro' (right path) is shown here with a poignancy made more acute by the bleak military circumstances which prevailed for the Republic around the time of the play's composition. The final line, '¡no pasarán!' (they shall not pass!) (p.95), shouted in unison as the soldiers exit, recalls, too, the conclusion of Mussot's *¡No pasarán!*, and it is interesting to note the very different moods which prevail at the conclusions of the two plays. Whereas Mussot's soldiers chant the words as, more or less, a political slogan, its inclusion at the close of *Tres soldados* reflects a much more battle-hardened determination, even desperation, to halt the enemy's progress. The differing dramatic moods evoked by the slogan suggest the panorama of experiences undergone by the *miliciano* and *teatro de urgencia*'s reflection of such a panorama through the portrayal of a wide range of issues designed to assist in the making of a victorious people's army.

The prominence lent by *teatro de urgencia* to the *miliciano* encouraged the emergence of a composite figure, but with varying shades of personality which reflected the exigencies of the moment in the demands of particular propaganda tasks. The various masks of the *commedia dell'arte* are useful as a means of exploring such a figure since the underlying principle was that of a basic character type which assumed particular forms in a range of dramatic circumstances. Although a simple chronology does not offer a complete explanation of the various facets of the character, the development of the Republican army mirrors to some extent the different roles played by the *miliciano*. As the army was forged from the popular militias, the *miliciano* grew as a character. The puppet-like automaton which appeared at the opening of Mussot's *¡No pasarán!* assumed more detailed attributes as more testing demands placed upon the *miliciano* reflected the increasingly complex nature of the army's organizational and training task. Such attributes manipulated images of the soldier which, depending upon the audience, were both idealized and realistic. The needs of the unwilling, ignorant or confused *campesino* were addressed so that he could be shown both how to conduct the struggle and its political meaning. In a more idealized fashion, the cult of the *miliciano*, which was so predominant in propaganda posters, was enhanced through the presentation in exemplary language of images of heroic sacrifice. The soldier was seen to be bonded with somewhat mystical essences such as the *pueblo* and the *patria*, qualities which enabled him to articulate a vision of the war as a revolutionary crusade for social justice and liberty.

It is notable how, in its presentation of the ordinary soldier, *teatro de urgencia* highlighted a figure which had been significantly absent from the Spanish stage. Apart from the Republic's proto-martyr, Fermín Galán, whose deeds had been controversially dramatized by Alberti,[30] the soldier had rarely received dramatic treatment on the Spanish stage during the decades prior to the Civil War. After the military disaster of 1898 plays relating to the situation in Cuba were produced, but the army rarely became the subject of serious or critical exploration. Protected by the strict Ley de Jurisdicciones (Jurisdiction Law) the military was a difficult institution to subject to dramatic treatment, since even the slightest criticism was liable to trial by court martial.[31] In focusing on the ordinary soldier as a dramatic character, *teatro de urgencia* was, of course, merely responding to the exigencies of the historical moment. Yet it also gave theatrical voice to a significant figure of Spanish society which had enjoyed no voice before the advent of the Republic and was to have none after its demise.

~ 6 ~

Training for Victory

The research which has taken place into Republican propaganda indicates that techniques of persuasion were numerous and employed a variety of media to disseminate Loyalist perspectives on the conflict. Abella, for example, describes the rapid growth of newspapers dedicated to raising consciousness and fostering the spirit of combat.[1] Posters and wall newspapers played a similar role, seeking to indicate to soldiers and civilians ideal conduct in such matters as discipline, hygiene and the raising of morale. *Consignas* (slogans) such as 'Madrid: ¡Hagámosle Inexpugnable!' (Madrid: make it impregnable!)[2] and 'Hay que eliminar a todos los vagos profesionales' (We must get rid of all the professional layabouts)[3] received prominent exposure in newspapers and public places. The Commissariat attached clear importance to what it described as 'propaganda gráfica' (visual propaganda) when it published detailed advice on the need to decorate front-line positions with a range of appropriate *consignas*. The sense of co-ordinated planning behind the Commissariat's pamphlet on the subject can be felt in its advice to commissars to prepare boards of 70 × 100 cm to display materials in preparation by the Commissariat.[4]

When one considers, too, the propaganda tasks carried out through collective activities such as recitals, library classes and cinema showings, an impression can be gained of significant sections of the population exposed to moral, political and military exhortation. The showing of the Soviet film *Los marinos de Cronstad* (*The Sailors of Kronstadt*) in Madrid, for example, was accompanied between reels by the projection of propaganda slogans applauding the work of the Milicias de la Cultura (Cultural Militias).[5] A similar development in a front-line context, where projection facilities were largely unavailable, was the publication of 'Charlas sencillas a los combatientes' (Simple Talks for Combatants), a pamphlet series designed to overcome the problem of widespread illiteracy. Through short narratives, presumably read by a figure such as a commissar, perspectives considered appropriate were encouraged and, almost certainly, discussion was fostered as a means of clarifying the topic's relevance to the *milicianos*' active service. In *Por qué los campesinos están interesados en vencer al fascismo* (*Why the Peasants have an Interest in Defeating Fascism*), for example, soldiers who might well have been rural labourers before the war, were offered an explanation of the talk's title in terms of *caciquismo* (local political bosses), inequitable land distribution and the opportunity of the war and revolution to eradicate past injustices:

> Una prueba de lo que el fascismo sería para el campesino la tenemos en lo que el fascismo es ya para los trabajadores del campo en la zona facciosa. Allí, los terratenientes salvajes, los usureros crueles, los explotadores de la tierra, siguen gozando de sus privilegios.[6]

> (We have proof of what Fascism would be for the peasantry in what Fascism is now for the rural workers in the rebel zone. There, the brutal landlords, the cruel moneylenders, the land exploiters carry on enjoying their privileges.)

Teatro de urgencia endorsed all of the above responses to the conflict since, despite inevitable questions of tactics or priorities, each sought to be coherent with the overriding *consigna* announced by the Council for the Defence of Madrid: 'lo primero es ganar la guerra' (First – win the war).[7] *Teatro de urgencia*'s own contribution to such propaganda was apparent in at least two ways. First, its comprehensive portrait of the enemy sought, as we have seen, an effective focus for military and civilian spectators which enabled the conflict to be presented largely as a foreign invasion. Second, its portrayal of the *miliciano* aimed to nurture military skills and attitudes necessary to victory. Images of the enemy and of the Loyalist soldier were perhaps the foremost elements of theatrical propaganda, but a third task had also to be attempted, one which stressed the panorama of civil and military issues presented by the conflict. The dramatization of *consignas* considered relevant, and their presentation before appropriate audiences, led, therefore, to a significant body of *teatro de urgencia* through which, in what an anonymous writer described as 'una buena lección dada desde el escenario' (a good lesson given from the stage),[8] drama was able to fuse with the numerous currents of Republican propaganda.

The principal *consigna* which *teatro de urgencia* sought to emphasize was that of duty. The transmission of such a notion was the overarching endeavour of propaganda writers, a theme which binds together a range of plays aimed at both military and civilian spectators. Presented as unflinching commitment to the Republic, duty is the essential quality of numerous characters whose purpose was to embody ideal behaviour and, through the plays' action, to offer audiences what was described at the time as 'un vivo motor de entusiasmo' (a vivid driving force of enthusiasm) and as an 'ensayo de movilización de espíritus' (attempt to raise morale).[9] Perhaps the clearest illustration of *teatro de urgencia*'s concern with duty can be felt, not in the Commissariat's guidance to writers of theatrical propaganda, but in aspects of advice concerning wall newspapers. Zanetti wrote, for example, of the need for such newsheets to lay great emphasis upon 'emulación' (emulation), highlighting and applauding not only obviously heroic acts, but also those individuals who showed themselves to be keen in study, hygienic or exceptionally disciplined.[10]

The most sustained exploration of devotion to duty, whatever its hazards for one's personal safety, is Mussot's *A la orden*. In this extremely rare text a loyal *alférez*, Ramos, and his superior, the Commander, provide what Mussot's prologue lauds as the noble figure of the 'auténtico héroe' (genuine hero), worthy examples of 'cuanto significa cumplimiento del deber' (how much the course of duty means).[11] Duty is, therefore, immediately established as the principal theme of the play. Although these two military figures are prominent in the author's understanding of duty in the play, the character Maruchi exposes herself to a similar degree of danger to the soldiers and, throughout the play's three scenes, therefore, the determined commitment of the Republicans is shared by soldiers and civilians alike. This may offer a partial explanation of why the play found its way into the repertoire of the Teatro Pavón in Madrid where, in May 1938, it was seen by rearguard audiences after its earlier presentation before front-line spectators.

The play's events occur on 21 July 1936 in Spanish North Africa where, as news of the military rebellion on the mainland begins to break, insurrectionist elements of the military garrison await their opportunity to participate in the uprising. Their plan is contingent upon the safe arrival of a naval vessel, potentially loyal to the Republic, delivering the soldiers' pay. Once this has been safely purloined, events are intended to move rapidly so that the rebels can, in the words of the Falangist Lieutenant, liberate Spain from 'esa horda roja, de foragidos, de ineducados, de ambiciosos, que pretenden que todos seamos iguales' (that red horde, of bandits, ignoramuses, envious graspers who want us all to be equal) (p.6). Unbeknown to the Lieutenant, however, his *novia*, Maruchi, is not the doting lover she seems. Although 'muy felina le pasa y repasa las manos por el cabello, el cuello y la cara' (very feline, she strokes his hair, neck and face) (p.5), the intention behind her fond behaviour to the Lieutenant reflects a strategic flattery which has already enabled her to elicit the information that a number of the garrison's officers are committed to the planned uprising. The Lieutenant's gullibility is in contrast to the brutality with which he views the Republic. His opponents, he declares, must be dealt with through 'una degollina que deje memoria eterna' (a massacre which will leave an everlasting memory) (p.6). He is unable, however, to see through what is, for the audience, Maruchi's obvious insincerity:

> Novia (*astuta, mimosa otra vez*): ¡Qué idiota eres! ¡Eres el falangista más obtuso de España! ¿Qué sé yo de política, ni de sublevaciones, ni de esas memeces? Con saber que te quiero me sobra, Pinocho... No dudes de mí, de tu Maruchi, que es una mujer que no cambiaría el mundo por tus besos. (pp.7–8)

> (*Novia* (*shrewd, affectionately again*): What an idiot you are! You're the most stupid Falangist in Spain! What do I know about politics, or insurrections or silly things like that? Knowing that I love you is more than enough for me, my little dish ... don't doubt me, your Maruchi, a woman who wouldn't swap your kisses for the whole world.)

Their conversation, in the corner of a bar, opens the play and establishes the background to the intended rebellion. As Maruchi leaves, with a mischievous 'adiós ... ¡mi bestia!' (goodbye ... whizzkid!) (p.8), the Lieutenant is joined by the Captain and, while they pore over the lists of the officers whom they believe committed to their plot, their discussion turns to Ramos, the *alférez* whose discretion is such that, according to the Lieutenant, it had for long been difficult to discern his attitude to a potential rebellion. The arrival of Ramos, and his apparent gratitude for being incorporated into the rebels' plans, pleases the Captain since, in his view, Ramos's youth provides the link between older officers who are fully committed to the uprising and younger ones who, he believes, will follow

Ramos's example and use the pretext of the rebellion as an opportunity for personal advancement through the ranks. Announcing the news which has reached him of the rebellion's success on the mainland during the previous forty-eight hours, the Captain senses that their own moment of glory is approaching. He has only one reservation: although the garrison Commander must possess the same information from the mainland, he has failed to declare his loyalties. Unwilling to make a move until the expected money is safely in his hands, the Captain anticipates his subsequent pleasure in executing the Commander and ushering in 'una nueva era: La Fascista' (a new era: the Fascist era) (p.13).

In the second scene of the play the Commander proffers his grateful admiration of Maruchi's courageous skill in eliciting vital information from the Lieutenant and confides that, although he has learned of the rout suffered by the uprising at the hands of the *pueblo* in Madrid and Barcelona, he intends to continue a waiting game so that it will prove possible to unmask all those whose loyalty is suspect and, thus, 'limpiar de miasmas la atmósfera' (clear the atmosphere of putrid matter) (p.14). Ramos's entry into the Commander's office, bearing news of the plotters' intention to await the consignment of money before raising the garrison, provides the opportunity to reveal the conspirators' identities. Before the details of his stratagem are made clear, however, the rebels approach with an ultimatum for the Commander. Alone on-stage, with his pistol on the table covered by a paper, he is accused at gunpoint, by the Captain and Lieutenant, of treachery for his failure to support the rebellion which he must be aware has occurred on the peninsula. Gradually turning the situation to his advantage, however, the Commander declares himself to be on the side of the uprising and, as proof of his integrity, reveals the communication he has received concerning the imminent arrival of the naval consignment:

> ¿Comprenden? Nada nos prohíbe recibir ese dinero del enemigo, hacernos del barco y ponernos después al servicio de España, de nuestra España. (p.8)

> (Do you understand? Nothing prevents us receiving this enemy money, getting hold of the boat and afterwards putting ourselves at the service of Spain, of our Spain.)

His ploy, successful in convincing the rebels of his sympathy with their cause, comes to fruition in the final scene of the play. As

Maruchi, impatient for news of developments, paces the Commander's office, he arrives and the full nature of his gamble becomes clear. In order for the rebels to identify each other, they have agreed with him that as they received their pay, a watchword should be spoken to the cashier. Since 'ignoran que los que no dicen nada al cobrar son sus carceleros' (they are unaware that those who say nothing when they are paid are their jailers) (p.22), the insurgents are outwitted and, having been paid, are identified, subsequently overpowered and placed under arrest. At the close of the action the Captain and the Lieutenant are escorted away to face military justice, and Ramos is ordered to send a telegram to the authorities declaring the insurrection defeated, the rebels' possessions distributed amongst the loyal forces and the garrison placed securely under the orders of the Republic.

An indication of the significance of duty in the play is felt in its very title and also in the notable sense of proud accomplishment with which, as the play concludes, the Republic is honoured through a chorus of *vivas*. Ramos himself frequently endorses the notion of duty when, on various entrances, his firm declaration, '¡a la orden!' (yes, *sir*!), suggests his eager readiness to serve. The Lieutenant's estimation of Ramos's abilities also serves to reveal the extent to which the *alférez* is a paragon of duty. Regarding him as 'inmejorable' (excellent) (p.9), the Lieutenant recommends Ramos to the Captain as disciplined, serious and, above all, as 'un cumplidor ciego del deber' (unflinching in carrying out his duty) (p.9). Portrayed as spending a great deal of time engaged in study, Ramos displays characteristic Republican diligence, although the Lieutenant confesses himself baffled to see Ramos 'pegado siempre a los libros' (always stuck in a book) since he fails to understand 'para qué romperse la cabeza de esa manera' (why [you should] rack your brains like that) (p.10).

Perhaps the most striking feature of the play's exploration of duty, however, is the extent to which the Republican characters are prepared to conduct themselves in a duplicitous manner in order to achieve their ends. Deception and lying, qualities which seem to undermine the idealized nobility traditionally associated with heroic figures of propaganda imagery, are fundamental aspects of the behaviour of Maruchi, Ramos and the Commander. Their sense of moral correctness, allied with the dedicated certainty of their commitment to the Republic, however, enables them to overcome reservations about deceit since duty to the cause is presented as the supreme virtue. The Commander is, thus, in Ramos's view, capable of telling a lie only 'en provecho de lo que a los tres nos une' (to benefit what unites us three) (p.21), the defence of the Republic and the defeat of Fascism. The Commander himself seems regretful, resigned to the course of feigned loyalty to the Fascist rising, but aware that no other action can serve the Loyalist cause. As he awaits, alone, the arrival of the Captain and the Lieutenant to usurp his authority in the garrison, he appears almost to despair of his involvement: '¡valen tan poco, tan poco, que casi no merecen mi preocupación!' (they are worth so little, so little, that they almost aren't worth my concern) (p.17).

The morality of the characters' actions is particularly intriguing with respect to Maruchi since her relationship with the Lieutenant is clearly one which suggests its physical nature. That the Lieutenant is so convincingly duped about her affections is due to the skill with which Maruchi plays, in effect, the role of camp prostitute. Her true feelings are revealed only in the second scene, when the Commander praises her determination to feign the role of besotted lover despite her personal disgust at behaviour which he carefully describes as being 'por muchos motivos . . . repugnante' (for many reasons . . . disgusting) (p.14). Her thoughts, like those of the Commander, rest ultimately upon the success of the greater cause and, lest she become despondent about her actions, he urges her to ponder the 'magnífico servicio' (magnificent service) (p.14) which she has done the Republic. Unlike Ramos, Maruchi is implicated more actively in the deceit. While his tactic enables him to appear somewhat aloof, playing the role of 'pundonoroso militar' (honourable soldier) (p.15) in order to enhance the rebels' view of him as an officer in the conventional mould of the Spanish military, Maruchi is required to do whatever is necessary to 'fingir cariño a un miserable . . . a un cretino' (feign affection for a scoundrel . . . a moron) (p.14). For the play's spectators the notion of sacrifice is acute with regard to Maruchi, since her concept of duty is so firmly rooted as to withstand actions which, in other circumstances, she would find self-destructive. Her wry comment that her relationship with the Lieutenant will form part of the 'martirologio revolucionario' (revolutionary martyrology) (p.13) indicates the depth of her commitment to a strategy which, while morally dubious, even indefensible, is presented as a vivid example of how 'los verdaderos antifascistas' (true anti-

Fascists) (p.2) must do their duty in spite of all qualms, 'cueste lo que cueste' (whatever the cost) (p.2).

Over its three scenes, described by Mussot as 'moments', *A la orden*'s presentation of the idea of duty displays a dramatic development which is more extensive than is generally the case with *teatro de urgencia*. The audience is encouraged to assimilate and practise a generalized notion concerning the need to embrace a sense of duty which should imbue all aspects of Republican life and work. Its rather conventional structure, a feature which might have recommended it for performance on the proscenium stage of the Teatro Pavón, ensures, however, that a *consigna* such as submission to duty is explored in a manner which is relatively naturalistic, even leisurely, in the pace and style with which events unfold. That this is unusual in *teatro de urgencia* concerned with the exploration of *consignas* is perhaps explained by the lack of specificity in the task with which the audience is confronted. The element of *deleite* might be felt to overshadow or outweigh that of *doctrina*, and the play would have functioned extremely well as an item of entertainment in a programme of organized recreation for soldiers. Its dramatic form, indeed, recalls Sender's *El secreto* which was a frequent choice for inclusion in such front-line *fiestas*.[12] The somewhat diffuse nature of the *consigna* explored by Mussot's play contrasts sharply with the majority of *teatro de urgencia* plays which, while similarly concerned to orientate their audiences with respect to appropriate values and behaviour, often arose from the need to produce propaganda in circumstances of the most pressing immediacy, circumstances which demanded a highly focused task to be urged upon sections of the population.

The defence of Madrid in November 1936 and the threat to Aragón in the spring of 1938 provided such circumstances, since Nationalist attacks prompted the urgent need for rapid enlistment into hastily organized shock battalions in order to check rebel advances.[13] The full titles of two plays mentioned earlier which were produced in response to such grave military developments, *Cuatro batallones de choque* and *Dos divisiones de la juventud*, not only suggest the manner in which *teatro de urgencia* sought to contribute at what emerged as moments of historical crisis, but also indicate the clarity of the plays' single-minded *consigna*. In *Cuatro batallones*, for example, the idea of duty is insisted upon through the specific focus of an enlistment so urgently required that, as the play's prologue declares, the recruits would be under fire even before the battalions were finally organized.[14] The play's call to arms was delivered through the simple dramatic device of constructing dialogue between social types whose commitment to the defence of the capital was perceived as lacking, but whose ages were within the optimum range for recruitment. The Fat Bourgeois, the Artist and the Affected Young Girl bemoan, therefore, the deprivations of the war, swapping anecdotes which list the inconveniences to which life is now subject. Deliberately unattractive, even ridiculous figures, their dramatic function was to discourage audience identification with them and, by implication, encourage the spectators towards affirmation of the need to enlist. Perhaps the most significant figure, however, was that of the Worker, since the play emphasized the very average nature of his character, one whose description tended to match the great majority of the play's audiences and which hinted at the atmosphere of the capital during the months following the outbreak of war. Seen as an honest labourer who earns his daily wage, the Worker's only shortcomings are a failure to realize that the danger of the time requires extraordinary effort, and that his union card is not to be used to excuse obligations or as a means of access to privileges. The exchanges between these characters establish their inadequate responses to the conflict and pave the way for the enlisted workers, a man and a woman who begin their role in the action by speaking from amongst the throng of spectators, to berate the others' failure to realize that, now more than ever, they should be learning how to handle a rifle or a machine-gun. The closeness of the enemy is seen to be such that even the Affected Young Girl, whose prime concern has been her inability to dress elegantly for fear that she may fail to blend with the current social mood, is urged to learn how to throw bombs since 'nos va a hacer falta en seguida' (we're going to need to do that immediately) (p.11). As each character is found to be failing Madrid in its hour of need, the focus switches to the spectators, those whose response to the play will determine whether the battalions enlist their target number of recruits. Having mounted the stage to challenge the other characters, the two enlisted workers close the action with an appeal for all men and women aged between twenty and fifty to enlist immediately, in the knowledge that, while they need not avoid their daily work, they will avoid the label of parasites which is visited upon the on-stage figures:

> Camaradas: el enemigo está cerca de Madrid. Tiene buenos elementos de combate que le ha proporcionado el fascismo internacional. Es preciso

que todos los antifascistas, hombres y mujeres, se dispongan a luchar con entusiasmo para que nuestro Madrid no caiga en sus manos ... (p.13)

(Comrades: the enemy is near Madrid. They have good combat equipment supplied to them by international Fascism. It's necessary for all anti-Fascists, men and women, to prepare to fight enthusiastically so that our Madrid doesn't fall into their hands ...)

This direct address with which the action concludes recalls other propaganda techniques such as posters, radio broadcasts and the slogans of street demonstrations, so that the *consigna* stands unambiguously apparent to the audience. Although the enlisted workers are incorporated into the action, the mood which the performers seek is more that of a spirited political meeting, of the play being interrupted in order to make an urgent announcement. Their viewpoints scornfully rejected, the non-enlisted characters are curtly dismissed from consideration. Such a forthright approach perhaps suggests the circumstances of near desperation which led to the play's composition and accounts for the rapid, even aggressive, nature of its language and the stark simplicity of its structure. The message of urgent enlistment is, thus, reiterated with great ferocity from the moment the enlisted workers impatiently barrack the indulgent complaints of the other characters. The conclusion of the performance, too, suggests the military gravity of the times and the relentless pressure of its events, when, eschewing the traditional conclusion to a performance, the actors are driven away to the next presentation on the back of their lorry/stage whilst singing the 'Internationale'.

Like *Cuatro batallones*, *Dos divisiones* is an energetic clarion call to enlist, delivered with similarly committed vigour. Yet its more expansive structure facilitates the inclusion of perspectives and techniques which the earlier play's brevity eschewed. As with *Cuatro batallones* the purpose of the play was to encourage recruitment, in this case to two divisions organized by the JSU which were to be placed at the disposal of the regular army.[15] Like *Cuatro batallones*, too, the majority of the action is a device which enables a direct exhortation to take place at the close of the play so that the call to arms is unmistakably heard. Initially, a chance encounter occurs between Sebastián, an aged worker, and Adela, a young JSU agitator whose current concern is to participate in the recruitment campaign. For Sebastián, his age and ill-health are a source of bitter regret since they prevent him combating 'los generales *renegaos* que han vendido nuestro suelo' (the renegade generals who have sold our land).[16] Adela, however, is eager to assure him that his 'trinchera está junto al torno' (trench is at the lathe) (p.50) and that he should take pride in the brave and dutiful active service of his son, Juan Carlos. As they are joined by Adela's comrade, Concha, the conversation turns to the subject of Spanish youth and the failure of some to live up to the example of Juan Carlos. For Concha, some seem so lacking in spirit that she declares them to have been born centenarians. As the three continue to chat in low voices, another dimension of the action opens with the entry on to the other side of the stage of two young people, described as Él and Ella (Him and Her). It becomes clear that their relationship is about to be broken since he has refused to volunteer for active service. She desires nothing more than to be left alone since 'me avergüenza haberme fijado en ti' (I'm ashamed that I ever set eyes on you) (p.54), while he fails to understand what he describes as her 'patrioterías' (flag-waving) (p.56) and is concerned only to pursue his own affairs, 'no habiéndome metido nunca en nada de política' (having never got involved in anything to do with politics) (p.54). As the focus of the dialogue crosses from one group to the other, the young couple's disagreement worsens while the conversation of the other characters turns to recall accounts which they have heard of Juan Carlos's bravery in combat. Such dedication is juxtaposed with that of the other young man, who is denounced as a coward by his *novia* before she finally walks out on him and leaves the stage.

A third dimension of the action now opens as Concha suddenly feigns a surprised awareness of the spectators. They are present, remarks Adela, to see the Guerrillas del Teatro who will, apparently, soon be performing. This device, found elsewhere in *teatro de urgencia*, by which a work's fictional status is challenged through the actors' seeming lack of awareness that they are performing a play, becomes the opportunity for a direct recruitment appeal to take place, since the two girls decide to take the opportunity of the presence of stage and spectators to initiate an improvised meeting in support of the JSU. Sebastián, too, declares that he wishes to address the crowd and the play concludes with each issuing an impassioned call to arms:

> ¡Jóvenes catalanes que todavía no habéis sido movilizados por el Gobierno! ¿No sentís ansias de igualar las hazañas de nuestros gloriosos soldados del aire, del mar y de la tierra? (p.57)

(Young Catalans who haven't yet been mobilized by the government! Don't you long to equal the exploits of our glorious soldiers of the air, sea and land?)

As though moved to return in support of the speakers, the girl who had earlier rejected her friend as a coward ascends the stage and also addresses the spectators, calling upon all her 'hermanas de Cataluña' (sisters of Catalonia) (p.57) to urge the enlistment of their menfolk in defence of 'la patria en peligro' (the endangered homeland) (p.57). With Adela's call for the building of 'la muralla de la juventud' (the wall of youth) (p.58), the action closes with the audience having been placed, as in *Cuatro batallones*, in the position of participants in a meeting who are invited to take a decision and act upon it in the immediate future beyond the play's conclusion.

Both *Cuatro batallones* and *Dos divisiones* are intended, of course, to exert a particularly direct influence upon male spectators. In the latter play, however, such an end is achieved through obliquely suggestive means. The idea of duty and enlistment in the play, for example, cannot be divorced from the question of *machismo* (masculinity) since the play's action reiterates the notion that honour and manliness are inseparable from participation in the Youth Divisions. Juan Carlos's exploits are, thus, a source of marvel for Concha as the girls reminisce about the early days of the conflict: 'días gloriosos aquéllos, ¿eh? ¡Mucho batallón, el batallón de las Juventudes! ¡Y mucho hombre, Juan Carlos!' (those were glorious days, eh? What a battalion, the Youth Battalion! And what a man, Juan Carlos!) (p.55). Adela recalls in particular an occasion when, surprised by the enemy as they were about to attack a rebel position, Juan Carlos urged his comrades forward with a cry of '¡adelante, camaradas, a la bayoneta!' (forward, comrades, with bayonets!) (p.55) even though they did not possess a single bayonet between them. Their success in taking their target is attributed to Juan Carlos's ability to lead the fight: 'a culatazos, a estacazos, con uñas y con dientes cuando es preciso' (with kicks and blows, with nails and teeth when necessary) (pp.55–6). The sense of Juan Carlos as a prodigious warrior, unceasingly engaged in the struggle of combat, is reinforced by his father's contentment that he rarely hears from his son by letter. Sebastián's proud response to the girls' enquiry after Juan Carlos evokes the image of a tight-lipped, grimly determined fighter whose letters home, while dutiful, are 'el consabido "estoy bien" y sanseacabó' (the usual 'I'm fine' and that's that) (p.54). This attempt to illustrate an idealized heroism is made in order to establish a contrast with the non-enlisted character who is found wanting by his *novia* precisely because he lacks the qualities displayed by Juan Carlos. While the latter is seen in terms of action, attack, nails and teeth, the former is despised for being 'por ahí tan campante, con tu cartero bajo el brazo' (so unconcerned – there with your briefcase under your arm) (p.56). For Adela, men who do not fight merit 'desprecio' (scorn) (p.53), an adjective with which the young man's *novia*, too, berates him as she accuses him of lacking manly dignity in failing to enlist.

The linking of military duty with sexual attractiveness, which is suggested here, is also a marked feature of Aparicio's *Los miedosos valientes*,[17] a play in which Juan and Pedro, two 'muchachos decididos' (decisive young men) (p.7) who have willingly enlisted, decide to shame those youths who have failed to display similar commitment. At the close of the play, the cowards transform themselves into brave fighters, but at the outset such individuals are seen by Juan as

> Gente insensata,
> Tan repleta de temores
> que cuando salen de casa
> van pregonando su miedo. (p.7)
>
> (Foolish people,
> so full of fears
> that when they leave home
> they go spreading them around.)

In league with Carmen and María, two local girls, the youths plan to frighten some of the cowards by covering themselves in white sheets to masquerade as spirits. The girls' role in the joke is to appear at the most appropriate moment and humiliate the cowards through ridicule. As they hide themselves, the cowards enter, a weak and dispirited trio who fall over with frightened shock when the two 'ghosts' appear and declare themselves to be spirits of military service which have been summoned to recruit them. Immediately, the cowards seek excuses. One is pigeon-chested, another left-handed and unable to handle a rifle, while the third claims to have been unwell since birth. As Juan and Pedro throw off their sheets, Carmen and María enter and the cowards are upbraided. María announces that no man could ever be appealing to her if he was not prepared to sacrifice everything for Spain, and as they form a circle around the cowards, the others sing a mocking song. Their spurning by Carmen and María is in direct contrast to the girls' banter with Juan and Pedro earlier in the play. Here playful attraction is evident, as is the girls' admiration for the strong-willed, forthright *milicianos*. Pedro's joking proposal of marriage, for example, is turned down, but with a flirtatious riposte as Carmen hints: 'si otra cosa precisáis' (if you need something else) (p.7). The image of masculine desirability which is presented in these two plays was a conscious recruitment strategy. The suggestion that enlistment is evidence of true *machismo* is strong, as is the opposite, that ignoring the call to arms is 'womanish' and undignified. Adela, for example, despises those who fail to enlist as callow youths and 'amerengados' (wimps) (p.53) still in need of a 'nodriza' (wet-nurse) (p.53). Willingness to fight was thus seen not only as a duty in some abstract sense but as a practical measure of manhood.

Theatrical propaganda such as this arose from circumstances in which conscription did not apply but where a pressing requirement was to bring men rapidly under arms. Alongside *teatro de urgencia* which stressed the obligation to serve were plays designed to complement recruitment calls by presenting *consignas* whose purpose was to illustrate the pitfalls and opportunities of life on active service itself. Judging by the evidence of first-hand documents, the role of *consignas* in soldiers' lives at the front seems to have been quite considerable. Mention has already been made of the use of posters, for example, and a particularly interesting example of how *consignas* may have been very directly involved in performance can be found in *En las trincheras* where, at the conclusion of the play and before the next item, the actor invites the audience to attend to 'unas consignas, unas consignas que en beneficio de nuestra guerra debéis tener siempre presentes' (some watchwords which in the interests of our war you ought always to bear in mind).[18] The Commissariat's publication of the *Manual del miliciano* (*The Militiaman's Handbook*) was perhaps the most comprehensive effort in this area, an attempt to furnish soldiers with guidance felt appropriate across a range of military, moral, political and religious issues. This alphabetically arranged handbook was designed for reading during the long hours of inactivity or waiting, and as an aid to discussion. The soldier was invited to meditate upon a range of perspectives presented through stimulating quotations from philosophy and history. Justice, liberty, education and morality could be explored alongside matters such as discipline, war and patriotism. The topic of 'deberes y derechos' (duties and rights) is particularly significant, declaring, in unambiguous terms, the accomplishment of duty as being the *only* right.[19]

The total number of plays written as a contribution to the dissemination of such *consignas* may perhaps never be accurately known. The Sindicato de Hospitales (Hospital Union), for example, was reported to be planning a play competition designed to stimulate *teatro de urgencia* dealing with the topic of military hygiene, but whether works were either submitted or performed is unknown.[20] Those works which do survive, however, offer a clear illustration of the extent to which theatrical propaganda consciously sought to participate in the cultural as well as the military education strategies which were initiated in the Republican army. A representative example may usefully be found in the anonymous play *Nunca falta un Judas* (*There's Always a Judas*) in which, through the criticisms levelled at card-playing as a soldiers' leisure activity, the author seeks to inculcate a number of lessons about desirable attitudes and behaviour on the part of combatants during the often extensive periods between battles.[21] As the play opens, four soldiers are gambling in a card-game which rapidly turns sour when accusations of cheating are levelled against Julián. His playing of the ace of spades arouses the suspicion of Emilio, who believes that Julián has played the same card earlier. As each man confronts the other, 'de modo chulo' (cockily) (p.16), a fist fight is threatened until Paco and Lucas separate the two men and the game resumes. As they continue to play, their comrade, Miguel, enters and is invited to join in. His refusal is not so much a puritanical disapproval of gambling or of card-playing, but of the inappropriateness of the occasion. For Miguel there is insufficient time for distractions unless they serve a purpose or at least do not prejudice morale or comradeship. The men's squabble is, to him, evidence that, particularly when gambling is involved, card games are likely to undermine the healthy spirit of a combat unit. The others' defence, that their efforts to kill time are harmless, provokes a litany from Miguel of the numerous tasks which confront them in order to 'entregar a otras generaciones una España entera, feliz y próspera' (hand on to other generations a Spain which is whole, happy and thriving) (p.16). His examples are intended, if borne in mind, to guarantee the battle-readiness of the *milicianos*. In particular, he seeks to impress upon his comrades the need to dedicate time to the care of their armaments and to the improvement of their weapon-handling skills. Their attitude to defence systems must be that all aspects of fortification are inadequate, capable of improvement in exactly the same manner that each soldier can find means to improve his own personal contribution to combat effectiveness. In what becomes increasingly like a lesson, Miguel also draws the soldiers' attention to matters which, while of a less directly military nature, display the prominence which the Republic attached to the notion of victory through cultural empowerment. Declaring that 'el libro es el mejor amigo' (a book is the best friend) (p.18), Miguel reminds the soldiers that spare time is available for self-improvement through study which will ensure better soldiers, sergeants and officers. Naturally, too, the acquisition of literacy skills is reiterated, so that the *milicianos* will be self-sufficient in their ability to write letters, and discriminating enough in their knowledge of the world to avoid the deceit which a 'chulo parlanchín, como Hitler o Mussolini' (cocky loudmouth like Hitler or Mussolini) (p.17) is accused of having practised upon German and Italian workers.

The effect of Miguel's words on the others is to encourage reflection followed by realization. As Emilio begins to deal the cards, Lucas becomes troubled by what he increasingly recognizes as their inactivity. Julián's brusque advice to ignore Miguel as one who 'se mata con los libros' (goes crazy with books) (p.18) merely through personal ambition, fails to convince Lucas. He is particularly impressed by Miguel's advice to avoid the use of scribes for letter-writing ' "pa" no necesitar que otro se entere de nuestras cosas' (so there's no need for another to know our business) (p.18) and to be able to communicate matters 'que se quedan "adrento" ' (that are personal) (p.18). As the others listen with increasing interest, Lucas wonders whether, if time that day had been more purposefully spent, 'no sabríamos manejarnos solos con la pluma' (we would not know how to get by with a pen on our own) (p.18). He determines to leave the game and dedicate himself to more useful activities, and his resolution is matched by Paco and Emilio. Together they plan to put their time to better use, leaving Julián, the apparent cheat, to swear angrily as the play ends that their 'disloyalty' proves that 'nunca falta un Judas en una procesión' (there's always a Judas in a procession) (p.18).

Miguel's role in the play is to confront the soldiers with orthodox Republican dogma upon a variety of germane military topics. The transmission of dogma is a significant notion since, in a play which recalls the tradition of the morality play, the biblical reference to Judas comes to refer, ironically, to Julián himself rather than his comrades and suggests that it is he who betrays them rather than vice versa. The idea of the morality tradition or the 'moral interlude' is also felt in the manner in which the play preaches, in effect, against sloth. The *Manual del miliciano* also invited the soldier to consider such matters when, under the heading 'parasitismo y ociosidad' (parasitism and idleness), *milicianos* were warned that 'la ociosidad corroe el corazón de los hombres y de las naciones, y los destruye como el moho al hierro' (idleness eats away at the heart of men and of nations, and it destroys them like rust on iron) (p.23). The impression is very reasonably gained that the author of *Nunca falta un Judas* was aware of, and seeking to reflect or inspire, similar *consignas* presented through other propaganda means. Miguel's observation that one's best friend is a book, for example, seems consciously to recall Bardasano's poster for the Jefatura de Sanidad del Ejército (Army Health Headquarters) declaring books to be the convalescent's best friend, while the play in general seems to illustrate much of the theme of 'Un vago es un faccioso' (A layabout is a rebel), a poster issued by the Public Order authorities of Aragón.[22]

A parallel example of efforts to inculcate soldiers with an appropriate sense of duty can be found in Herrera Petere's *Torredonjil*, a play which in strikingly vivid, often moving verses, aims to instruct *milicianos* on the need to treat rural communities and *campesinos* with respect. Published by the Commissariat, the play seems, like *Nunca falta un Judas*, to enjoy a clear relationship with propaganda efforts in other media. It would be reasonable to assume that Herrera, himself a commissar, was aware of the Commissariat's pamphlet *Cómo deben comportarse los soldados en los pueblos próximos al frente* (*How Soldiers should Conduct themselves in the Villages close to the Front Line*)[23] and that, whichever was written first, the play and the pamphlet shared an influence which may result from common authorship. *Torredonjil* deals with an encounter between two *milicianos* and a rural labourer as the soldiers arrive in the village of the play's title. Unshaven and dirty after long days at the front line, the *milicianos* despise the town for the lack of comfort it offers them. With its rubbish-strewn street, bugs and mosquitoes, they declare it to be a pigsty and its inhabitants to be like pigs. While they mock the *pueblo*, one of its inhabitants appears, an elderly Peasant who sets about gathering sheaves of corn. Although they mock him, too, as a badly dressed bumpkin, he ignores their insults. Demanding to know his name, the soldiers meet only silence as he continues with his work and the *milicianos* joke that perhaps ringing a cow bell will summon him. Increasingly angered by his unresponsiveness, the First Soldier roughly asks whether he understands their language. Unmoved by their taunts, and with simple dignity, the Peasant finally requests '¿qué deseas compañero?' (what would you like, comrade?) (p.18) and, in the brusque dialogue which follows, the soldiers demand wine and refreshment after the strains of combat duty. The Peasant's protestation that there is nothing in the town infuriates the First Soldier, who asserts his right to the village's provisions, given the sacrifices and physical hardship he has endured:

> En la llanura desierta
> creí que caía muerto,
> el aire en la tierra hervía
> como caldo en los barbechos,
> sartenes eran los llanos. (p.18)

> (On the deserted plain
> I believed I was dropping dead.
> The air on the land was boiling,
> like steam on the fallow fields.
> Frying-pans were the plains.)

Threatening the Peasant with a pistol, the First Soldier is restrained by his comrade and criticized for behaviour which he deems unworthy of a soldier whose purpose is to defend the *pueblo*. His assumption that service in the trenches of itself merits special treatment is mistaken, asserts the Second Soldier, since the war is fought not only at the battle front but in the towns and villages, and by demonstrating that the *milicianos* are 'cultos y humanos' (educated and humane) (p.19). The fight on behalf of the *pueblo* must, he insists, be carried out by drawing the army and the rural population together in mutual respect and, in contrast to the First Soldier, he addresses the Peasant in a manner designed to serve as an example to his comrade:

> yo te digo, yo te ruego
> que me digas dónde está
> aquí la fuente del pueblo,
> desde ayer va que no como,
> desde ayer va que no bebo. (p.19)

> (I say to you, I beg you
> to tell me whereabouts here
> is the village fountain.
> Since yesterday I've been without food,
> since yesterday I haven't quenched my thirst.)

The contrast between the two soldiers is underlined both in their differing behaviour to the Peasant and in the Second Soldier's choice of water rather than wine. His respectful request, too, provokes a change of heart on the part of the *campesino* who, although the village no longer has wine, becomes eager to share his own purchase since 'por las buenas soy muy amable' (to good people I'm very kind) (p.20). For him, the First Soldier had recalled the bullying tactics

> de esos del antiguo ejército,
> aquellos que cuando iban
> de prácticas por los pueblos
> nos trataban como a fieras,
> no respetaban derechos. (p.20)

> (of those of the old army,
> those who when they went on
> manœuvres around the villages
> treated us like wild animals,
> not respecting rights.)

As they quench their thirst and toast the *pueblo*, the Peasant reveals that Torredonjil has not only lost its wine, but also its hens, goats, sheep and the personal possessions of many inhabitants. Those responsible, he laments, are Republican soldiers who, en route through the town, have left it 'sin resuello' (breathless) (p.21) and its inhabitants uncertain if the *milicianos* are truly on the side of the people. For the First Soldier the Peasant's tale is a sad one, but for the other *miliciano* the village's treatment is 'canallesco' (rotten) (p.22), and, as he ponders the matter, he remembers his commissar's advice that the Republic's soldiers' own families were day labourers, factory workers or shepherds, bound together by poverty and 'negros insomnios de hambre' (the black sleeplessness of hunger) (p.22). That the *pueblo*'s struggle is also that of the soldiers becomes increasingly clear to him, and in his eloquent description of the hardships of peasant life is felt a more general picture of the injustice and exploitation whose elimination was presented as bonding all workers in common endeavour:

> Todo, todo al campesino
> le era hostil, la tierra, el cielo,
> el aire de la llanura,
> ardiente brisa de fuego.
> De fuera le viene engaño,
> de dentro cuentos de miedo,
> desconfianza marrullera,
> incultura y aislamiento. (p.23)

> (To the peasant, everything, everything
> was hostile, the land, the sky,
> the air of the vast plain
> a burning breeze of fire.
> Deceit comes to him from outside,
> from within, tales of fear,
> dirty suspicion,
> ignorance and isolation.)

Like the conclusion of *Nunca falta un Judas*, the play ends with a sense of realization, in this case that the soldiers must become the champions of the *pueblo* both in battle and in the respect shown to the villagers. Such insight also comes to be shared by the First Soldier, endorsing his comrade's words through his own recognition that, if it is not for the well-being of the *pueblo*, waging the war is futile. That his earlier behaviour had been inappropriate is now a source of apology and, in his understanding of what has occurred, is found the essential lesson of duty which *teatro de urgencia* sought to inculcate:

> Hemos venido a reírnos
> y salimos aprendiendo.

> Y ahora creo es lo mejor
> predicar con el ejemplo. (p.23)

> (We came for a laugh
> and we leave learning.
> And now I think it's best
> to practise what you preach.)

With relish, they join the peasant in gathering the corn, certain that the struggle to the death in the trenches is carried on 'pecho a pecho' (shoulder to shoulder) (p.24) with the rural labourers and, in a suggestion of the unity now found between the men, a final tableau is struck in which images of battle blend with those of the harvest:

> Torredonjil, tus cosechas,
> tus gavillas de centeno
> voy a cargar con mis manos
> negras de pólvora y fuego. (p.23)

> (Torredonjil, your harvests,
> your bundles of rye,
> I'll gather with my hands
> black with powder and fire.)

Whatever the actual relationship between Herrera's play and *Cómo deben comportarse los soldados en los pueblos próximos al frente*, the similarities are very striking. The image of harvest-gathering which is used to symbolic effect in the play seems to find a reflection in the proud report from the Extremadura front which opens the pamphlet. Here, the activity of the Sixty-Third Brigade in gathering the corn is lauded for its role in ending the queues for bread and, as an indication of the fruitful unity of soldiers and *pueblo*, village women have responded with another form of gathering, of thirty sewing machines, in order to manufacture clothes for the *milicianos*. The pamphlet also warns soldiers that, in another echo of the play's concerns, the *campesino* must not live with 'el temor de que le van a robar el ganado y las gallinas' (the fear that he is going to be robbed of cattle and chickens) and that the Republican soldier is no less than 'un hijo del Pueblo que defiende la libertad, el pan y la justicia de todos los españoles que trabajan' (a son of the people, who defends the liberty, bread and justice of all the Spaniards who work). The Peasant's view of the First Soldier's early behaviour as reminiscent of the old army, is perhaps reflected in the pamphlet's discussion of the relationship between the earlier army and the *pueblo*. Military manœuvres were, it is suggested, seen by the *campesinos* as a plague in which soldiers, inculcated with sentiments of distaste towards rural labourers and their life-style, descended upon villages as if upon a conquered country.

The prominent emphasis upon teaching which is felt in both *Nunca falta un Judas* and *Torredonjil* reflects the manner in which, despite the huge organization and communication problems involved in executing a propaganda strategy, a number of themes related to education were coherently reiterated through a variety of means. Soldiers were invited to consider the concept of duty within a wide moral, social and political framework in order, as the *Manual del miliciano* suggests, to do all that is 'honrado y bueno' (honourable and good) (p.14). Nor was it only the military who were exposed to such influences. As the title of Mussot's lost play, *La retaguardia también es frente* (*The Rearguard is also the Front Line*), indicates, the exhortation of the rearguard population was necessary since its morale and effort were logically viewed as other battlegrounds upon which the conflict would be decided.

A number of matters had to be addressed in this respect. In *Despedida de reclutas*, for example, the back of the playing area was decorated with the *consigna* '¡aumentad la producción!' (increase production levels!),[24] a call which was echoed in numerous *teatro de urgencia* references to the obligations of factory workers. In *Lección y escarmiento*, a worker declares himself to be shoulder to shoulder with the soldiers since in his factory 'trabajaremos aquí como se lucha en los parapetos: hasta el último respiro de nuestras fuerzas' (we'll work here as one fights on the barricades: until the last gasp of our strength).[25] A particularly useful illustration of the manner in which theatrical propaganda focused upon the duties of civilians is found in Hernández's *La cola* (*The Queue*) since the play incorporates three of the issues clearly felt to be most significant in establishing and maintaining a correct perspective on the part of the rearguard.[26] In a rapidly moving sketch, therefore, the action combines *teatro de urgencia*'s frequent reiteration of the blood spilt in the trenches on behalf of the *pueblo*, the avoidance of alarmist or uncivil behaviour and the unmasking of cowards and those who seek to avoid their duty.

The setting of the play is a queue in which four 'deslenguadas' (foul-mouthed women) battle to become first in line to buy coal. Their hasty entrance in quick succession on to the stage, tearing at each other's shawls in an effort to gain the head of the queue, initiates an extended, colourful passage of threats and insults. The first woman's determined stance is established in an opening line which also serves to illustrate the vivid, spirited rhythm of the play's dialogue: 'aunque me tiraras de las tripas más que el mantón, no entrarías en la carbonería antes que mi alma' (even if you grab me by the guts rather than the shawl, you wouldn't get into the coalyard before me) (p.409). The violence of their language and the energetic, rapid delivery demanded of the performers provide a sense of tumultuous disorder which is interrupted by the arrival of the Mother, who seeks to shame them by comparing their disreputable squabble with the fight being carried on in the trenches. Denouncing the 'bonito cuadro de mujeres' (pretty picture of women) (p.412), she now becomes the target of the women's sharp-tongued ferocity as she is curtly ordered '¡vaya a ver los del Museo del Prado, si éste no le agrada!' (go and see the ones in the Prado Museum if this one doesn't appeal to you!) (p.412). As they upbraid the Mother for her interference, she defends herself with eloquent vigour, retorting that the women's ill-tempered anger would be better spent in the trenches as part of the battle effort. Again the Mother is ridiculed since the battle front is arrogantly declared to be the domain of men, a viewpoint whose indulgence is roundly criticized since, asserts the Mother, the men are not making such huge sacrifices in order for the womenfolk to scratch each other and squabble. Where, asks the Mother, will the women find the strength to mourn their battle dead if their energies are squandered in petty argument? With smug satisfaction the 'deslenguadas' are pleased to declare their husbands and sons to be 'donde no llegan balas' (where bullets don't reach) (p.412), safely ensconced in a variety of comfortable positions. Two are out of harm's way working on rearguard committees responsible for the running of life's daily needs. Another hints with enigmatic pride that she fears little for her husband's well-being since they have both arranged for him to be 'resguardado y enchufado' (protected and with friends in high places) (p.413).

These revelations anger the Mother and lead her to denounce the men as cowards and the women as little better. Continuing to mock her, now dismissing her as eccentric through age, the women are unmoved even by the Mother's powerful exhortation to them to compare their own selfishness with the heroism of other Spanish women who have proudly given their sons to the struggle 'con dolores de parto y con orgullo de haber amamantado cuerpos de valentía' (with birth pangs and with the pride of having suckled courageous bodies) (p.413). By contrast, the 'deslenguadas' offer only 'la lengua podrida del egoísmo y el ocio' (the rotten language of selfishness and idleness) (p.413). Suddenly, the Alarmist enters, wide-eyed with fear, urging all to the basements to avoid an apparently imminent bombing raid. With cries of '¡doscientos muertos, mil heridas, medio Madrid en ruinas!' (two hundred dead, a thousand injured, half Madrid in ruins!) (p.414), she exits in search of her sons, rapidly followed by the panic-stricken 'deslenguadas'. Alone on-stage, the Mother despises the cowardice and the alarmism which exaggerate the air raids. For her, the other women are unworthy to tread the ground upon which has fallen the blood of 'hijos de tantas madres' (sons of so many mothers) (p.414), including that of her own two sons. As the bombing raid turns out to have been a figment of the Alarmist's fearful imagination, the other women return, shaken by the shock which they have received. As they criticize the Alarmist for her irresponsibility, they too are roundly criticized by the Mother in a final speech which demands exemplary behaviour from the capital's citizens, since the world is felt to be watching 'la capital del mundo honrado' (the capital of the honourable world) (p.415), a city in which the spilt blood of its inhabitants transforms 'sus piedras en corazones' (its stones into hearts) (p.415).

It is perhaps significant that only the Mother is given a substantial number of lines after the return of the other women. After the panic sown by the Alarmist's imagined air attack, the 'deslenguadas' seem crestfallen and, to an extent, they begin to adopt something of the mother's sense of civic duty. Denouncing, for example, 'estas sembradoras de alarmas' (those who sow panic) (p.414), one of the women, in her customary frank manner, bluntly suggests cutting out their tongues. For the Mother, however, both the behaviour of the Alarmist and that of the other women are equally undesirable. While one alarms the city, the others indulge in riotous behaviour and bring disorder to the capital. The silence of the women is intriguing after their earlier loquacity. Their apparent lack of response might suggest an unrevised script which, in rehearsal, might have been changed to include lines to clarify the women's response to events. There seems little doubt, for example, that the play was never actually performed. Alternatively, one is tempted to conclude that silent endorsement of the Mother is intended from the actresses through gesture, posture or grouping on the stage. What is clear is that the final harangue is, of course, actually aimed at the audience and that Hernández might well have felt that, in terms of propaganda clarity, the role of the 'deslenguadas' having ended, the most appropriate conclusion was the customary *teatro de urgencia* one of a character's discourse upon the meaning of the action. The Mother's sense of the events' meaning certainly suggests an appeal to the spectators as she urges the duty of all to dignify Madrid through their behaviour. Addressing all those engaged in the defence of the capital, she denounces those who degrade the city through 'acciones y actitudes bajas' (base acts and attitudes) (p.415) and calls on the inhabitants to 'andad, gallarda y diáfanamente, entre sus calles y sus cañones, entre sus muertos y los bombardeos enemigos' (walk, valiant and shining, amongst its streets and its cannons, amongst its dead and the enemy bombardments) (p.415). With the characteristic emphasis upon duty as example, the behaviour of the capital's citizens is presented as something which will be emulated by the other towns and villages of Spain and, perhaps turning to the other women on-stage, her final word, 'compañeras' (comrades) (p.415), seems to invite their incorporation into the task of making the city 'como un gigante mudo y sereno, seguro de la victoria' (like a silent and serene giant, certain of victory) (p.415).

The dating of the composition of *La cola* to 5 January 1937 might suggest a number of explanations of the emotionally charged, intense admiration of Madrid which is felt in the play. Perhaps most significant was the relatively recent, and unexpected, failure of the city to capitulate to the advancing Nationalists. The status which this heroic resistance assumed in Republican mythology is legendary and was frequently reiterated in *teatro de urgencia*. A period of intense optimism was ushered in with the turn of the year, and there seemed firm grounds for believing that the war could be won. Noticeably absent from the play, therefore, is an emphasis upon the dangers of defeatism. This was one of the persistent themes of theatrical propaganda concerned with the dissemination amongst civilians of notions of duty and, amongst plays dealing with the conduct of life in the rearguard, therefore, Hernández's play is untypical in that it seems unconcerned to stress the maintenance of belief in victory.

Defeatism, which might be considered a powerful weapon of war, was a subject which *teatro de urgencia* had to tackle, since a bulwark was required against the obvious dangers of the collapse of the will to resist. The campaign of street theatre which was mounted in Barcelona in the early months of 1938 suggests that, since at least two plays survive which were written and produced in order to address the issue directly, the matter had become one of considerable urgency. The full title of the first of these plays, *Lección y escarmiento del derrotismo* (*Lesson and Warning about Defeatism*), indicates in itself the very firm attitude which was felt necessary to challenge the possibility of crumbling morale. The warning which is offered in the play is more akin to a threat, that the defeatist is a traitor and will be dealt with as such. The lurking danger, too, of fifth-columnism could not be ignored and in the second play, *¡Aplastar a Franco!*, there is a strong suggestion that those accused of defeatism in the play are hoping for a return of the pre-war social and economic regime.

This latter play has a particularly interesting class aspect to it since the two well-dressed individuals who are the principal characters are clearly figures of some financial and industrial pre-eminence. The suggestion implicit throughout is that they are, in effect, trapped by circumstances in the Republican zone. As the play begins, the men sip coffee while seated in a bar. In their elegant, well-made suits and with their English newspaper, the two men are far from the *mono* uniform and sandals favoured by many *teatro de urgencia* Republicans. Their conversation is a catalogue of deprivations resulting from the war. Such 'privaciones horrorosas' (dreadful deprivations)[27] include the lack of sugar for coffee, the absence of visits to the bullfight and no longer being able to enjoy café life with a good cigar. Recalling earlier times summons the memory, too, of the factories which one of the men had owned, the shameful demands of his workers and the sums of money which had been spent by his son, a 'verdadera cabezaloca' (real headcase) (p.9). Their unease at the atmosphere of the times is emphasized through the fear expressed by one of the men as the other unfolds his English newspaper. Suspecting a hostile reaction from soldiers to the foreign press, he urges him to close the paper, but his companion scorns the idea that common soldiers might be able to read English and confides with a quiet sneer: 'los oficiales de antes eran más cultos' (the officers from before were more educated) (p.10).

As they discuss the possibility of foreign diplomatic moves to end the 'infierno de guerra' (hellish war) (p.10), they are interrupted by the Young Girl who, dressed in the *mono* outfit of a worker, wonders whether she might share their table. With a gallant smile, one assents, suggesting that for ladies 'hay un buen sitio en todas partes' (there's a comfortable seat everywhere) (p.11). Such flattery does not impress the Young Girl, who is visibly exhausted from long hours of factory work. Although she does not have time to relax, she is not despondent but thinks rather of the much worse deprivations suffered by her brother who, at the front line, has been injured three times but whose combat spirit is undiminished. During the conversation which strikes up between the three, the men hark back to an earlier time of apparent simplicity and correctness which, by implication, the war has interrupted. Women's role in substituting for men by working in the factories is seen as 'bonito' (nice) (p.13), but, since they regret the Young Girl's absence from home and from her *novio* (boy-friend), their true opinion is felt to be the opposite. For the men, the changes brought by the conflict are 'desorden brutal' (an incredible mess) (p.12) which could be rectified through the concessions of a negotiated settlement brokered by the European powers.

With her fists clenched tightly upon the table, the Young Girl is unable to contain her anger, and she interrupts to denounce the men as the hidden enemy whose true purpose in counselling mediation as a means of halting the war is to restore the old order of landowners, capitalists and treacherous generals. For her, the conflict's meaning concerns the working class's ability to keep open 'el camino de su porvenir' (the route of its future) (p.14), and this can be achieved only through total victory. The alternative, of compromise, she energetically declares equal to defeat. As she speaks with passion of the workers' implacable commitment never to accept the defeat of the *pueblo*, her voice grows louder and other workers gather around in support. The atmosphere becomes explicitly threatening when, grabbed by the arm by the Worker, the man who had spoken of the need for compromise is asked whether he does not in fact agree with the Young Girl's viewpoint. Trembling, he enthusiastically assents to the need to 'aplastar a esas canallas' (crush those swine) (p.16) and, although this answer grimly satisfies the Worker, his attention then turns to the foreign newspaper carried by the man. Although he does not understand its language, the Worker is certain that there will be found those who do and, stepping forward, a young man informs the crowd that the newspaper's report concerns the attempts of British

Conservatives to seek a rapid end to the war through the partition of Spain. In response, another worker unfolds a Spanish newspaper which announces hundreds of enemy losses in a recent Republican victory. This latter news is applauded by all as an illustration of the route to victory and, as the Young Girl calls upon all to destroy both Franco and those who defend him, the workers take hold of the reactionary man and he is dragged forcibly from the scene.

The violence of the play, both in the ferocity of its language and the implicit fate of the man who, at the conclusion, is taken from the stage, suggests the severity and the fear with which defeatism was viewed in Republican quarters. There is a sense of barely contained hysteria which is felt not only in the Young Girl's dialogue, but also in the stage directions themselves. The advice to the actor playing one of the defeatists, for example, calls, in essence, for him gradually to raise his voice, but is vividly accompanied by the author's loathing for what the character represents. His reactionary thoughts are described as proclaiming hatred towards the millions of men whose commitment to the war does not vacillate and who are 'dispuestos a morir, si es preciso' (prepared to die, if necessary) (p.12). The Young Girl displays similarly aggressive sentiments in her tirades against the men. Her interruption of the pessimistic talk is accompanied by the rough grabbing of the man's hand, followed by a seventy-line speech which is a vitriolic outburst scorning the prospect of defeat or compromise when the *pueblo*, 'seguro de su porvenir y de su fuerza' (certain of its future and of its strength) (p.15), is implacable in its determination for victory. Even more ferocious in the denunciation of defeatist attitudes is the figure of the Worker in *Lección y escarmiento* who, in a similar manner to that of the Young Girl, berates his friend for becoming disillusioned with the possibility of victory. Grabbing him by the lapels, the Worker subjects him to an outpouring of angry insults for being 'un ser asqueroso' (a disgusting person).[28] The Friend thus becomes an insect who would be crushed underfoot if he were not so loathsome, a 'canalla incapaz de estar entre los hombres' (swine incapable of being amongst men) (p.38), and is finally taken to prison after provoking blows from actors playing outraged members of the audience.

The play is similar in structure to *¡Aplastar a Franco!* in that a conversation is established in a bar and the various participants offer perspectives which lead ultimately to the fierce denunciation of those who are perceived as undermining the war effort. The dialogue is initiated by the Worker, the Friend and a Woman who, whilst seated in a café, are joined by the Soldier who asks permission to share their table. The Friend's pessimism is evident from his forlorn expression and he is unmoved by the Woman's advice to 'hacer frente con alegría y confianza a las cosas' (face things with happiness and confidence) (p.33). For him, optimism equals self-deception since, of late, the enemy has attacked and advanced unchecked. The Worker resents this 'temor de las gallinas' (chicken fear) (p.34) and urges instead greater unity and the example of good conduct in order to provide the army with all that it requires to overcome recent setbacks. The arrival of the Soldier with his enthusiasm for combat and belief in victory does nothing to assuage the Friend's fears, since 'las cosas no están para hacerse ilusiones' (things are not looking hopeful) (p.35). The ensuing argument pits the gloom of the Friend against the belief and purpose of the others. For him, the Soldier's comrades have fallen in vain since the Republic is still endangered, even a forty-hour day will not suffice to provide war materials, and the role of foreign powers in support of the enemy makes victory a foolish illusion. The other characters, like the Young Girl, make powerful, increasingly angry appeals to counter the Friend's negative interpretation of the Republic's situation. The Worker recalls the grave circumstances of the battles for Madrid, Guadalajara and the Jarama, occasions when with fewer men and weapons the Republic had managed to drive off the enemy. For him: '¡como entonces, ahora también se les cerrará el paso!' (like then, now too we'll block their path) (p.36). The Woman declares that, if the *milicianos* are overcome, the women will take over the machines in order to free others for the fight and will defend Spain, bread and the liberty of their children by taking up the tools of work. The heart which the Soldier derives from this sense of common purpose, of their being fused together in united effort, is reflected in the chorus of *¡vivas!* which breaks out, perhaps from the spectators but certainly from amongst the actors planted amongst the audience. Turning upon the Friend, the Worker accuses him of being 'lo más parecido a un traidor' (the nearest thing to a traitor) (p.37), a defeatist whose proper place is in jail with 'los fascistas de su calaña y de su espíritu' (the Fascists of his own kind and character) (p.38). The Friend's protestations that he is not a Fascist count for nothing as the others, including the Waiter, call for his incarceration. The beating, from what is described as 'el público' (the public) (p.38) and which he receives as he is dragged from the stage, is meted out since defeatism and support of the enemy are presented as synonymous.

The element of warning which characterizes these two plays encapsulates a central issue of *teatro de urgencia* and propaganda in general. The energy with which the 'anti-Republican' figures are attacked both in *¡Aplastar a Franco!* and *Lección y escarmiento* tends to undermine the image perpetrated elsewhere, at times even in the same play, of a populace united and fervent in the conviction of victory. The misgivings and fears about the conflict, even outright opposition to it, which were inevitably held to some degree by much of the population, were certain to exert an influence upon the conduct of the war both in the front line and in the rearguard. As the Friend protests at the close of *Lección y escarmiento*, 'veo las cosas de otra forma' (I see things differently) (p.37), a viewpoint whose individualism had to be discouraged in the search for the disciplined unity of effort which was the best guarantee of victory. This potential gap between the real and the ideal, between what the Republic might hope for from its citizens' determination to resist and what it might fear, was the mainspring of the lessons, tasks and slogans which were dramatized to offer a highly direct means of communication with men under arms and the civilian population which supported them.

The use of drama in this respect seems to have been a more varied phenomenon than might be anticipated, since to inculcate the notion of citizens' duty was a task which had a broad range of manifestations. Duty was portrayed, for example, almost as an abstract concept, an article of Republican faith in a play such as *A la orden*. More specific propaganda tasks led, at moments of grave military danger or in circumstances of military training, to the presentation of highly focused sketches such as *¡Hacia la victoria!*, plays which illustrated a lesson whose purpose was to demand some immediate course of action on the part of spectators as a result of their assimilation of the action's significance. Within the context of the enlisted population, *teatro de urgencia* contributed distinctively to both cultural and military education strategies through plays which sought to explore ethical values as well as those whose purpose was to orientate soldiers with regard to the conduct of battle. Civilians, too, were subject to the dramatized presentation of *consignas* intended to offer guidance to the population with regard to issues arising from life's daily needs in circumstances of harsh conflict, and with regard to the civic values felt appropriate to aid the conduct of the war. In terms of style, *teatro de urgencia* which explored the demands of duty lacked the varied dramatic approaches which are found, for example, in its portrayal of the enemy. Its variety with regard to the former, however, lies in the number of differing tasks, all crucial, which it sought to address to a range of target audiences in circumstances of considerable political fluidity. Through its manipulation of images of desirable and undesirable behaviour, *teatro de urgencia* fused, too, with other manifestations of Republican propaganda and, as with these, a range of artistic, educational, civil and military undertakings were made in order to exhort citizens to victory.

~ 7 ~
Celebrating the People

The discussion of *teatro de urgencia* in earlier chapters focused on aspects which might well be regarded as indispensable to a kind of drama concerned with wartime propaganda. Images of the enemy, for example, were central to the effectiveness of such theatre, offering audiences an analysis of the war's meaning which reiterated the notion of foreign aggression as a predominant explanation of the conflict. A similarly important inclusion was the portrayal of the Loyalist combatant since it provided a means of military training through dramatized illustration and presented heroic images of soldiers as a spur to the rearguard's own war effort. The exhortation of civilians through drama was also significant since it was necessary to transmit the notion of civic duty as fundamental to the conduct of daily life in the circumstances of war.

To these three essential features of *teatro de urgencia* must be added consideration of the role alloted to the *pueblo* since this was a phenomenon held in high esteem by Republicans. Forcefully asserted in the fundamental articles of the 1931 Constitution of the Republic, for example, was the absolute sovereignty of the *pueblo*. The justice and liberty of all was to be guaranteed, it was declared, by state organs whose powers 'emanan del pueblo' (derive from the people).[1] Theatrical propaganda emphasized the conflict as the defining moment of the *pueblo*'s persistent battle against its traditional enemies: hunger, unemployment, inequitable land distribution, the Church and *caciquismo* (local political bosses). Writers of *teatro de urgencia* shared the perception that the mobilization and education of the *pueblo* were the keys to victory and that the purpose of the conflict was the future well-being of the *pueblo*. One also finds in theatrical propaganda a deep respect for the *pueblo*, a profound admiration which is often expressed with considerable lyricism. Alberti's image of rural labourers heading towards combat as immense seeds to be sown in the deep furrows of the trenches is characteristic of numerous images of the *pueblo* as a life-source which is doggedly determined, long-suffering and yet passionately inspired:

Muchos no saben nada. Mas con la certidumbre
del que corre al asalto de una estrella ofrecida,
de sol a sol trabajan en la nueva costumbre
de matar a la muerte para ganar la vida.[2]

(Many know nothing. But with the certainty
of one who runs to seize an offered star,
from sunrise to sunset they work in the new tradition
of killing death in order to win life.)

This kind of celebration of the *pueblo*'s relentless, pervasive dedication was not unique to the Civil War but characterized the language of many on the Left in the decades prior to the conflict. Sender, for example, writing in 1932, declared confidently that the influence of the *pueblo* was destroying traditional understanding of culture as a consequence of what he perceived to be the objective truth and inevitable momentum of socialist ideas.[3] Similarly, in *El novelista y las masas* (*The Novelist and the Masses*), he commiserates with those who have not had what he suggests is the good fortune to have been born into a family with a proletarian mentality, and he applauds what he describes as the 'esencia activa' (active essence) of the *pueblo*.[4] Such admiration of the *pueblo* as a gathering political force and as a repository of certain essential but intangible qualities was also, as we have seen at the outset, a dominant feature of the prewar social dramatists. Writers such as de Orriols and Martín had sought to express working-class struggle from the perspective of the *pueblo* as a means of rousing revolutionary consciousness.[5] For them, figures such as Dicenta's Juan José came to occupy centre stage as a prelude to a similar dominance in the economic and political sphere. From a less explicit political perspective, Unamuno, too, in *La regeneración del teatro español* (*The Regeneration of the Spanish Theatre*), had identified any potential spirit of renewal in the Spanish theatre as arising from the *pueblo* through the marriage of literary genius with some kind of popular essence to produce a drama equal to that of the seventeenth century.[6]

Belief in the *pueblo* was expressed in *teatro de urgencia* in terms which elevated it to a status recalling that of a religious icon. The fervent devotion of the true believer is typical of many characters' responses. The Lieutenant in *El cuartel*, for example, dismisses as trivial the wounds he has suffered to his hands since 'la alegría de ver al pueblo triunfante me compensa de todas las amarguras pasadas' (the joy of seeing the people triumphant makes up for all past bitterness).[7] His *novia*, too, pays homage to the *pueblo* in language which recalls that of worship, seeing the *pueblo* as the saviour of the Lieutenant and seeking a means to acknowledge its beneficial powers: 'yo amo al pueblo . . . pero no sé que podría hacer yo por el pueblo' (I love the people . . . but I don't know what I myself could do for the people) (p.22). As an educated young girl who has been brought up, she asserts, merely to write poetry and music, she feels unable to serve the *pueblo*. The Lieutenant's response emphasizes the sense of the *pueblo*'s deification when he enthusiastically endorses his *novia*'s skills as a worthy offering:

> Pues eso es lo que tienes que dar al pueblo: versos y músicas. ¿Crees tú que el pueblo no quiere más que pan? Está igualmente hambriento de luz y de belleza. (p.22)
>
> (So that's what you have to give to the people: music and verse. Do you think the people don't want more than bread? They're equally hungry for light and beauty.)

The feeling of a religious bond, of the people seeking to nourish or serve a secular god is powerful, not only in this example, but throughout *teatro de urgencia*. The *pueblo* became a unifying focus for Republicans, a means of asserting all that bound them together against a common enemy. The word *pueblo* itself is appropriately fluid, suggesting a trinity which combines tangible notions of people and place with the less tangible idea of shared assumptions about the world derived from deeply felt common experience.[8] One is reminded of Gemier's perception of the role of theatre. For him, the original meaning of the word religion as 'that which binds us together' was to prove central to his understanding of theatre.[9] In somewhat similar terms, the Commander in Mussot's *A la orden* speaks of the common values, beliefs and aspirations of Republicans as 'lo que . . . nos une' (that which unites us),[10] a bond whose depth merits sacrifice even of life itself, for the triumph of the *pueblo*.

A fruitful manner in which to initiate a detailed exploration of this sense of a united community is to examine *teatro de urgencia* which emphasizes the tribal quality of the drama. A crucial notion in this respect is that of self-affirmation since the Republic saw itself as a community under threat and responded by seeking to affirm its particular identity. The title *España no es Austria* hints at this need to express a unique self since, in differentiating between Nazi-annexed Austria and Spain, the spirit of resistance was fostered and, through this, pride in the independence of the Spanish people. The play is a dialogue between characters who are included for the various Republican perspectives they bring to the action. A Commissar, an Old Man, a Young Girl and a Woman discuss the progress of the war with a young, female Agitator and, with exemplary vigour and dedication, demonstrate their commitment to the *pueblo*, their refusal to countenance negotiated compromise to end the war, and their determination that they will not suffer the fate of the Austrians and see their homeland taken from them.

At the centre of the action is a captured Italian pilot who is forced on to the stage and subjected to the verbal abuse of the other characters for his role in the destruction of their land and loved ones. Surrounded by these angry members of the *pueblo*, he becomes emblematic of the enemy and the focus of communal hatred. The Mother, who has lost her daughter in the war, curses his blood and, as she declares '¡maldita sea la teta de fiera que te dieron!' (damn the monster's breast which suckled you!),[11] his character assumes bestial, dehumanized proportions. For the Old Man, the Italian has emerged from a black womb to steal the community's possessions and the land which has been made glorious by the sweat of the *pueblo*. Displayed to the crowds by the Agitator, the Italian is publicly denounced as the tool of a criminal, Mussolini, and as one who has come to sow ruin as a means of delivering the people's liberty to his master. The outraged response of the characters emphasizes the tribal nature of the drama as each vows to defend the land. The Mother, for example, urges the menfolk to ensure that 'los asesinos de mi hija no estarán jamás entre nosotros' (my daughter's killers will never be amongst us) (p.46), while the Woman declares that the invaders will be vanquished since from 'toda nuestra tierra sale el coraje para machacaros a todos' (all our land the courage appears for you to crush them all) (p.46). The importance of the Italian as a conduit for the feelings of the *pueblo* is marked by the manner in which he is directly addressed at the climax of the characters' harangue. With a cry of determination to avenge their dead, the crowd demands '¡que sepa tu amo que España no es Austria!' (let your master know that Spain isn't Austria!) (p.46).

The sense of the community threatened from without, and thus bonding together in an act of collective affirmation of itself, is keenly felt in the play. Territory, as suggested by the title, is staked out for defence against an enemy who is portrayed as a rapacious alien speaking a language described as cursed, bearing black flags and with sharp machetes to slice off the hands of children as they raise their clenched fists in defiance. To protect the territory becomes the task of the *pueblo* and, in this particular play as in *teatro de urgencia* in general, resistance is described in terms of a wall, human steel against the invader:

> ¡toda nuestra tierra está en pie, se hace de hierro enterizo, se hace muro y hoja de acero para que no la pasen las bayonetas italianas! (p.43)

> (all our land is ready, it becomes all iron, it becomes a wall and sheet of steel so that the Italian bayonets shan't pass.)

The furious abuse to which the Italian is subjected offers actors and audience alike a means of overcoming the enemy. As they vehemently berate their prisoner the action acquires symbolic significance since the enemy is vicariously repulsed by denunciation. Such a concrete act is important in the ritual possession of territory since the enemy is seen to be in some sense driven off. Significant parallel actions can be found elsewhere in *teatro de urgencia*. In *Defendemos la tierra*, for example, the Italian general's dress uniform is fouled by villagers hurling mud on it.[12] Similarly, as we saw earlier in *¡No pasarán!*, the enemy's uniform is triumphantly plundered as a symbolic acknowledgement of the *pueblo*'s victory over the military rebellion.[13]

The feeling of a community seeking self-affirmation as a means of rendering its defences impregnable is prominent in *teatro de urgencia* since it enabled a clear distinction to be drawn between those fortunate enough to be incorporated into the Republican family and those who, willingly or otherwise, occupied the other zone. The tribal nature of the drama, and its wartime task, demanded that the *pueblo*'s perception of itself as engaged in a battle on behalf of justice and liberty should be enhanced by the portrayal of life outside the *pueblo* as a bleak, cruel tyranny. The affirmation of the values enshrined in the *pueblo* therefore involved theatrical propaganda which itself illustrated what the *pueblo* was *not* and highlighted the apparent barbarism against which it urged relentless struggle. Perhaps the most characteristic example of this is *El pueblo fascista*, a play in which spectators were presented with images and ideas which emphasized the *pueblo* under Fascism in terms which suggest that the cycle of nature itself has been fractured by the visitation of a blight upon the land. A *campesino* who has succeeded in fleeing to the Republic recalls for some *milicianos* how, where once there had been little else but ploughs in the village and joyful anticipation of the next harvest, the land has now withered and been abandoned:

> nadie labra, nadie siembra,
> nadie rastroja ni ara.
> Sólo lechuzas de noche
> y cuervos por la mañana
> buscan piltrafas sangrientas
> entre los surcos y matas.[14]

> (nobody farms, nobody sows,
> nobody harvests or ploughs.
> Only owls by night
> and crows by day
> look for bloody scraps
> amongst the furrows and bushes.)

His picture of the *pueblo* is of a sullen, silent village in which the inhabitants are more like chained animals than human beings since, in fear, they have taken to their homes to avoid execution by the Falange. In a significant indication of the manner in which the Republic was careful to distinguish between its anticlericalism and accusations of being anti-religious, the men of the *pueblo* have sought the safety of the convent where, within its walls, they are

> mirando hacia las estrellas
> o a su terruño, abrazados,
> sin escuchar los lamentos
> de heridos y torturados,
> de mujeres sin marido
> y de huérfanos descalzos. (p.4)

> (looking towards the stars
> or at their own plot of land,
> holding each other tight,
> without listening to the cries of
> the wounded and tortured,
> of husbandless women
> and barefoot orphans.)

It is from such a hellish nightmare that the *campesino*, like many refugees who appear in *teatro de urgencia*, has fled. His desire is to reach what he describes as 'nuestra tierra' (our land) (p.2), the true *pueblo*, land which he proudly declares to have been given by the Republic for cultivation by those who, in the past, have had nothing. At the close of the action, as the peasant and the *milicianos* silently embrace, the *campesino* is reincorporated, as it were, into the tribe and, in the manner of swearing an oath, the peasant undertakes the struggle to free his *pueblo* by liberating Spain itself.

Such affirmation of the values of the *pueblo* involved the manipulation of images such as these so that the Fascist zone was seen as all that was contrary to the well-being of the *pueblo*. This was accompanied by a much broader vision, glimpsed across a range of plays, which sought to communicate the spirit of life in the Republic. A portrait emerged of the community and its life-style, one which reveals the persistent significance of the notion of the *pueblo* in Republican eyes. Alongside self-affirmation, therefore, theatrical propaganda focused on self-representation so that the *pueblo* was, in effect, presented to itself through drama. As we have already seen, *teatro de urgencia* stressed the role of the *miliciano* as that of the crucial individual. Its portrayal of the *pueblo* offered a necessary balance by emphasizing the crucial collective. The transmission of appropriate Republican values was thus attempted through the exploration of the community's various perceptions of the conflict. In this sense the plays represent the mood of the times, examining viewpoints and tensions within the populace, celebrating achievement or castigating failure to display the dignity which is commonly associated with the portrayal of the *pueblo*.

Such an approach involved the presentation of a wide range of characters from a broad span of ages, occupations and classes. However, perhaps the most appropriate manner to examine the nature of the *pueblo* is to explore the ways in which, from amongst this collective, three significant representative groups were portrayed in theatrical propaganda. Broadly speaking, a generational approach is fruitful since it offers an impression of the way in which *teatro de urgencia* addressed itself to the entire community. The dramatic presentation of the elderly, women and children illustrates, therefore, some of the range of experiences which confronted the people during the war and to which propaganda needed to address itself in order to provide suitable perspectives upon issues. Bearing in mind the widespread absence of able-bodied men, these three groups represented significant members of the community. The elderly were often seen as elders in the tribal sense, as possessing wisdom and knowledge which had a contemporary validity. Likewise, women occupied a unique status through the variety of functions which were combined within their dramatic role. Variously seen as mother, fighter and lover, women in *teatro de urgencia* offer an insight into their complex significance within Spanish society. Particularly striking is their lamentation over the deaths of their menfolk, overt grieving which seems prohibited to male characters since it implies lack of strength. By contrast, however, women acquired traditionally male attributes when assuming the role of agitator or rearguard combatant. Aub's Woman in *¿Qué has hecho?*, for example, sees the deaths of her own family more as a spur to further fighting and there is undoubted significance in Aub's choice of a name for the character, Juana Herrero Martín, which combines suggestions of maleness and metallic hardness. The third representative group, children, was one invariably seen in relation to its parents' war effort and, in this sense, added to the varied roles adopted by women. As one might expect, for practical reasons children tended to appear less frequently in theatrical propaganda, but their participation was often used to awaken the conscience of their parents and, through their presentation in a forthright and optimistic manner as the young hope of the people, children eagerly sought to contribute to the war.

The first of these groups, the elderly, assumed considerable authority by virtue of their association with work and struggle. The Old Man of Bleiberg's *Sombras de héroes* sees in his bombed *pueblo* the destruction of a whole lifetime's daily sweat, while, despite his seventy years, Hernández's Refugee spurns what he sees as the charity offered to those displaced by the war. Preferring to work for a pittance gathering olives from dawn, for him work is never demeaning if it is done with honour: 'lo mismo me da cavar olivos que recoger la peor basura' (it's the same to me whether I dig olive trees or collect the worst rubbish).[15] Nor is the willingness of the elderly to struggle perceived only in civilian terms, since their enthusiasm for active combat is undimmed despite their advanced years. The aged Sebastián, in *Dos divisiones*, regrets that he is no longer twenty and in good enough health to enlist. Adela, however, in the same play, recalls his contribution during the improvised resistance of the early days of the conflict as ferociously energetic:

'batiendo el cobre como un jabato por montes y llanos' (working tirelessly, like a daredevil, in the mountains and the plains).[16] In Hernández's play, too, the Refugee desires only to have marched with the militias. The role of the elderly in seeking to vanquish the July rebellion also gave a historical dimension to the war by offering an impression of the *pueblo*'s long struggle against oppression. The Old Man of *España no es Austria*, for example, is ready to defend the land with his hoe in the same manner that his grandfather participated in the resistance to Napoleon with stones and knives. He recalls, too, the first days of the uprising, describing how others had laughed when he had begun to clean his old shotgun, but that with others like his, and with sticks and knives, they had overcome the *señoritos*:

> les hicimos rendirse en el Casino y de nada les valieron sus rifles nuevos, ni sus pistolas ametralladoras, ni el piquete de la Guardia Civil. (p.42)
>
> (we made them surrender in the casino, and their new rifles, their automatic pistols and their Civil Guard squad were worthless to them.)

The elderly's unflinching reaction in the face of adversity was a yardstick against which other, perhaps younger, men's contributions to the war could be measured. Hernández's Refugee had opposed what he saw as the cowardly abandonment of his *pueblo* by the rest of the townsfolk. Those who had trumpeted their bravery had been, he regrets, the first to run. His own spirit of resistance is, by contrast, powerfully expressed in the image of him planning to defend his home by standing alert behind the door, brandishing a bullwhip with which to lash any Fascist who might attempt to cross the threshold. The persistent emphasis placed by the elderly upon resistance using whatever means come to hand enhances the mood of courageous valour which surrounds them, and reinforces the manner in which they are associated with natural or agricultural objects. The weapons of modern warfare held by the enemy are opposed by poles, axes and hoes, basic implements intended to highlight the selfless bravery of those who wield them.

This association of the elderly with agriculture and the land was the source of the wisdom they were presented as possessing. A revealing example of this can be found in the figure of Tío Jeromo in *Defendemos la tierra*, a character whose relationship with the land is such that he is described as fallow in complexion and as a lean, strong example of a 'vida entera de labrador humilde' (humble farm-worker's whole life) (p.79). His sense of self-worth is intricately bound up with what he perceives as the respect owed to those who cultivate their own land and, through his character, one is keenly reminded of the great significance which the Republic attached to land distribution. The action of the play concerns a group of *campesinos* who feed some *milicianos* and a Nationalist soldier who has managed to flee to Republican lines and is being escorted to headquarters. The interest shown by the peasants in the nature of life in the opposing zone is particularly acute in the case of Tío Jeromo and, in a manner described as obsessed, he reflects upon how the enemy have treated the land. Questioning persistently but politely, he demands of the fugitive soldier:

¿Y la tierra? ¿Qué han hecho con la tierra los invasores? ¿Nos la han *quitao*? ¿Nos *l'han robao* o qué han hecho? (p.82)

(And the land? What have the invaders done with the land? Have they taken it from us? Have they robbed us of it or what?)

The soldier, García, recounts a tale of greater exploitation of the *pueblo* than ever by absentee landlords who no longer offer true day labour but only 'un *puñao* de calderilla que no alcanza para comprar un pedazo de pan negro' (a handful of loose change not sufficient to buy a piece of brown bread) (p.82). Smallholders, he declares, have been expelled from the land which they had made productive but which is now absorbed into great estates worked by enforced Portuguese labourers. His picture, of a land enslaved and plundered by foreign interests, is greeted with helpless despair by Tío Jeromo, who contrasts it with the respect earned by those who work their own land. For him, there is nothing more sacred than the land itself and, in a characteristically rural image, he becomes 'más serio que un ajo' (more serious than a clove of garlic) (p.85) and lapses into a brooding silence.

The play's emphasis on the wisdom and active role of the elderly in defending the land is brought fully into focus at this point as, in his deep preoccupation with the fate of the *pueblo* in the opposing zone, Tío Jeromo is unable to share in the ludicrous antics of one of his fellow peasants, Patarra. Having donned the dress uniform of an Italian general which García had been carrying when he made his escape, Patarra jokes that now that he has quit his peasant garb he will be able to appropriate the patch of earth which Tío Jeromo has been engaged in sowing. In a clearly symbolic action, Tío Jeromo defends his land in the way which the play's title urges upon the spectators, and the elderly, in their own way, are seen as active contributors to combat duty. Since the land is, for Tío Jeromo, 'más que la madre de nuestra madre' (more than our mother's mother) (p.86), its defence is paramount and his powerful expression of its meaning chimes accurately with the orthodox view of it presented in all Republican propaganda. Patarra is warned that he must not take a step towards the ploughed furrows while wearing the enemy uniform since he would be treading upon the land that had given them birth and raised them, and where they would rest their bones. Rather than watch the enemy enslave the *pueblo* or tear them up like a bad root, he swears that he will see himself killed and buried at the foot of the furrows. To permit the enemy to contaminate and steal the land would leave the *pueblo* not only without territory but without honour, and he seizes his hoe to threaten Patarra that the uniform must not encroach upon his earth. With Patarra's resigned abandonment of the joke so as not to antagonize the old man, the action concludes with the symbolic expulsion of the enemy. Significantly, it is not the young *milicianos* who have achieved this victory but the elderly civilian. As the shots and explosions of approaching battle are heard, the real expulsion of the enemy is demanded and the departing soldiers reassure Tío Jeromo and the peasants that, as with the general's uniform, the enemy shall not pass.

The steadiness and resolve displayed by the elderly members of the *pueblo* was undoubtedly the most prominent feature of their characters, to such an extent that a single character type in the manner of a *commedia* mask can be easily discerned. A different picture emerges when one considers the presentation of women members of the *pueblo*. Particularly noticeable here is the way in which, across a range of plays, female characters adopt a number of different roles in line with the demands of changing social and political circumstances. Such a development is noteworthy in that, by and large, the conventional role allotted to women in the drama of the earlier part of the century varied little. Mussot draws attention to this in the prologue to *Mi puesto* when, as we have seen, he characterizes the traditional female dramatic role as that of the affected young girl who suffers desperate pangs of love for the handsome, penniless young man she can never marry since her father has arranged her wedding to a wealthy old man.[17]

This rather passive role perhaps recalls the Lieutenant's advice to his *novia* at the close of *El cuartel*, that she write verses and music in honour of the *pueblo*. The suggestion of marginalized participation in the war effort implicit here was not, however, typical of *teatro de urgencia* and, initially, women were portrayed as active combatants, on a par with men in the struggle to defeat the military rebellion. Adela, in *Dos divisiones*, offers such an impression when another character recalls how she had exposed herself to danger in the task of carrying boxes of munitions to the front line during fierce fighting. Similarly, a production photograph of *Cuatro batallones* shows the Obrera Alistada (Enlisted Female Worker) side by side with her male counterpart exhorting civilians to defend the capital.[18] Indeed, the actress's role in the play is to challenge the conventional stereotype represented by the Affected Young Girl whose interest in the war is detached, extending to little more than a sense of inconvenience that the social calendar has been disrupted. While the girl confides that, as a result, she can only dream of all the dresses she would have shown off, the enlisted worker is seen in the photograph wearing the non-gender *mono* outfit, strictly utilitarian garb suited to the weapon-handling which she urges upon all the female spectators.

A particularly revealing illustration of the new demands placed upon women during the early weeks of the conflict occurs in Balbontín's *Pionera* (*Girl Pioneer*), performed during the last week of October 1936.[19] The play combines dramatic roles more traditionally associated with women, such as Amalia, an emotional portrait of an ailing, invalid mother desperate to hear news of her *miliciano* son, and Sole, a *miliciana*. Amalia's fretful concern for Rafael, her son, is rather mawkishly redolent of melodrama. Haunted by dreams that every stray bullet has found its way to his chest and that he lies injured and calling for his mother, she fears being unable to help him:

> Le tiendo la mano con angustia, y no llego adonde él está. ¡Hijo de mis entrañas! (*tose con marcada fatiga*). (p.4)
>
> (I hold out my hand to him in anguish, and I can't reach to where he is. My own dear child! (*she coughs with obvious tiredness.*))

Sole, by contrast, represents something of the new spirit of the times, entering the play with a cry of '¡salud y República social!' (greetings and long live the Social Republic!) (p.12) and bringing an independent, assertive air to the action. Although she fails to escape the occasional sentimentality of the play, Sole's character stands out amongst the female characters of the play since it is pitted against calls from the other women for her to behave in a conventional manner. A neighbour, Bernarda, for example, upbraids her for indulging in fantasy by wearing the *mono* uniform and insists that her place is in the home darning socks. With characteristic patience, Sole explains that her outfit is not a fashion accessory to stroll through the city, but to enable her to fight at the side of Rafael. She confesses herself unable to understand, since there are sufficient women to sew and to fight, why 'se ha de frenar a la que sienta afanes de lucha' (you have to hold back those who are eager to fight) (p.13). Her choice of words is interesting for its implication of the release from accepted social roles which the war had brought, and she insists upon the need for women to offer an example, through their service at the front line, to the thousands of men who have adopted a low profile rather than enlist. In a line which has startling force even today, she declares: 'cada mujer que cae en el frente es un latigazo en la cara de los hombres que huyen' (each woman who falls at the front is a whiplash in the face of the men who flee) (p.14).

The gradual emergence of the Popular Army from the earlier militias led to the withdrawal of women from front-line fighting, and their new role was reflected in the altered emphasis of theatrical propaganda. In accepting the changed priorities with exemplary grace, Adela in *Dos divisiones* draws attention to features of the soldier which suggest the more male-dominated image associated with combatants, particularly in characteristic poster imagery: 'las armas, por ahora, para los jóvenes, para los sanos, para los fuertes' (weapons, for now, for the young, the healthy, the strong) (p.50). It is not clear why these three qualities are peculiarly masculine attributes but, undoubtedly, the cult of the *miliciano* which is apparent in many aspects of Republican propaganda became overwhelmingly male in tone. Whether *milicianas* in general approved of such developments is unclear, but perhaps the Young Girl in *España no es Austria* reflects a strain of contemporary opinion when she voices her desire to be a man and embrace combat duties. For her, all her chores are insignificant in comparison to active service, and she wonders aloud what it is that makes her worth less than her *compañero* (male companion), Fermín.

Women's new, rearguard role was encouraged through plays which portrayed them as supporting figures whose task was to undertake all non-military activities. The tools of production were to be shared amongst the women, declared the Woman of *Lección y escarmiento*, in order to encourage men to the front line. In similar fashion, Adela explains the role of women as that of producing whatever is needed and in the quantities required, declaring that tools, pens and words are also combat weapons. Both she and her friend Concha put this into effect through their work with the JSU, like the Female Agitator of *España no es Austria*, to maintain morale and encourage greater levels of production in war industries. Such work was carried out beyond the normal call of duty, since other employment continued. The figure of the Girl who, in *¡Aplastar a Franco!*, works eight hours daily in a factory before attending meetings designed to foster political awareness displays a characteristic diligence in this respect. Despite exhaustion and the loss of her *novio* during the Aragón campaign, her refusal to lose heart is typical of the indefatigable spirit which, by and large, it was suggested women in the rearguard possessed. Both as daughters and as mothers they have an air of Socialist Realist art about them, a civilian equivalent of the similar technique with which the *miliciano* was portrayed in poster art of the time. María, in *Despedida de reclutas*, illustrates the unflinching clarity and political orthodoxy common to such figures when she applauds the suggestion that the only regret of the mother of one of the new recruits is not having more sons to give to the cause. For her, this recalls her own mother, who is also declared to be acutely conscious of the struggle's meaning – a democratic republic free of foreign tyranny.[20] Similarly, the Woman who harangues the audience in Aub's *¿Qué has hecho?* perceives the sacrifice of war with a hard-edged absence of overt emotion. To a member of the crowd who asserts his lack of commitment to the war since it has claimed the lives of his wife, his children and home, she retorts with uncompromising grimness that the time has come, therefore, for his own stance against its progress.

There is a hard edge to this image of women in *teatro de urgencia* and this derived perhaps from the predominantly urban feel to the examples cited. The emphasis is upon factory production and street meetings, with an accompanying strident, harsh tone to the plays. One senses the loud clamour and harsh violence of cities under aerial attack, and a tone of desperation in those who urge resistance at all costs. However, a less hard, more explicitly maternal role was also adopted for the portrayal of women, especially in those plays with rural settings. The sharp eloquence of a character such as the Woman of *¿Qué has hecho?* was thus accompanied by yet another female dramatic contribution to the representation of the *pueblo*. In this case, the image which emerged was one which emphasized loss and suffering, as though women were the conduit for the overt expression of the whole community's grief.

Perhaps inevitably, this image predominantly concerned women whose loved ones had directly suffered at the hands of Fascism. With its recurrent emphasis upon separation, disappearance and the unknown fate which might befall husbands and sons, such plays must have seemed acutely relevant. The frequence of dramatic types in *teatro de urgencia* is obvious, but those female characters concerned with the exploration of loss become more than types and seem, rather, to embody more profound experiences. It is for this reason, possibly, that the language of such plays alters from the steely prose of works such as *España no es Austria* to a more poetic register which permits the communication of a greater range of feeling.

The depth of such experiences can be glimpsed, for example, through the role of the Mother in *Pedro López García*, a woman who loses her shepherd son, Pedro, to the Nationalist army when he is forcibly enlisted by a brutal Sergeant. As discussed earlier, her despairing anger at his loss leads her to denounce the Sergeant with insults for which she is threatened with death. When she invites him to do his worst it is in the knowledge, she asserts, that 'te estaré chillando al oído lo que te mereces' (I will be at your ear, screaming what you deserve).[21] The sense of gnawing conscience which such an image evokes is extended throughout the play since, after ordering the woman's death at the hands of his soldiers, the Sergeant is plagued by guilt at this and numerous other brutal acts. His own crisis of conscience is paralleled by that of Pedro who, in the trenches, is visited at night by his mother's spirit urging him to overcome his fear and cross to Republican lines. The emotional depth of the play is unusual in *teatro de urgencia*, and yet it loses none of the keen propaganda edge associated with the genre. Its relative profundity derives from the spiritual dimension of the Mother's role which acts as the catalyst for the psychological crises of the two men. The force of her character is acute when, as a ghost, she reassures her son that he is not alone since she remains with him. The richness of such an idea is enhanced by the manner in which, subsequently, the Mother is seen to metamorphose into the figure of the Land. The appearance of this character, declaring that it is Pedro's mother, is accompanied by the symbolic action of the Mother enfolding herself in its skirts as the Land speaks to Pedro of the deep bond which unites him with them and which will inevitably force him to desert and seek the trenches of his true brothers.

The relationship between mother and son is presented, therefore, as one which involves the land itself, an essential and unbreakable union which lends to the figure of the mother a status which suggests Mother Earth. As she vanishes, Pedro's mother murmurs that what he has heard is 'el viento de la noche' (the wind of the night) (p.99) and the Land/Mother figure describes itself as all that exists in nature, everything which gives meaning and substance to Pedro's life. This image of women as a life-source seeking to nourish their sons is particularly prominent in Bleiberg's *Amanecer*, a powerful expression of maternal grief at the destruction of the *pueblo*.[22] In many ways the play is an allegory of nature in which the Mother Earth figure emerges from night, death and the grief of loss to deliver new life one springtime dawn in the form of her young child. The play's action concerns the attempt of a refugee Woman and her son to flee the Fascist zone. Exhausted and uncertain of their best route in the darkness, they rest and, as she explains to her son the need for their desperate journey, a life story emerges which seems emblematic of *teatro de urgencia*'s vision of the *pueblo*'s own life and suffering. When day breaks, she discovers herself between opposing trenches and, dashing with her child towards the *milicianos*, she is fatally wounded by a *requeté*'s bullet. As she dies she is assured by the Republican soldiers that they will care for her son and the action draws to a close as the *milicianos* place flowers upon the sheet with which they cover her body.

The Woman grieves since she and her son are the only survivors of her family and her emergence from the night's darkness is, thus, both literal and metaphorical. The loss of her family is seen in terms which again emphasize the relationship between mothers, the *pueblo* and the land since her husband and children were, she recalls, as strong as trees and as healthy as ripe apples. Now, however, they are shrivelled and cold. Their deaths, through bullets in the back while they slept, were executions while they were dreaming of the ripening harvest. Her account of life in the *pueblo* recalls that of *El pueblo fascista* – a plague has descended upon the land in the form of violent terror and ruthless exploitation by German troops and brutal Falangists. Wandering the streets in search of bread she sees only tearful, sad faces and hears only groans of pain. The notion of the *pueblo* as a paradise which has been usurped is felt, not only in the imagery of thriving nature made rotten by the blight of Fascism, but in the young son's nightmare that a black serpent is eating away at his mother's eyes.

The dark, brooding mood which dominates the early part of the play arises from memory and the recollection of loss. While day approaches, however, the tone and image alter as the Woman embraces her surviving child and promises him a different future since 'también la sangre da sus frutos' (blood also bears fruit) (p.30). As the dawn light promises to break, her vision for the child is one of abundant nature, of a garden always in flower or 'una llanura siempre cubierta de frutos' (a grove always covered in fruit) (p.30). The past is seen in terms of death, as blood and ashes, but the future resembles youth bursting from the injured womb of its mother and filling her heart with sunlight. Such an image seems prophetic of her death since, as she expires, it is as though she has delivered new life through, and to, her child:

> Mira, toda la vida es tuya . . . aquí mismo, bajo mis pies, hasta más allá de miles de horizontes, la nueva España surge entre la niebla, la España de los españoles, de los obreros y de los campesinos. (pp.30–1)
>
> (Look, all of life is yours . . . here itself, beneath my feet, even to beyond thousands of horizons, the new Spain emerges from the mist, the Spain of the Spaniards, of the workers and the peasants.)

The embracing of the son by the *milicianos* and his incorporation amongst them as a new brother is presented as the acceptance of new life which must be cared for and nurtured. Their promise to tend him and love him as his mother did is seen as a sacred duty, an undertaking for which no sacrifice will be too great. As the spring flowers – poppies and daisies – seek to break through the soil of the trenches despite the enemy's fire, the child, too, blends into the image of new life overcoming death to recall sweetness and to promise 'un bienestar muy próximo' (well-being in the near future) (p.33).

The fusion of so many images of nature, earth and motherhood in *Pedro López García* and *Amanecer* transforms the plays' female characters into icons which represent some profound notion of the *pueblo* and its meaning, particularly in the lives of their soldier sons. One is reminded of Catholic iconography in the cult of the Madonna, a grieving mother, often associated with flowers, who prays for the redemption of her son. The religious suggestion here is not inappropriate since the concept of a Republican deity is central, for example, to Alberti's *Cantata* and his portrayal in it of the figure of Spain as a woman. A kind of divine status accrues to her through the obeisance offered by other characters. The sense of worshippers who perceive themselves both as part of the deity and as humbly obedient supplicants of it can, for example, be readily glimpsed in the words of the International Soldier:

> aquí nos tienes, claros, anónimos, dispuestos
> a ser como pedazos de tus mismas entrañas.
> En tu aurora queremos ser lumbre de esa aurora.
> Tú ordenas, tú diriges, tú castigas, tú mandas.[23]

> (here you have us, clear, anonymous, ready
> to become part of your womb itself.
> In your dawn we want to be light of that dawn.
> You order, you direct, you punish, you command.)

This godlike figure of Spain fuses within her role, too, various icons central to the dramatic presentation of the *pueblo* and, as a result, the impression of something more significant than a totem emerges – a powerful symbol with the language and emotional force of a deity is seen to combine essential *teatro de urgencia* images of the suffering mother, fraternal love, heroic sacrifice and the national territory itself.

As has already been seen, the action of the *Cantata* involves the ritual unification of Spain with one of her sons, a Nationalist soldier who comes to perceive himself as deceived into betraying the maternal figure of Spain by fighting against her. His reincorporation into the ranks of the *milicianos* leads to the removal of Spain's funeral vestments and, with the descent of flowers and the flight of doves, the ritual ends with a processional exit. As even this brief summary suggests, the presence of Christian ritual is very marked in the *Cantata*, to such an extent that it blurs the distinction between theatrical event and sacred ceremony and enhances the perception of women in the work as purveyors of some divine essence. The powerful female presence of Spain itself, for example, is enhanced by the group of Spanish Women, led by the figure of the Mother, who bid farewell to the International Brigade soldiers by embracing them as sons and delivering to them the flags of their various regiments. The ritualistic language which accompanies their gesture recalls, as in *Amanecer* and *Pedro López García*, the endurance of memory and the unique status of the bond between mother and son:

> Manos de madres, manos de mujeres
> os la entregan, hijos. Que a los vientos
> de las estrellas patrias y a los soles
> siempre ejemplar ondule su recuerdo. (p.197)

> (Mothers' hands, women's hands
> pass them to you, sons. May their
> exemplary memory always wave
> in the winds of patriotic stars and suns.)

It is a moment of great significance, blending ideas of benediction by some holy icon and the transmission of the sacrament, and it is important in this respect that the language and imagery which surround Spain reinforce such a religious mood by evoking the cult of Our Lady. Thus, in a manner reminiscent of the Woman of *Amanecer*, Spain is spoken of in terms of dawn and the heart, of being 'el mar más dichoso' (the most fortunate sea) (p.198) and 'la estrella de la mañana' (the morning star) (p.198). Significantly, too, whereas at the opening of the cantata her heart was felt to be pierced by nails, at the end the traditional bleeding heart of the Madonna has been so transformed by reunification with her prodigal son that '¡que de mis pechos salten dos ríos de esperanza!' (from my breasts spring two rivers of hope) (p.201).

It is an indication of the chameleon-like nature of *teatro de urgencia* that, in fulfilling its task of presenting the necessary variety of social perspectives on the war, the image of women discussed above could be radically transformed so as to offer a quite contrary impression of their view of the conflict. The unstinting support for resistance which we have seen to characterize the attitude of women involved, of necessity, the surrender of their sons to combat. This was presented as a sacrifice made with dignity and resolute belief in their sons' role as liberators of the *pueblo*. Inevitably perhaps, a female image emerged which was intended to balance such an exemplary display of duty. In this respect, consideration of the role of children in theatrical propaganda becomes apt since, against youthful desire to seek adventure or to see action against a despised enemy, was ranged a maternal instinct for protection of the young.

Hernández pits two such attitudes against one another when, in *El hombrecito* (*The Little Man*), the Son, a young man, rejects his mother's pleas that he remain at home with her and chooses to fulfil his burning desire to see a tank on fire, smoking cannon and the enemy mortally wounded.[24] It is important to take such bellicose, destructive comments within the rather humorous sketch-like nature of the play, and as the sentiments of a youth of fifteen seen as irrepressibly eager to serve the *pueblo*'s cause. The simple action of the play, a dialogue between mother and son, becomes the opportunity to paint a picture of the young man's view of his own emerging manhood and, as a consequence, his perception of duty with regard to combat. His attitude to the war is thus seen as a model of orthodoxy. One has the impression that it was intended, however, not for the encouragement of recruitment through presentation before youth audiences, but as a stimulus to mothers to understand the need to surrender their sons to the war.

Much of the rather subtle humour of the play arises from the actual maturity of the youth in comparison to his mother's highly strung over-protectiveness. Her concerned calls to ask where he is as she enters the play, for example, are a tiresome irritation to him since, in an appropriately domestic image, he asserts that he is not going to get lost like a sewing needle. Ironically, it is she who is more fearful of enemy attack, and despairs about when (not if) the enemy's bombs will fall upon them. The son's calming response is to remind her of the shell which had landed in a neighbouring orchard but failed to explode, and to say that the enemy is more concerned to attack the local barracks. The childlike relationship which the mother seeks to preserve is felt in his desire to break the umbilical connection suggested by his feeling that 'estoy harto, madre, de ir atado a tu falda' (I'm fed up, mother, with going around tied to your apron strings) (p.418). By contrast, his litany of complaints about involvement in household chores reflects his true desire, expressed in martial imagery, to join his father in the front line. His sense of shame, therefore, at finding himself constantly amongst women, queuing for bread and milk, is pitted against his enthusiasm to carry at least a drum, if not a rifle, into battle.

Contrasting imagery such as this is employed for the two characters throughout the play, serving to reveal the manner in which, despite his years, the youth already reveals many of the qualities of the characteristic *miliciano*. Blood rushes to his heart with anger, for example, when he hears the explosion of bombs and he recognizes that the war will be lost: 'si habemos [*sic*] hombres cruzados de brazos' (if we have men with their arms folded) (p.419). Such language evokes that of the heroic soldier and his forthright denunciations, in plays such as *Los sentados* and *Los miedosos valientes*,[25] of lukewarm commitment to the war by men of fighting age. No such accusation could be levelled against the youth who, in a conscious recall of the story of David and Goliath, declares that he will fight with a sling if he does not have a rifle, with his teeth if he lacks a sling and that, failing teeth, he will spit at the enemy until he has no saliva. The angry mood of battle is markedly different from his mother's vision of her child, at work in the garden, cultivating the wallflowers and pruning the acacias. Such a protective image suggests a paradise, but, for the son it is, without victory, merely an illusion and, in the prospect of defeat, he sees rather the hell of the *pueblo*'s earlier life-style:

> el hambre será más grande que nunca y todos seremos como bueyes . . . mi padre volverá a no tener trabajo y ni tú ni yo alegría. (p.419)
>
> (there will be greater hunger than ever and we will all be like oxen . . . my father will go back to having no work and you and me no happiness.)

The suggestion of the younger generation clamouring to enlist complemented the similar eagerness to contribute to the fighting displayed by its elderly counterpart in the *pueblo*. If the latter were seen to look back, finding its resolve in the example of earlier struggles, the children were seen to look forward, embracing the current struggle regardless of its hazards. As he determines to leave, the son offers his clenched fist in defiance of the enemy and declares it to be his salute 'hasta que no me quede aliento dentro de la vida' (until there's no breath left in my body) (p.420). His strength as a source of life and brave energy is also felt in his rejection of the fear of death. His mother's disbelief that he can commit himself so fearlessly to the possibility of death is answered with a blunt refusal to recognize its power: 'no la conozco, y quiero ver si la asusto yo a ella' (I'm not acquainted with it, and I want to see if I can frighten it) (p.420).

The jauntiness of the son's spirit, though obviously naïve and untested, was, none the less, intended to arouse amongst mothers and the wider community a recognition of the inevitability of children of a certain age being required to fight. The youth's insistence at one point in Hernández's play that he is effectively sixteen, provokes an emotional denial from the mother since this would bring closer his enlistment. That this was an issue of increasing topicality as the war progressed there can be little doubt since, towards the end of the conflict, the Republic had felt it necessary to enlist the *quinta* (call-up) of 1941.[26] A useful propaganda tactic, therefore, was the presentation of children themselves as eager to serve the *pueblo* in the manner of *El hombrecito*. Aub adopts such a tactic in *¿Qué has hecho?* through the figure of the Youth, aged fourteen, who eagerly confesses to the Woman that he has done nothing that day to aid victory since his family refuses to permit him to contribute. Summoned to the stage, he announces his desire to serve as a pilot and is indignant at his parents' objections since, given that so many others are fulfilling their duty, he sees his place clearly in the front line. The same eagerness, energy and somewhat rebellious spirit which typified the Son in Hernández's play, is found in the Youth. The Woman's unwelcome advice that his best service to the Republic is achieved through continuing his school education is greeted, for example, with a humorously impatient refusal to listen to the advice of his elders:

¡Ah! ¿Pero es que usted también . . .? No quiero oírla. (*Da un salto del tablado a tierra y se va.*)[27]

(Oh! So you too . . .? I don't want to hear it. (*He jumps off the stage onto the ground and goes away.*))

The relationship between mothers and their male children, of whatever age, is so prominent a feature of *teatro de urgencia* because of the notion of maternal sacrifice and the intricate nature of the role of mother as an icon. The young males leave their mothers behind, but, in a rare inversion of this idea, Balbontín's *Pionera* demonstrates how the female child takes her father with her, leading him out of despair and towards combat. The child in question, Lina, is the Young Pioneer of the play's title who, dressed in her *mono* uniform, returns to her parents' Madrid home to announce proudly that she has been selected to recite a *romance* about the war in a *fiesta* that afternoon, and to request her father to descend to the street when the Young Pioneers' procession passes their home. Although they disguise it from the child, the mood of her parents, despite their committed socialism, is one of despondent resignation and fear about the war. Their worries over the well-being of their *miliciano* son Rafael have a deleterious effect on Amalia, the mother, who is dying. The news of their son's grave wounding and imminent death is concealed from her, but she dies and the double blow brings the father, Julián, to consider suicide. Lina, unaware of events, returns home to beg her father to come down into the street and, believing her mother to be sleeping, urges her father to do as other children's parents are, by joining the socialist battalion which is leaving for the front line.

Although she plays quite a minor role in the action, Lina is central to the propaganda intention of the work – to celebrate the Popular Militias and issue a call to arms. The play's title belongs to her, and the *romance* of the same name, a stirring commendation of youthful commitment to the war, is recited by Lina during the course of the action. As with the boys of *El hombrecito* and *¿Qué has hecho?*, she longs to see combat but, as she asserts in her poem:

> Como soy tan niña,
> no me atendió nadie,
> cuando, a grandes gritos,
> reclamaba un máuser. (p.6)

> (Since I'm such a little girl,
> nobody listened to me,
> when, at the top of my voice,
> I demanded a Mauser.)

The girl's *romance* is a vivid illustration of the relish with which children were presented as viewing the conflict and the way in which they were prepared to join with the adults in repelling the enemy. The poem is structured around an image which contrasts the physical smallness of children with the grandness of spirit which they bring to the prosecution of the war. Since the child of the poem is so young she has been prevented from accompanying her father to fight in the *sierra*, but she imagines herself being carried proudly upon his shoulders towards the battle. She longs to have been both bigger and stronger so that she might have saved him from a fatal bullet by acting as a human shield. As captain of the Young Pioneers, however, she bears the standard of her troop and, declaring herself transformed into a powerful giant, she defiantly asserts:

> ¡Que nadie
> vuelva a echarme en cara
> mi niñez inane! (p.7)

> (Let no one
> throw in my face again
> my unworthy childhood!)

Calling upon her fellow Pioneers and those children who have lost their fathers to the war, she urges vengeance upon their murderers and promises that, if the adults call them, the children, too, will serve at the front line since

> También nuestros puños
> sirven de acicate. (p.8)

> (Our fists also
> serve as a spur.)

The child's desire to play a role in the combat is seen as one which brings the vigour and powerful idealism of youth to the older generation. To Lina's father, life has become evil and hateful since, both at the front line and in the rearguard, the bravest and best die. His own existence, he suggests, is like life within a tomb. Such dark, gloomy imagery is in stark contrast to the images which surround his daughter. She is described as being like a ray of dawn light and as a revitalizing force who urges her father to breathe 'el aire fresco de fuera' (the fresh air outside) (p.22). The symbolism of this fresh world outside the home becomes the focus of the play's political message, since it is to the world of the street, with its marching, recruitment and celebration of the *pueblo*, that Lina wishes to lead her father. Her repeated desire for him to descend to the street is an invitation to join the people's struggle. As in *El hombrecito*, however, it is the fretful concern of the mother which urges the male to avoid combat. Lina, thinking her mother to be asleep, urges her father to take the opportunity which this presents, to join the Pablo Iglesias battalion. As the play draws to a close, the mood of life triumphing over death strengthens as Julián resolves to enlist, choosing to leave behind the world of the home with its associations of spent life. In a final image which suggests the earlier one of the daughter carried proudly aloft upon her father's shoulders, the two leave together to participate in the struggle as 'hijos y padres, por la defensa de Madrid, por el triunfo del pueblo' (children and parents, for the defence of Madrid, for the triumph of the people) (p.23). The child has brought renewed strength to the adult and demonstrated through example that, as suggested in the girl's *romance*, the clenched fists of youth are also weapons of combat.

The play concludes with the symbolism of the generations in unison, and this draws attention to the notion, common to the exploration of the *pueblo*, of the whole community seeking unity with which to secure victory. The dramatic presentation of the elderly, and of women and children, was a central element of such a portrait, with women in particular offering an illustration of the wide range of perspectives addressed by the propaganda. The very fluid nature of their role in a number of plays associates them, as we have seen, with what are presented as essential, spiritual qualities of the *pueblo* and, notable in this respect, is the manner in which they are linked with the appearance of mythical or mystical characters. Such figures seem to speak in the plays with overarching authority, sanctioning characters' actions or offering a kind of religious blessing upon the events which, unseen, they have witnessed. Bleiberg uses such a device at the close of *Sombras de héroes* when the figure of the Voice of Spain enters to conclude the action with a kind of benediction upon the dead *miliciano* and to call upon the *pueblo* to avenge the Republic's defeat in the Basque country. It is not clear whether the character is to be played as a woman, yet this seems appropriate, given the mood of sorrowing grief which is initially felt in the *romance* which the figure recites. Past defeat is cast aside, however, in a call to wreak vengeance upon the enemy which seems to emanate from a figure reminiscent of an Old Testament prophet or even a divine figure:

> ¡Vengad el crimen del Norte!
> ¡Que España tiene un ejército!
> ¡Que los héroes muertos gritan:
> el triunfo ya sólo es nuestro!²⁸

> (Avenge the crime of the North!
> Spain has an army!
> The dead heroes shout:
> Victory is ours alone!)

A similarly striking example of such a figure occurs at the close of *El hombrecito* when the Mother's reluctance to surrender her child to the war is transformed into active endorsement of his enlistment. An unseen, godlike voice which she feels comes from within her, serves to take the place of the loneliness she senses at her son's loss. This Voice of the Poet speaks like a divine being, urging mothers not to hinder their children's recruitment but, rather, to give birth to 'gigantes para la hazaña' (giants for the heroic deed) (p.421) and to sew flags for their sons to carry upon their victorious shoulders. The Mother's fear in the play for her child's death is replaced by the Voice of the Poet's heroic assertion that the mothers' sons may fall but that they will not die. They will find themselves, rather, united with the Voice of the Poet in what is suggested as a kind of Valhalla:

> No morirán, yo lo digo:
> caerán, sí, pero no muertos.
> ¡Madres, quedarán conmigo
> de relámpagos cubiertos! (p.421)

> (They will not die, I declare:
> they will fall, yes, but not dead.
> Mothers, they will remain with me
> covered in glory!)

The feeling of the sons' embrace by a divinity is reminiscent of Pedro López García and the sense that, in crossing to Republican lines, he has been absorbed by the figure of the Land which had earlier urged his desertion. Even more so than the Voice of the Poet, the Land is portrayed as a figure whose authority cannot be denied or ignored and, in speaking to the shepherd/soldier Pedro, the deep bond between the *pueblo* and the Spanish earth which seems to underpin much of the war's meaning is made clear. The land is thus seen as the immense total of all that exists. Life itself, in a strikingly Beckettian image, becomes merely a chance moment of light between two infinite darknesses. The power of the land, by contrast, is greater than the infinite vastness of the night sky upon which Pedro gazes, and yet it is also seen as a tiny seed which breathes life through roots and stalks and brings the golden sheen to grains of wheat.

Much of the importance of mystical figures such as these lay in their flexibility as dramatic creations. In the case of the Voice of the Poet, its appearance in the action serves to dislocate the style of the play so that its prose realism alters to a heroic verse which speaks with stark authority to the Mother of her duty towards the *pueblo*. In turn, she adopts much of the verse's tone and, in an image which seems entirely characteristic, describes her son as a seed which will become bread to nourish all the sons who will issue from their mothers' wombs. The appearance of the Land in *Pedro López García* brings about a similar change of style. Again, the fundamental realism of the work breaks down since, as with the Mother, there is a sense that the figures which speak to them are, in some crucial sense, projections of the characters' own thoughts upon, and understanding of, the conflict. The internal world of the characters seems to have been rendered external in order to make more explicit the fundamental bond which is persistently seen to link the *pueblo*, the war and the land for which it is fought.

Perhaps the most important contribution which characters such as the Land and Spain made to the portrayal of the *pueblo*, and to *teatro de urgencia* in general, was to provide elements of the extensive metaphor by which the war's meaning was communicated through propaganda. Images of seeds and plants, of birth and childhood, extend themselves outwards in the language and characterization of the plays, culminating in the appearance of mystical figures with their images of the cosmos and of heaven turned into hell by war. Within this overarching metaphor, theatrical propaganda attempted to convey a vision of the *pueblo* which would serve to galvanize its spirit, celebrate its successes and admonish failure to defend it against attack. There is, perhaps, an occasional air of romantic adulation of the *pueblo* which might lead one to imagine a naïvety on the part of the plays' authors. Their vision, however, while undoubtedly based on the high esteem in which *teatro de urgencia* held the *pueblo* and all that it signified, was propaganda. As such, it indicates a certain mistrust of the people who are generally so lauded in the plays or whose shortcomings are so easily corrected.

In its affirmation of the *pueblo*, theatrical propaganda was following in the path of earlier dramatists. As we saw at the outset, socialist writers prior to the Civil War had attempted a similar task to that of *teatro de urgencia*, to explore the ways in which the people could become master of the land rather than its slave. That this attempt largely failed was due to a question of dramatic form. As the debate amongst socialist thinkers discussed earlier demonstrates, the Left did not have, prior to the Civil War, a dramatic aesthetic capable of reflecting satisfactorily their view of the *pueblo*.[29] The desire for the *pueblo*'s self-affirmation through drama could only remain a desire since they did not possess the form through which they might create a people's drama free of bourgeois notions of quality. By contrast, *teatro de urgencia* was able to offer a confident affirmation of the *pueblo* since it utilized a forceful, malleable dramatic form which was, crucially, a form created on the *pueblo*'s own terms.

~ *Conclusion* ~
A Lost Theatre Recovered

The picture of *teatro de urgencia* which has emerged is characterized by two notable and contrasting features. As a *theatrical* development it was diffuse and rather fragmented, yet as a body of *drama* it was clearly unified in terms such as theme, language and character. These two features serve as helpful guidelines to encapsulate *teatro de urgencia*, lending greater clarity to a phenomenon which is at times indistinct. Viewed as theatre, *teatro de urgencia*'s development was marked by numerous initiatives designed to achieve a number of important aims. A repertoire had to be encouraged, for example, which would provide the various groups with dramatic material considered appropriate for presentation, and the intended audiences for such a repertoire had to be reached despite the changing and difficult circumstances of war. These were tasks of great magnitude and, when one considers the varied organizations which nurtured *teatro de urgencia*, a somewhat disparate, rather complicated impression characterized its theatrical development. Given the highly generalized nature of current commentary on *teatro de urgencia* I hope that my discussion of such development in chapters 2 and 3 contributes towards offering a more detailed perception. Viewed as drama, a contrast is felt, since the analysis of *teatro de urgencia* through recovered texts has facilitated a discussion which is, from the outset, more concrete. What emerges from this perspective is a kind of drama which, despite the absence of a central, controlling organization, displays many shared features. The common purpose of the drama encouraged similar approaches to the portrayal of particular groups such as, for example, the rebel soldier, the *miliciano* or the German and Italian officer class. Vocabulary and imagery, too, share numerous common features which derive from the fundamental, frequently reiterated themes of *teatro de urgencia* – the conflict as a foreign invasion and the Republic as guarantor of the liberty and well-being of the *pueblo*.

I have drawn attention to these two features, of theatre and of drama, to assist in ordering discussion of a phenomenon which was characterized less by clear structures than by improvisation, by seizing appropriate initiatives and seeking the means to carry them through to desired goals. In this respect *teatro de urgencia* clearly echoes Irene Falcón's perception of the work of Nosotros as a rapidly improvised response to the political tasks which the group perceived to be significant at any given moment. This emphasis upon improvisation was prevalent in *teatro de urgencia* whether it is viewed from the perspective of theatre or of drama. Its brief appearance in the Madrid theatres, for example, arose from a desire for a radical political theatre which, at that early stage of the war, could only be met through a drama characterized by rapid composition, minimal demands and the capacity to address issues of great immediacy. Dramatic qualities such as these were, however, essential strengths of the genre when, later in the war, *teatro de urgencia* was required to fulfil training tasks with soldiers. The sense of improvisation is particularly marked here, offering an impression even of improvised playwrights, as commissars and others turned their hands to dramatic composition as a means of inculcating ideas or demonstrating appropriate military practice.

A particularly revealing illustration of this notion of improvisation can perhaps be felt in the title of the CCT's journal, the *Boletín de Orientación Teatral*. This short-lived publication contained articles and information about current theatre initiatives, the history of drama and the role of theatre in society. The title's emphasis upon orientation is intriguing and offers an insight into perceptions about theatre which were held at the time by those, such as Alberti and León, who were prominent in undertaking theatrical activities. One senses a mood of tentative exploration which seems an appropriate reflection, not only of theatrical developments in the Republic, but of many other aspects of its social and cultural life. It is a title much concerned with the theatre's direction at a significant turning-point and hints at much which enables us to embark upon a fruitful conclusion to this study by examining how *teatro de urgencia* may be understood, both as drama and as theatre, in relation to three significant issues of orientation and direction: those of its provenance, of its wartime task and of how those involved in its creation sensed its future possibilities.

Viewed from a theatrical perspective, *teatro de urgencia* undoubtedly had a confident sense of its own orientation with regard to its immediate origins. As indicated in the earlier chapters, writers on the Left had encountered the agitprop aesthetic through their experience of political theatre elsewhere in Europe, and had actively sought to apply it to their own circumstances. In comments which seem almost prophetic of *teatro de urgencia*'s intentions, Alberti, for example, had suggested in 1933 that a theatre of the masses could be created in Spain only through the adoption of techniques which recall the work of Piscator or the Blue Blouse. His call for troupes of eleven actors to 'realizar la cruzada por toda España' (carry the crusade through all Spain) was intended to bring a theatre of political agitation to what he saw, like Unamuno, as the natural source of the Spanish theatre – the *pueblo*.[1] Although details are tantalizingly few, it is now clear that agitational theatre of this kind was prominent in Spain during the peacetime years of the Republic, seeking, in Alberti's view, to be a tendentious theatre concerned to denounce economic and social injustice.

Such a forthright oppositional orientation, so marked in works such as Aub's *El agua* and Alberti's *Farsa*, altered when the agitprop theatre encountered the new demands placed upon it by the Civil War. Its sense of its wartime duty was varied, and a number of new directions were established which arose naturally from circumstances in which it was judged a useful tool to employ in pursuit of particular ends. At the outset *teatro de urgencia* served to offer a call to arms and to provide an initial repertoire for some of the recently socialized theatres of the capital. As the conflict deepened, however, a wider range of tasks became apparent. The term 'theatre in education' seems appropriate to describe some of these tasks and perhaps its foremost example was Mussot's *Mi puesto*. Plays such as this derived largely from initiatives within the army and their emphasis was upon military training through a drama oriented towards the clarification of a complicated issue or the perception of how to achieve a specific military goal. Entertainment, too, was regarded as a significant task, not only for the purposes of distraction, but for the important sense of bonding which might be encouraged through the satirical lampooning of the enemy. The overarching concern of *teatro de urgencia* was, of course, the consolidation of the Republic as a political and military entity and, inevitably, the orientation of theatrical propaganda altered. The pre-war agitational stance was abandoned and emphasis was placed instead upon duty to the state and the civic responsibilities of its citizens.

It was perhaps similarly inevitable that *teatro de urgencia*'s perception of its future orientation as theatre was less certain than its sense of its immediate task. There did exist, however, an important awareness of its transitional nature. The prologue to *Un teatro de guerra* offers useful insights in this respect, with its suggestion that the anthology reflects a kind of theatre which is a 'buen ensayo' (good attempt), an experiment which contains within it the germ of a more sophisticated theatre.[2] In similar fashion, the creation of the Guerrillas del Teatro to perform *teatro de urgencia* was viewed as an initial phase in a more ambitious programme of theatrical innovation.[3] Given the much-rehearsed regeneration argument, there is considerable poignancy in the apparently uncomplicated strategy to institute a theatre which combined both popular appeal and high quality. The absence of such a theatre had persistently frustrated Spanish artists and intellectuals, but the Guerrillas' intention was to pave the way for it through the success with which they would capture the affection of the masses. By encountering *teatro de urgencia* in the streets and squares, citizens of all ages and backgrounds would become intelligent, critical spectators and, in a subsequent phase of the Guerrillas' development, would eagerly demand more challenging works. Prominent amongst such works, it was imagined, would be *Fuenteovejuna*, a play much admired during the years of the Republic as offering an important expression of the *pueblo*. There was obvious contemporary political significance in the *pueblo*'s collective action in the drama, but there seems too, even in the earlier production of the play by Lorca and La Barraca, to have been great significance in the *pueblo* as *audience* for the play.[4] It is as though, for those associated with *teatro de urgencia*, in the act of viewing this particular work the *pueblo* created again the popular theatre of earlier centuries. The future orientation of the post-war theatre seems to have been predicated upon a notion such as this, that the repertoire would be revitalized through the rediscovery of an earlier relationship between stage and audience. Such a view recalls, of course, Unamuno's explanation of the ills of the Spanish theatre and draws attention once more to the enormous significance which the idea of the *pueblo* held for Republicans.

This concern to draw upon the drama of the Golden Age was matched by *teatro de urgencia*'s interest in a number of dramatic sources which it eagerly appropriated. One has a distinct impression that its perception of its provenance as drama was strikingly clear. Its theatrical debt to the kind of 'poor' theatre favoured by earlier European experiments with political theatre was mirrored, for example, in its extensive use of the sketch format. Such a form, with its direct, agitational style and its emphasis on the communication of an unambiguous political message, became a principal dramatic method of *teatro de urgencia*. Perhaps its most prominent example was *Cuatro batallones*. Derived to a great extent from Piscator's recommendation of a utilitarian, 'trivial' form, its usefulness to Republican propagandists lay in its adaptability, its capacity to absorb whatever political lesson it was required to teach, and transmute it into an accessible dramatic illustration.

Like many popular art forms, *teatro de urgencia* also demonstrated awareness of popular traditions and drew upon them whenever they could prove useful vehicles for contemporary propaganda. As has been suggested, this predominantly entailed a keen focus on the potential offered by Golden Age dramatic forms. In the same manner that *teatro de urgencia* practitioners and commentators were aware of its part in the tradition of travelling theatre and the *corral* (courtyard) stage, so too were they aware of its appropriation of the earlier indigenous drama. Dieste, for example, consciously exploits such forms in *Nuevo retablo*, recasting Cervantes's original in a Civil War setting to derive satirical humour from the discomfiture of reactionary characters who seek to prove themselves free of Marxism by claiming to see what is not in fact there. Aub, too, recognized the fruitful possibilities of utilizing the drama of the Golden Age to enhance the *teatro de urgencia* repertoire. *Pedro López García* bears the subtitle 'auto' and skilfully blends a contemporary setting with images and characters recalling earlier religious drama which enacted a perennial struggle between good and evil. Similarly, Aparicio emphasized the common links between *teatro de urgencia* and the popular drama of previous centuries. His call for a repertoire which seized the opportunity to exploit the Golden Age canon of short plays was one which recognized the intrinsic quality of such plays but was also aware of their capacity, through adaptation, to comment upon or reflect contemporary circumstances.[5]

Aparicio also displays an awareness of *teatro de urgencia*'s place in a continuing tradition of popular dramatic forms when he urges the presentation and adaptation of *sainetes* (one-act farces) and Lorca's small-scale dramas. In encouraging such initiatives, Aparicio might well have had in mind examples of similar work by Ontañón and Dieste. For his satirical farce, *El bulo*, Ontañón had drawn upon the knockabout comedy and humorous word-play of the *sainete*. Likewise,

Dieste's *Al amanecer* juxtaposed the traditional form of romantic drama with contemporary images such as the obviously symbolic invasion by *milicianos* of the play's elegant drawing-room setting.

The variety of dramatic forms which characterizes *teatro de urgencia* suggests, I believe, its mood of energetic improvisation, a mood which is consistent with that found in other areas of Republican culture and society. In terms of the theatre as an institution and as an industry, the popular revolution desired by the Left suffered significant failures. In terms of drama, however, 'popular' and 'revolution' were concepts which fared well. The dominant emphasis on the *pueblo* in so many cultural spheres brought to the fore past dramatic forms whose roots undoubtedly lay in the popular culture of the *pueblo*, and these forms fused with those derived from contemporary revolutionary agitation. This does not make *teatro de urgencia* 'lo popular' (the folk tradition) but I do believe that a persuasive case can be made to regard it as a unique contribution to the tradition of popular drama.

The use of popular dramatic forms suggests *teatro de urgencia*'s sense of its wartime task to have been one which reflected the period's emphasis upon the collective and the community. Machado's comment that the best works are often those of more than a single author recalls the anonymous roots of popular culture, but it also usefully illustrates something of *teatro de urgencia*'s chameleon-like quality of using whatever materials seemed appropriate to achieve its aims.[6] Alberti drew attention to such a quality when, in his call for an extensive repertoire of *teatro de urgencia*, he described such work as utilitarian, effective and necessary.[7] His emphasis eschewed the notion of a pure style and lay, rather, upon the conscious exploitation of a range of genres and stylistic approaches as demanded by the propaganda intentions of the task. Particularly important was Alberti's use of the word 'necessary' in his recommendation of *teatro de urgencia*. In the same way that the Guerrillas del Teatro were regarded as the first step on a journey towards a more substantial and ambitious theatre, there was a similar awareness that, as drama, *teatro de urgencia* was a means to an end rather than an end in itself. The evidence of events in the Madrid theatres in the summer and autumn of 1936 confirms such a view, since groups such as Nueva Escena and the GTP had a clear idea of the kind of radical European and classical repertoire which was their goal. The TAP, too, displayed similar clarity of purpose. Indeed, the title of the group is itself an indication of the distinction which they made between work of challenging complexity and the cultivation of a popular audience for such work through initially more accessible dramatic forms.

If the ambitions of such groups with regard to a renaissance of Spanish drama and theatre were to be realized, *teatro de urgencia* was, therefore, as Alberti had stated, a necessary element of the Republic's cultural and political orientation. As drama it offered demonstration, education and laughter, and urged patriotism and duty. It sought to educate its audience for a theatrical future which was sophisticated. Such a future depended, however, upon military victory. It was this crucial goal which provided the impulse for a drama of fundamental simplicity and stark political clarity, directed at spectators for whom, in many cases, dramatic performance was itself a new experience. Spender records his lack of enthusiasm as a writer for the 'propagandist heroics' of the Civil War and suggests that Alberti experienced similar feelings.[8] There is undoubtedly truth in this view, but, interpreted carelessly, it could give a misleading impression of the extent to which Alberti and others concerned with *teatro de urgencia* understood themselves to be involved in a phase of artistic creation which was transitional. They were clearly aware of the limitations of *teatro de urgencia* as drama, but were also aware that, in the circumstances of military struggle, these limitations were actually exploitable and necessary strengths.

Through the focus of the term 'orientation', useful conclusions have been possible, I hope, as to how *teatro de urgencia* perceived its origins, its task and its future both as theatre and as drama. Such a focus offers a means to encapsulate a phenomenon which was clearly resistant to neat categorization. It was, in my view, a drama which, fundamentally, had a sure grasp of what it wished to achieve, despite the difficult circumstances imposed upon it by the war. Yet, paradoxically, the war was the reason for its existence and perhaps, therefore, one of *teatro de urgencia*'s essential elements was the very struggle it experienced to reach audiences and impress itself upon them. The Republic's defeat meant that it did not have a life beyond the conflict, but this was not, in any case, intended. *Teatro de urgencia* had a purpose which did not extend beyond the war other than, as discussed earlier, to act as a conduit for new forms of drama and theatre and, crucially, for new audiences. In this respect it can be viewed as a neglected aspect of the twentieth century's various attempts to regenerate Spanish drama and theatre.

Conclusion: A Lost Theatre Recovered

An interesting illustration of how we might usefully understand *teatro de urgencia*'s position in relation to twentieth-century Spanish and European theatre can be found in the work of the Spanish theatre group, Tábano. In 1979, Tábano presented *El nuevo retablillo de las maravillas* (*The New Little Tableau of Wonders*), a piece of radical, agitational theatre developed from Cervantes's play. The work, like Dieste's 1937 adaptation of the same play, appropriates an earlier popular form for the purposes of contemporary satire. However, whereas Tábano's work, like that of other recent Spanish agitational groups, has been both admired and documented, this has not been the case with *teatro de urgencia*.[9] My impression has been, rather, that commentators have regarded Republican propaganda theatre as a somewhat irrelevant aspect of their drama's history, and even as an embarrassing diversion in the literary careers of writers such as Alberti, Hernández and Aub. I would suggest, by contrast, that *teatro de urgencia* forms part of a dramatic tradition whose origins are ancient but which is still vigorous today, and which is particularly prominent in times of great social and historical crisis. The writers of *teatro de urgencia* were aware that they were engaged in experimentation which demanded the resources of both new forms and old traditions. Like Tábano, they utilized the powerful roots of their own culture to illuminate the meaning of contemporary struggle. The widely held view of the Civil War years as a fallow period of Spanish theatre history needs, in my view, a degree of revision which incorporates *teatro de urgencia* as a strikingly significant experiment.

Since it was a drama which formed part of a popular tradition *teatro de urgencia* tended to function without records, with rudimentary forms of printing or publication and with little concern for its own documentation. It is for these reasons that it effectively vanished in 1939. It is possible, however, that further evidence of *teatro de urgencia* may be found through archive research and that future researchers will continue to reconstitute a detailed dramatic and theatrical picture. The archives of small *pueblos* and the records of army units may well yield interesting results, while, as mentioned earlier, research needs to be undertaken into the possible existence of *teatro de urgencia* written in Catalan and the other peninsular languages. There is clearly much to be done to enable *teatro de urgencia* to take its place alongside the various other elements of Republican culture which have been painstakingly recovered after more than half a century of neglect and disregard.

Notes

Introduction

[1] See F. García Pavón, *El teatro social en España* (Madrid: Taurus, 1962), p.120. See also Francisco Mundi Pedret, *El teatro en la guerra civil* (Barcelona: PPU, 1987) and Robert Marrast, *El teatre durant la guerra civil espanyola* (Barcelona: Institut del Teatre, 1978).

[2] See Ramón J. Sender, *Teatro de masas* (Valencia: Orto, 1932).

[3] For information about the work of Piscator, Brecht and the Living Newspaper see ch.1, note 33. For the Red Megaphones see *Agit-Prop to Theatre Workshop: Political Playscripts 1930–50*, ed. by Howard Goorney and Ewan MacColl (Manchester: MUP, 1986), pp.xxi–xxxii. For the Unity Theatre see Raphael Samuel, Ewan MacColl and Stuart Cosgrove, *Theatres of the Left 1880–1935: Workers' Theatre Movements in Britain and America* (London: Routledge, 1985), pp.59–64.

[4] María Teresa León, *Huelga en el puerto* and Miguel Hernández, *El refugiado*, in *Teatro de agitación política 1933–39*, ed. by Miguel Bilbatúa (Madrid: Editorial Cuadernos para el Diálogo, 1976), pp.55–79 and pp.93–104.

[5] Rafael Alberti, 'Teatro de urgencia', *Boletín de Orientación Teatral*, 1 (1938), 5. Subsequently, *BOT*. See also Rafael Alberti, *Prosas encontradas*, ed. by Robert Marrast (Madrid: Ayuso, 1973), pp.193–6.

[6] Interview with Germán Bleiberg, London, May 1980. See also Germán Bleiberg, *Sombras de héroes*, in *Teatro de urgencia* (Madrid: Signo, 1938), pp.97–127. This rare volume can be located in the archives of the Fundación Juan March, Madrid. References throughout are to this edition. The play can also be found in *Teatro de agitación política 1933–39*, pp.105–32.

[7] *BOT*, 1, 5.

[8] Rafael Alberti, *Radio Sevilla*, El Mono Azul, 45 (1938), 6–8. Subsequently, *Mono Azul*. References throughout are to the original journal. However, the more easily available facsimile reproduction has been consulted. See *Radio Sevilla*, in *El Mono Azul* (Liechtenstein: Detlev Auvermann, 1977), pp.176–8.

[9] See *Teatro juvenil* (Madrid: Diana, 1938). This volume can be located in the archives of the Fundación Pablo Iglesias, Madrid.

[10] Álvaro de Orriols, *España en pie* (Barcelona: Librería Falums, 1937).

[11] *Teatro de urgencia*, p.7.

12. See Antonio Aparicio, 'El teatro en nuestro ejército', *Comisario*, 4 (1938) (repr. Marrast, *El teatre*, pp.279–82) (p.280).
13. See 'Un teatro del ejército para el ejército', *Boletín de Información y Orientación Política*, 13 (1938), 22–4. Subsequently, *BIOP*.
14. Vsévolod Vishnévsky, *An Optimistic Tragedy*, in *Four Soviet Plays*, ed. by Ben Blake (London: Lawrence & Wishart, 1937), pp.81–176. All further references to the Teatro de Arte y Propaganda will be to the TAP.
15. See José Monleón, *El Mono Azul* (Madrid: Ayuso, 1979), p.102. Further references are given after quotations in the text. The magazine's title, *The Blue Monkey*, refers to the nickname given to the characteristic blue boiler suit worn by many Republicans during the Civil War.
16. Santiago Ontañón, *El saboteador*, in *Teatro de urgencia*, pp.53–87 and José Antonio Balbontín, *El cuartel de la Montaña* (Madrid: Sociedad General Autores de España, 1936). Subsequently, *El cuartel*.
17. See Pablo de la Fuente, *Sobre tierra prestada* (Santiago de Chile: Nuestro Tiempo, 1949), pp.236–41 (repr. Marrast, *El teatre*, pp.285–7) (p.286). For the play see Santiago Ontañón, *El bulo*, in *Teatro de urgencia*, pp.17–52.
18. Rafael Dieste, *Al amanecer*, *Hora de España*, 15 (1938), 99–119. References throughout are to the original journal. However, the more easily available facsimile reproduction has been consulted. See *Al amanecer*, in *Hora de España*, 5 vols. (Liechtenstein: Detlev Auvermann, 1977), 3, pp.495–515.
19. Antonio Sánchez-Barbudo, 'Nueva Escena', *Mono Azul*, 10 (1936) [n.p.].
20. Luis Mussot, 'La evasión de los flamencos'. Typescript in my possession but see ch.2, note 53. Subsequently, *La evasión*. Further references are given after quotations in the text.
21. Miguel de Cervantes, *El cerco de Numancia*, in *Teatro completo* (Barcelona: Iberia, 1966), pp.67–133. For Alberti's adaptation see Rafael Alberti, *Numancia* (Madrid: Turner, 1975).
22. *BIOP*, 13 (1938), 22–4 (p.22).
23. Rafael Alberti, *Bazar de la providencia*, in *Bazar de la providencia: dos farsas revolucionarias* (Madrid: Editorial Octubre, 1934), pp.5–15 and Ramón J. Sender, *El secreto*, *Nueva Cultura*, 5 (1935), 10–13. References to this journal throughout are to the original version. However, the more easily available facsimile reproduction has been consulted. See *Nueva Cultura* (Liechtenstein: Topos Verlag, 1977).
24. For further information see P. Broué and E. Témime, *The Revolution and the Civil War in Spain* (London: Faber, 1970), chs.11 and 12.
25. The Commissariat was established in order to exert political control over the armed forces through the medium of political commissars. For details of communist domination of the Commissariat see E. H. Carr, *The Comintern and the Spanish Civil War* (London: Macmillan, 1984), pp.39–40 and 63–4.

1. The Emergence of an Aesthetic

[1] Erwin Piscator, *El teatro político* (Madrid: Cenit, 1930). For the reception in Spain of European experiments with proletarian art see, for example, Miguel Alejandro, 'Antología de los poetas de la revolución: 1. Vladimir Mayakovski', *Nueva Cultura*, 5 (1935), 66–7. See also 'Por una literatura proletaria', *Octubre*, 1 (1933), 21 and 'Por una literatura proletaria: encuesta', *Octubre*, 2 (1933), 32. References to *Octubre* throughout are to the original journal. However, the more easily available facsimile reproduction has been consulted. See *Octubre* (Liechtenstein: Topos Verlag, 1977).

[2] María Teresa León, 'La guerra, el teatro, la revolución y la industria', *BOT*, 3 (1938), 5.

[3] María Teresa León, *Memoria de la melancolía* (Buenos Aires: Losada, 1970), p.267.

[4] 'Carta de Moscú', *Nueva Cultura*, n.s. 1 (1937) [n.p]. This particular issue of the journal was published without page numbers.

[5] *BOT*, 3 (1938), 5.

[6] Antonio Ramos Oliveira, *Nosotros, los marxistas: Lenin contra Marx* (Madrid: Editorial España, 1932), pp.208 and 210. For socialist attitudes to culture see Luis Gómez Llorente, *Aproximación a la historia del socialismo español (hasta 1921)* (Madrid: Cuadernos para el Diálogo, 1972). My discussion is derived from Gómez Llorente's painstaking study. See also *València, capital cultural de la República (1936–1937): antologia de textos i documents*, by Manuel Aznar Soler and others (Valencia: Generalitat Valenciana, 1986).

[7] Miguel Hernández, *Teatro completo* (Madrid: Ayuso, 1978), p.405.

[8] Miguel Seisdedos, 'El teatro socialista. Mi opinión', *El Socialista*, 24 October 1928, p.4.

[9] García Pavón, *Teatro social*, pp.36–50 and G. G. Brown, *A Literary History of Spain: The Twentieth Century* (London: Ernest Benn, 1972), pp.111–12.

[10] Joaquín Dicenta, *Juan José* (Madrid: Cátedra, 1982), p.108.

[11] Gonzalo Torrente Ballester, *Teatro español contemporáneo* (Madrid: Guadarrama, 1968), p.94. For detailed discussion of some of the issues raised by the social dramas see David George, '*Poor Man's Bread*: a Spanish version of Hauptmann's *The Weavers*', *Theatre Research International*, 12 (1987), 23–38 and H. B. Hall, 'The working man in late nineteenth-century drama', *Bulletin of Hispanic Studies*, 28–9 (1951–2), 173–85.

[12] García Pavón, *Teatro social*, p.37.

[13] See ibid., p.65 for references to such plays, many of which, even at the time of García Pavón's investigation, had been lost.

14 José Fola Igúrbide, *El Cristo moderno* (Barcelona: Maucci [n.d.]). Further references are given after quotations in the text.
15 Arturo Cortada Rodríguez, *Águilas negras o los misterios de los conventos* (Madrid: Boreal, 1936). Further references are given after quotations in the text.
16 Álvaro de Orriols, *¡Máquinas!* (Madrid: Boreal, 1936).
17 Angela Bhattacharya, 'The social theatre in Spain: 1895–1915' (unpublished doctoral dissertation, University of London, 1975), p.90.
18 Brown, *Literary History*, p.112.
19 *Brecht on Theatre*, ed. by John Willett (London: Methuen, 1979), p.37.
20 Brown, *Literary History*, p.110.
21 L. Rodríguez Alcalde, *Teatro español contemporáneo* (Madrid: Epesa, 1973), p.5.
22 Brown, *Literary History*, p.110.
23 Ibid., p.111.
24 Lunacharsky's views are discussed in Lars Kleberg, *Theatre as Action* (London: Macmillan, 1980), p.9.
25 Luis Araquistáin, 'Socialismo y poesía', *El Socialista*, 1 May 1925, p.8.
26 Luis Araquistáin, *La batalla teatral* (Madrid: Mundo Latino, 1930), p.27.
27 Seisdedos, 'Teatro socialista', p.4.
28 Sender, *Teatro de masas*, pp.114–15. Further references are given after quotations in the text.
29 María Francisca Vilches de Frutos, 'Las ideas teatrales de Ramón J. Sender en sus colaboraciones periodísticas', *Segismundo*, 35–6 (1982), 211–23.
30 *Brecht on Theatre*, p.8.
31 Miguel de Unamuno, 'La regeneración del teatro español', in *Teatro completo* (Madrid: Águilar, 1959), p.1,137.
32 *BOT*, 3 (1938), 5. See also *Teatro de agitación política 1933–1939*, pp.29–42.
33 For information about the Junta see Hipólito Escolar, *La cultura durante la guerra civil* (Madrid: Alhambra, 1987), pp.20–2. For Russian and German theatre see David Bradby and John McCormick, *People's Theatre* (London: Croom Helm, 1978) and Michael Patterson, *The Revolution in German Theatre: 1900–1933* (London: Routledge, 1981).
34 The manuscript of *Russlandstag* is in the possession of the Akademie der Künste, Berlin. My account is derived from Christopher Innes, *Erwin Piscator's Political Theatre: The Development of Modern German Drama* (Cambridge: CUP, 1972), pp.27–9.
35 John Willett, *The Theatre of Bertolt Brecht* (London: Methuen, 1959), p.146. Geis's remark was made with reference to Brecht's *Mann ist Mann*, which Geis produced in 1926.
36 Max Aub, 'Piscator y una nueva valoración del teatro', *Nueva Cultura*, 3 (1935), 6–7 (p.7). Further references are given after quotations in the text.

[37] 'El teatro en España: los actores parados', *Octubre*, 4–5 (1933), 39.
[38] Christopher Cobb, 'Teatro proletario – Teatro de masas. Barcelona 1931–1934', in *Literatura popular y proletaria*, ed. by Jorge Urrutia (Seville: Universidad de Sevilla, 1986), pp. 247–67 (p.248). For detailed information about cultural debate at this time, see also Christopher Cobb, *La cultura y el pueblo: España 1930–1939* (Barcelona: Laia, 1981) and César M. Arconada, *Obra periodística: de Astudillo a Moscú*, ed. by Christopher Cobb (Valladolid: Ámbito, 1986).
[39] Irene Falcón and Christopher Cobb, 'El grupo teatral "Nosotros"', in *Literatura popular*, pp.261–79. Further references are given after quotations in the text.
[40] Jesús Parrado Vaamonde, *¡Guerra, a la guerra!*, *Nueva Cultura*, 12 (1936), 18 and 23. Further references are given after quotations in the text.
[41] *Literatura popular*, p.263.
[42] Santiago Ontañón, 'Francisco Mateos y su arte', *Mono Azul*, 47 (1939), 107–19 (p.113).
[43] Erwin Piscator, *The Political Theatre*, trans. by Hugh Rorrison (London: Methuen, 1980), p.47.
[44] Max Aub, *El agua no es del cielo*, in *Obras completas* (Mexico: Águilar, 1968), pp.230–40. Subsequently, *El agua*. Further references are given after quotations in the text.
[45] Rafael Alberti, *Farsa de los reyes magos*, in *Bazar de la providencia: dos farsas revolucionarias*, pp.17–33. Subsequently, *Farsa*. Further references are given after quotations in the text. For discussion of the play see Gregorio Torres Nebrera, *El teatro de Rafael Alberti* (Madrid: Sociedad General Español de Librería, 1988), pp.148–54.
[46] *Literatura popular*, p.270.
[47] See Eric Bentley, *Seven Plays by Bertolt Brecht* (New York: Grove Press, 1961).
[48] *Brecht on Theatre*, p.6.
[49] José Monleón, *Tiempo y teatro de Rafael Alberti* (Madrid: Primer Acto, 1990), p.139.
[50] Max Aub, *Proyecto de estructura para un teatro nacional* (Valencia: Tipografía Moderna, 1936).

2. The Development of Teatro de urgencia

[1] Christopher Cobb, 'The educational and cultural policy of the Popular Front government in Spain, 1936–9', in *The French and Spanish Popular Fronts: Comparative Perspectives*, ed. by Martin S. Alexander and Helen Graham (Cambridge: CUP, 1989), pp.240–53 (p.240).
[2] See, for example, García Pavón, *Teatro social*, pp.119–21, Ángel

Berenguer, *El teatro en el siglo xx (hasta 1939)* (Madrid: Taurus, 1989) and Francisco Ruiz Ramón, *Historia del teatro español: siglo xx* (Madrid: Cátedra, 1984).

[3] Mordecai Gorelik, *New Theatres for Old* (London: Dobson, 1940), p.9.

[4] María Teresa León, *Juego limpio* (Barcelona: Seix y Barral, 1987), pp.167–8.

[5] Letter from Rafael Dieste, 28 August 1979.

[6] Letter from Luis Mussot, 7 March 1980.

[7] Luis Mussot, 'Mi puesto está en las trincheras'. Unpublished typescript in my possession. Subsequently, *Mi puesto*. Further references are given after quotations in the text.

[8] Pablo de la Fuente, *El café . . . sin azúcar*, in *Teatro de urgencia*, pp.135–50. Subsequently, *El café...*

[9] Luis Mussot, '¡No pasarán!'. Unpublished typescript in my possession. Subsequently, *¡No pasarán!*. Oliva mistakenly attributes this play to José Antonio Balbontín. See César Oliva, *El teatro desde 1936* (Madrid: Alhambra, 1989), p.32. For further information on Mussot, see Luis Miguel Gómez Díaz, 'Luis Mussot: su labor teatral durante la guerra civil', *Anales de Literatura Española Contemporánea*, 18 (1993), 519–37.

[10] Mundi Pedret suggests that the play might have been published in an author's edition available from Balbontín's house at Barquillo, 20 in Madrid since this was printed on the cover of another of Balbontín's wartime plays, *Pionera*, performed at the Teatro Maravillas from 31 October 1936. Mundi Pedret had clearly been unable to locate *El cuartel*. See Mundi Pedret, *El teatro en la guerra civil*, p.92. My later discussion of *El cuartel* derives from a copy I located in the University of Colorado Library.

[11] The Alliance of Anti-Fascist Intellectuals had been formed in early 1936 as an umbrella organization for writers and artists of the Left actively committed to the Popular Front as a means of revolutionary change. Subsequently, Alliance. For further information see Monleón, *El Mono Azul*, pp.16–17.

[12] Dieste, *Al amanecer*. Alberti's play, long considered lost, has recently been published. See Rafael Alberti, *Los salvadores de España*, *Cuadernos Hispanoamericanos*, 485–6 (1990), 11–20. Subsequently, *Los salvadores*. Prior to this the play had been widely discussed. See, for example, Hub Hermanns, *El teatro político de Rafael Alberti* (Salamanca: Universidad de Salamanca, 1989), pp.157–60. For a review of its first performance see Sánchez-Barbudo, 'Nueva Escena', *Mono Azul*, 10 [n.p.].

[13] See Marrast, *El teatre*, p.25.

[14] 'El teatro en España: los actores parados', *Octubre*, 4–5 (1934), 39.

[15] Ronald Fraser, *Blood of Spain: An Oral History of the Spanish Civil War* (New York: Pantheon, 1979), p.137.

16. Interview with Mussot, Madrid, 10 April 1980. All further references to the Grupo Teatro Popular will be to the GTP.
17. For details of the take-over see 'El comité del Grupo Teatro Popular se incauta del Fontalba', *ABC*, 26 July 1936, p.32. The Marquis is denounced as an exploiter of art and as having no right to possess 'lo que de este momento es de los productores de arte' (that which from now on belongs to the producers of art).
18. 'Cómo se está empezando a organizar cooperativamente la vida del teatro', *Mundo Gráfico*, 4 November 1936, p.12. For further information about take-overs see Burnett Bolloten, *The Grand Camouflage* (London: Pall Mall Press, 1968), pp.48–54.
19. 'Van a desaparecer la obscenidad y la grosería de los escenarios', *ABC*, 15 August 1936, p.13.
20. 'Actividad de la Alianza: sección de teatro', *Mono Azul*, 8 (1936) [n.p.].
21. Sender, *El secreto*, *Nueva Cultura*, 5 (1935), 10–13. The play was also published, perhaps in an anthology entitled *Teatro revolucionario*, by Ediciones de la 43 Brigada. Despite exhaustive searches, both in Spain and South America, I have been unable to locate the volume.
22. Interview with Dieste, La Coruña, 15 April 1980.
23. Fernando Collado, *El teatro bajo las bombas en la guerra civil* (Madrid: Kaydeda, 1989), p.417. Further references are given after quotations in the text. The TAP was an element of the Alliance. The Madrid authorities leased the Teatro de la Zarzuela to the group between September and December 1937 and a number of productions of classic European drama were mounted.
24. For the work of La Tarumba see 'La Tarumba: los títeres al servicio de la guerra', *Ahora*, 12 May 1937, pp.7–8. In the Archivo Histórico Nacional, Salamanca, an anonymous article is catalogued as 'La Tarumba: guiñol satírico al servicio de la guerra'. It bears the reference: Sección: Prop. Núm: 93 but also the words 'no está' (missing).
25. From 16 October 1937, for example, Vishnévsky's *La tragedia optimista* was presented and from 26 December 1937 Alberti's adaptation of Cervantes's *El cerco de Numancia*. See Introduction, note 21.
26. The Consejo Central del Teatro was created in August 1937 to oversee the artistic and cultural aspects of all theatrical activity. Subsequently, CCT. See Marrast, *El teatre*, pp.245–6 for details of the decree by which it was established. Its authority and influence in the Madrid theatres seem to have been less than intended by virtue of the power of the UGT and CNT. Mussot recalled in an interview on 21 April 1980 that only syndicate power mattered and that, as regards the intention of government decrees in relation to the theatres, 'esto fue un deseo' (this was a desire).
27. 'Para recreo de los leales', *ABC*, 29 July 1936, p.30.
28. 'La función para los soldados del frente', *ABC*, 30 July 1936, p.35.

[29] 'Para solaz del espíritu de los heroicos soldados', *ABC*, 2 August 1936, p.31.
[30] 'Teatros, cinematógrafos y conciertos en España y en el extranjero', *ABC*, 4 August 1936, p.43.
[31] 'Informaciones y noticias teatrales en Madrid', *ABC*, 5 August 1936, p.35.
[32] 'La TEA prepara obras para el frente', *ABC*, 18 August 1936, p.16.
[33] See Marrast, *El teatre*, p.97.
[34] *Memoria del patronato de Misiones Pedagógicas* (Madrid: [n.pub.], 1934), p.93.
[35] Ramón J. Sender, *The War in Spain* (London: Faber and Faber, 1937), p.98.
[36] 'Actuación de la Tribuna', *ABC*, 29 August 1936, p.13.
[37] '¡Aquí Madrid, Altavoz del Frente!', *Mundo Gráfico*, 21 October 1936, p.11.
[38] Letter from Dieste, 28 August 1979.
[39] For information about the wealth of research which has taken place in this area see, for example, Aznar Soler, *València*, and Escolar, *La cultura durante la guerra civil*, ch.1, notes 6 and 33.
[40] Letter from Mussot, 4 February 1980.
[41] See ch.1, note 28.
[42.] Anon, *Cuatro batallones de choque: teatro en la calle* (Madrid: Quinto Regimiento [1936(?)]). Subsequently, *Cuatro batallones*. Further references are given after quotations in the text. Marrast, *El teatre*, p.20 suggests that this play was the work of Mussot's GTP but, in conversation, Mussot made it clear that this was not the case. It is possible that the play was performed by the Compañía Teatro Popular which had performed *El cuartel* and was linked to the Communist Party. A copy of *Cuatro batallones* is in the Marx Memorial Library, London. A performance photograph, showing cast and audience giving the clenched fist salute can be found in *Milicia popular: diario del 5º regimiento*, 4 November 1936, p.6.
[43] For an interesting example of such posters, which also illustrates some of the play's techniques see 'Obreros de la Construcción: alistaos en los batallones de fortificación', in *The Palette and the Flame: Posters of the Spanish Civil War*, ed. by John Tisa (London: Collet's, 1980), p.29.
[44] For the siege of Madrid see Hugh Thomas, *The Spanish Civil War* (London: Penguin, 1977), pp.478–81.
[45] 'Un teatro del ejército para el ejército', *BIOP*, 13 (1938), 22–4. Further references are given after quotations in the text.
[46] Interview with Mussot, 21 April 1980.
[47] Letter from Mussot, 4 February 1980.
[48] Aparicio, 'El teatro en nuestro ejército', in Marrast, *El teatre*, pp.279–82. Further references are given after quotations in the text.

[49] Anon., *En las trincheras* ([Valencia(?)]: Subcomisariado de Propaganda, [1937(?)]). Further references are given after quotations in the text. This collection can be found, catalogued as 1.299 and intriguingly stamped 'Recuperación de Documentos Rojos' (Recovery of Red Documents), in the Archivo Histórico Nacional, Salamanca.

[50] See Introduction, note 9.

[51] All the Teatros del Frente series seem to have carried this imprint.

[52] Gabriel García Narezo, *¡Hacia la victoria!* ([Valencia(?)]: Subcomisariado de Propaganda, [1937(?)]) and José Herrera Petere, *Torredonjil*, in *Teatro para combatientes* ([Valencia(?)]: Subcomisariado de Agitación, Prensa y Propaganda, 1937; repr. Madrid: Editorial Hispamerca, 1977), pp.17–24. For Herrera Petere's theatrical activities see Gonzalo Santonja, 'Herrera Petere y el teatro de agitación', *Triunfo*, 2 July 1977, pp.52–3. I am grateful to Nan Green of the International Brigade Association for a copy of this article.

[53] Anon., *Guadalajara-Italia* ([Valencia(?)]: Subcomisariado de Propaganda, [1937(?)]). To this list should also be added Mussot's *La evasión de los flamencos* and *A la orden de la República*. As published editions these two plays have disappeared.

[54] For further information see Collado, *El teatro*, p.483.

[55] Marrast, *El teatre*, p.259 reproduces the decree which officially established the groups. For more information see 'Arte de guerra y para la guerra', *Frente Rojo*, 30 December 1937, p.9.

[56] El Búho was a student theatre company directed by Max Aub which worked in the Valencia region both before and during the war. For information about this and Aub's theatre in general see Rafael Prats Rivelles, *Max Aub* (Madrid: Epesa, 1978), pp.33–6 and Estela R. López, *El teatro de Max Aub* (Barcelona: Uprex, 1976), p.37. For another theatre group which possibly offered similar work to the Guerrillas del Teatro see 'La labor de Arte y Cultura', *Mundo Gráfico*, 22 September 1937, p.10. An article in *Pasaremos*, 16 (1937), 4 indicates that La Barraca had spent 'unos días en Torija, Trijueque, Gaganejos representando diversas obras ante las fuerzas de nuestra División' (a few days in ... performing various works before our Division's forces). Almost certainly this repertoire did not extend beyond Golden Age interludes.

[57] Anon., *España no es Austria*, in *Un teatro de guerra* (Madrid–Barcelona: Nuestro Pueblo, 1938), pp.41–8. Further references are given after quotations in the text.

[58] Anon., *Lección y escarmiento del derrotismo*, in *Un teatro de guerra*, pp.33–9. Subsequently, *Lección y escarmiento*.

[59] Anon., *Tres soldados en una batalla*, in *Un teatro de guerra*, pp.89–95. Subsequently, *Tres soldados*. Further references are given after quotations in the text.

[60] *Un teatro de guerra*, pp.5–6.
[61] See ch.1, note 39.
[62] See Marrast, *El teatre*, pp.76–8. The Guerrillas del Teatro were housed in the basement. The building was the palace of the Marquis of Heredia Spínola and had become the Alliance's base after having been taken over during the early weeks of the war.
[63] Antonio Aparicio, *Los miedosos valientes*, *Mono Azul*, 46 (1938), 7–8.
[64] De la Fuente, *El café...*, p.149.
[65] The Alliance established a Cine-Teatro-Club in its headquarters and had planned a full programme for 1938 to 'dar a conocer en sus sesiones todas aquellas obras, tanto pasadas como actuales, que merezcan ser recordadas . . . por sus valores literarios, documentales o artísticos' (to make known through its sessions all those works, past and current, which are worthy of revival . . . by virtue of their literary, documentary or artistic value). Chamber music sessions alternated with lectures on cinema. Six plays are mentioned as planned for production but it is unlikely that more than the Molière was performed. Lectures included 'Documentales de la guerra de España' by Julio Angulo and 'Buster Keaton y su arte' by Pedro de Neyra. This information derives from a pamphlet, in very fragile condition, catalogued as VE1158/18/R886979 in the Biblioteca Nacional, Madrid.
[66] 'Actividad de la Alianza: sección de teatro', *Mono Azul*, 8 (1936) [n.p.].
[67] 'Notas', *Mono Azul*, 47 (1939), 126.
[68] León, *Juego limpio*, p.167.
[69] For operations in the Ebro sector see Thomas, *Spanish Civil War*, pp.818–19.
[70] See note 66 above.
[71] See Introduction, note 9.
[72] Alberti's speech was later published. See *BOT*, 1 (1938), 5. Further references are given after quotations in the text.
[73] *Teatro juvenil*, p.5.
[74] Hernández, *El refugiado*, in *Teatro completo*, pp. 423–9. All future references to the Juventudes Socialistas Unificadas will be to the JSU.
[75] For further information about such performances see Marrast, *El teatre*, pp.207–8.
[76] Letter from Miles Tomalin, 3 September 1979.
[77] Letter from Dieste, 31 March 1978.
[78] The text which survived is *El moro leal*. Señor Dieste kindly tracked this down in Barcelona, having recalled that it had been published during the Civil War in a bilingual magazine, *Nova Galiza*. I am grateful to him for providing me with a photocopy of the play. It has subsequently been published in Rafael Dieste, *Teatro: 2* (Barcelona: Laia, 1981), pp.95–105.
[79] See ch.1, note 37.
[80] Piscator, *Political Theatre*, p.47.

[81] See Bradby and McCormick, *People's Theatre*, p.45.
[82] See ibid., p.32.

3. Staging the Political Drama

[1] Francisco de Luis Martín, *La cultura socialista en España 1923–1930* (Salamanca: Universidad de Salamanca, 1993), p.32.
[2] José Templado, *Literatura de la posguerra: el teatro* (Madrid: Cincel, 1981), p.24 and Ruiz Ramón, *Historia*, p.251.
[3] Sender, *Teatro de masas*, p.18. Further references are given after quotations in the text.
[4] Balbontín, *El cuartel*. Further references are given after quotations in the text.
[5] The Montaña barracks were besieged by Loyalist supporters in the days immediately following the military insurrection. Its capture was regarded as the 'taking of the Bastille' which signalled the start of the Civil War. Inside, the Loyalists found 50,000 rifles, which were distributed to the popular militias. See James W. Cortada, *A Historical Dictionary of the Spanish Civil War 1936–1939* (London: Greenwood, 1982), p.312.
[6] Bertolt Brecht, *The Messingkauf Dialogues* (London: Methuen, 1977), p.51.
[7] Armand Gatti, 'Armand Gatti on time, place, and the theatrical event', *Modern Drama*, 25 (1982), 69–81 (p.71).
[8] Letter from Mussot, 7 March 1980.
[9] 'Las Guerrillas del Teatro: comediantes en las calles, en los frentes, en los pueblos', *El Sol*, 11 March 1938, p.13. Further references are given after quotations in the text. For an interesting poster announcing the formation of the theatre groups see Collado, *El teatro*, p.462.
[10] Aparicio, for example, writing towards the end of the conflict asserts that most divisions of the army had performance troupes independent of visiting groups. See Marrast, *El teatre*, pp.279–82 (p.279). In conversation, Dieste felt this was exaggerated. An indication of the kinds of activity which took place is given by the national competition to encourage *teatro de urgencia* which was set up by the Ejército Popular de Albacete. Prize money of 12,000 pesetas was offered but the outcome of the competition is unknown. See Collado, *El teatro*, p.322.
[11] Anon., *Dos divisiones de la juventud*, in *Un teatro de guerra*, pp. 49–59 (p.56). Subsequently, *Dos divisiones*. Further references are given after quotations in the text.
[12] Anon., *Defendemos la tierra*, in *Un teatro de guerra*, pp.79–89 (p.79). Further references are given after quotations in the text.
[13] Alberti, *Radio Sevilla*, *Mono Azul*, 45 (1938), 6–8. Further references are given after quotations in the text.

14 General Gonzalo Queipo de Llano (1875–1951) commanded the Nationalist Army of the South and administered most of Andalusia. Called 'the radio General' for his nightly broadcasts, he used caustic, taunting propaganda to demoralize the Republican militias. Interestingly, in view of Alberti's play, Cortada describes Queipo as having the air of an 'incompetent Hispanic general in a comic opera'. See Cortada, *Historical Dictionary*, p.411.

15 The play was in the repertoires of the Guerrillas del Teatro of the Army of the Ebro and the puppet theatre of the Army of the Centre's Eighth Division.

16 Letter from Dieste, 31 March 1978. Collado also saw a Guerrillas troupe since he describes it, scathingly, as 'algo montado sobre viejas bambalinas y telones cursis' (something mounted on old backdrops and tacky curtains). See Collado, *El teatro*, p.159.

17 Interview with Mussot, 7 March 1980.

18 Mussot, *La evasión*, p.1. Further references are given after quotations in the text.

19 See Marrast, *El teatre*, p.259.

20 See León, *Juego limpio*, p.167.

21 See *BOT*, 1 (1938), 5.

22 Anon., *Despedida de reclutas*, in *Un teatro de guerra*, pp.17–25 (p.17). Further references are given after quotations in the text. *Teatro de urgencia*'s frequent awareness of the largely illiterate nature of its audience is felt when, the actor having erected the banner, a voice from the crowd calls for it to be read aloud for those who cannot read.

23 Anon., *Barco de traidores*, in *Un teatro de guerra*, pp.25–33 (p.25). Further references are given after quotations in the text.

24 Luis Mussot, 'A la orden de la República'. Typescript in my possession, but see ch.2, note 53. Subsequently, *A la orden*.

25 García Narezo, *¡Hacia la victoria!*, p.3.

26 A characteristic example of such a programme would be that of the TAP which, at the Teatro de la Zarzuela on 12 December 1937, presented two *teatro de urgencia* works, Ontañón's *El bulo* and Bleiberg's *Sombras de héroes*, as part of a meeting of the CCT which also included an invited audience of social and political organizations.

27 Anon., *En las trincheras*. See ch.2, note 49.

28 Anon., *El pueblo fascista*, in *En las trincheras*, pp.2–5 (p.5). Further references are given after quotations in the text.

29 It is important in this respect to bear in mind the unfavourable circumstances for performance which must occasionally have arisen. Strong winds, poor weather and ineffective spectator sightlines are all factors which obviously hinder the success of this kind of theatre.

30 Anon., *España no es Austria*. Further references are given after quotations in the text.

[31] Max Aub, *Juan ríe, Juan llora*, in *Obras completas*, pp. 294–8 (p.297).
[32] See, for example, *¡Que nos quitan nuestra tierra!*, in *Teatro juvenil*, pp.7–10.
[33] Anon., *Pueblos de vanguardia*, in *Un teatro de guerra*, pp.71–9 (p.79).
[34] See *Memoria del patronato*, pp.93–101.
[35] For a detailed study of La Barraca's theatrical practice see Luis Sáenz de la Calzada, *La Barraca: teatro universitario* (Madrid: Revista de Occidente, 1976).
[36] Anon., *Cuatro batallones*, p.9.
[37] Anon., *Lección y escarmiento*. Further references are given after quotations in the text.
[38] Max Aub, *¿Qué has hecho hoy para ganar la guerra?*, in *Obras completas*, pp.285–91. Subsequently, *¿Qué has hecho?* Further references are given after quotations in the text.
[39] Mussot, *Mi puesto*. Further references are given after quotations in the text.
[40] See ch.1, notes 1 and 24. My discussion is indebted to Kleberg's thorough analysis of performance theory.
[41] See, for example, Bertolt Brecht, *The Measures Taken and Other Plays* (London: Methuen, 1994).

4. Attacking the Enemy

[1] For the relationship between war and propaganda in this context see Francis Thorpe and Nicholas Pronay, *British Official Films in the Second World War* (Oxford: Clio Press, 1980) and Peter Buitenhuis, *The Great War of Words: Literature as Propaganda 1914–18 and After* (London: Batsford, 1989).
[2] Spain had no first-hand experience of modern warfare on its mainland soil. Cox offers an excellent account of the implications of this. See Geoffrey Cox, *Defence of Madrid* (London: Gollancz, 1937), pp.26–37.
[3] For a detailed discussion see E.Comín Colomer, *El Quinto Regimiento de milicias populares* (Madrid: Editorial San Martín, 1973).
[4] See Rafael Abella, *La vida cotidiana durante la guerra civil española: la España republicana* (Barcelona: Editorial Planeta, 1975), pp.299–319. Further references are given after quotations in the text. For an indication of the importance which Republicans attached to the related issue of literacy campaigns see 'La guerra contra el analfabetismo', *Ahora*, 22 October 1937, p.6.
[5] *BOT*, 1 (1938), 4.
[6] Monleón, *El Mono Azul*, p.222.
[7] See Marrast, *El teatre*, p.280.
[8] José Herrera Petere, *La voz de España*, in *Teatro para combatientes*, pp.25–31 (p.28).

[9] For a more detailed discussion of such propaganda techniques see Sam Keen, *Faces of the Enemy* (New York: HarperCollins, 1988).
[10] Bleiberg, *Sombras de héroes*, p.115. Further references are given after quotations in the text.
[11] Germán Bleiberg, *Amanecer, Cuadernos de Madrid*, 1 (1939), 25–34 (p.31). Further references are given after quotations in the text. References throughout are to the original journal. However, the more easily available facsimile reproduction has been consulted. See *Amanecer*, in *Cuadernos de Madrid* (Liechtenstein: Detlev Auvermann, 1975), pp.25–34. The play has also been published in *Teatro de agitación política 1933–39*, pp.105–32.
[12] Anon., *Defendemos la tierra*. Further references are given after quotations in the text.
[13] Max Aub, *Pedro López García, Hora de España*, 19 (1938), 81–100. Further references are given after quotations in the text. References throughout are to the original journal. However, the more easily available facsimile reproduction has been consulted. See *Pedro López García*, in *Hora de España*, 5 vols. (Liechtenstein: Detlev Auvermann, 1977), 4, pp.372–92. For a more detailed discussion of the parallels between *teatro de urgencia* and Christianity see my 'Drama, religion and republicanism', in *Contemporary Theatre Review* (London: Harwood, 1996), 7, pp.47–59.
[14] Rafael Alberti, *Cantata de los héroes y la fraternidad de los pueblos*, in *Teatro* (Buenos Aires: Bajel, 1942), pp.180–201. Subsequently, *Cantata*. Further references are given after quotations in the text.
[15] Toledo, 'The Fascist hordes are trying to invade our land', in *The Palette and the Flame*, p.135.
[16] Anon., *La muerte y la vida*, in *En las trincheras*, pp.5–8. Further references are given after quotations in the text. The play was also printed in *Somosierra: órgano de la 26 Brigada*, 10 January 1939, p.7. This can be located in the Hemeroteca Municipal, Madrid.
[17] Rafael Dieste, *Nuevo retablo de las maravillas, Hora de España*, 1 (1937), 65–79 (p.69). Subsequently, *Nuevo retablo*. Further references are given after quotations in the text. References throughout are to the original journal. However, the more easily available facsimile reproduction has been consulted. See *Nuevo retablo de las maravillas*, in *Hora de España*, 5 vols. (Liechtenstein: Detlev Auvermann, 1977), 1, pp.65–79. The play can also be found in *Teatro de agitación política 1933–39*, pp.165–205.
[18] José Luis Clairac, *¡Unidad!, Por qué luchamos (boletín interior de la 38 brigada)*, 24 August 1937, p.2.
[19] Balbontín, *El cuartel*, p.17. Further references are given after quotations in the text.
[20] Dieste, *Al amanecer*. Further references are given after quotations in the text.
[21] Alberti, *Radio Sevilla*. Further references are given after quotations in the

text. Some line drawings which offer a useful insight into the performance style of the play can be found in *BOT*, 6 (1938), 2.
22. Monleón, *El Mono Azul*, p.263.
23. Pierre Duchartre, *The Italian Comedy* (New York: Dover Publications, 1966), p.228.
24. For the Punch and Judy tradition see George Speaight, *Punch and Judy* (London: Boston, 1970).
25. Mussot, *¡No pasarán!*, p.5.
26. For the traditional pantomime see Gerald Frow, *'Oh, Yes It Is': A History of Pantomime* (London: British Broadcasting Corporation, 1985) and David Mayer, *Harlequin in his Element* (Cambridge, Mass.: Harvard University Press, 1969).
27. Aub, *El agua*, p.239.
28. Alberti, *Los salvadores*, p.15. Further references are given after quotations in the text.
29. Anon., *El pueblo fascista*, pp.2–5. Further references are given after quotations in the text.
30. De la Fuente, *El café* . . . Further references are given after quotations in the text.
31. Anon., *¡Aplastar a Franco!*, in *Un teatro de guerra*, pp.9–17. Further references are given after quotations in the text.
32. Ontañón, *El bulo*. Further references are given after quotations in the text.
33. For Portugal's role in the conflict see Thomas, *Spanish Civil War*, pp.359–60.
34. See 'La Tarumba: los títeres al servicio de la guerra', *Ahora*, 12 May 1937, pp.7–8.
35. Play competitions appear to have been quite common, although it is possible that these initiatives often remained no more than planned projects. Little evidence survives of the results of such competitions, and so it is unclear to what extent they encouraged a substantial degree of new writing. In the first issue of the *BOT* the Hospital Workers' syndicate is reported to have been planning a competition for works which dealt with military hygiene, but no references occur in subsequent issues. See *BOT*, 1 (1938), 7.
36. Interview with Bleiberg, May 1980.
37. Anon., *En las trincheras*, in *En las trincheras*, pp.8–12 (p.8). Further references are given after quotations in the text.
38. Dieste, *El moro leal*, in *Teatro: 2*, pp.95–105. Further references are given after quotations in the text.
39. See Thomas, *Spanish Civil War*, p.373.
40. See *Teatro de urgencia*, p.8.
41. See Monleón, *El Mono Azul*, p.242.

5. Forming the Soldier

1. *The Palette and the Flame*, p.26.
2. Ibid., p.31.
3. 'Una visita al cuartel de Hortaleza', *Pasaremos*, 16 (1937), 4.
4. Michael Alpert, 'Soldiers, politics and war', in *Revolution and War in Spain 1931–1939* (London: Routledge, 1993), pp.202–25.
5. Mussot, *Mi puesto*, p.24.
6. García Narezo, *¡Hacia la victoria!*, p.4. Further references are given after quotations in the text.
7. Anon., *Defendemos la tierra*, p.88.
8. Mussot, *¡No pasarán!*, p.1. Further references are given after quotations in the text.
9. *Manual del miliciano* (Barcelona: Editorial Labor, 1937), p.214.
10. Mussot, *¡No pasarán!*, p.6.
11. Aub, *Pedro López García*, p.99.
12. *Manual del miliciano*, p.214.
13. See ch.2, note 48.
14. See Marrast, *El teatre*, p.280.
15. Anon., *Pueblos de vanguardia*, in *Un teatro de guerra*, pp.71–9. Further references are given after quotations in the text.
16. *¡Que nos quitan nuestra tierra!*, in *Teatro juvenil*, pp.7–10. Further references are given after quotations in the text.
17. Mussot, *Mi puesto*, pp.8–9.
18. Ibid., p.6.
19. Miguel Hernández, *Los sentados*, in *Teatro completo*, pp.431–7 (p.433).
20. Bleiberg, *Sombras de héroes*. Further references are given after quotations in the text. For an illuminating account of Bleiberg's involvement in the war and how certain personal experiences may have found reflection in the play, see Germán Bleiberg, 'Páginas de un diario: sobre la guerra en el norte', *Hora de España*, 15 (1938), 54–66.
21. *Teatro de agitación política 1933–39*, p.7.
22. Bleiberg, *Amanecer*. Further references are given after quotations in the text.
23. Information furnished by Bleiberg in interview, London, May 1980.
24. Interview with Bleiberg, London, May 1980.
25. Anon., *Lección y escarmiento*. Further references are given after quotations in the text.
26. Anon., *Barco de traidores*. Further references are given after quotations in the text.
27. Anon., *Despedida de reclutas*. Further references are given after quotations in the text.
28. Ontañón, *El saboteador*. Further references are given after quotations in the text.

29 Anon., *Tres soldados*. Further references are given after quotations in the text.
30 Rafael Alberti, *Fermín Galán*, in *El poeta en la calle* (Madrid: Águilar, 1978), pp.631–747.
31 See Bhattacharya, 'Social theatre', p.90.

6. Training for Victory

1 See Abella, *La Vida cotidiana*, pp.219–317.
2 Ibid., p.124. *Consigna* has a range of meanings – task, watchword, undertaking – and has connotations of training or propaganda. In subsequent references the Spanish word will be used.
3 Ibid., p.139.
4 *Propaganda en los frentes: carteles y rótulos* (Valencia: Subcomisariado de Propaganda, [1937(?)]). The edition was printed without page numbers.
5 See P. Vich, 'La cultura en los frentes', in Cobb, *La cultura*, p.430.
6 *Por qué los campesinos están interesados en vencer al fascismo* ([Valencia(?)]: Subcomité de Agitación, Prensa y Propaganda, [1937(?)]). The edition was printed without page numbers.
7 See Kantos, 'The first task is to win the war', in *The Palette and the Flame*, p.30.
8 See *BIOP*, 13 (1938), 22–4 (p.24).
9 *Un teatro de guerra*, p.6.
10 V. Zanetti, 'El mural de un batallón', in Cobb, *La cultura*, pp.445–7.
11 Mussot, *A la orden*, p.2. Further references are given after quotations in the text.
12 The play was performed by the theatre group of the Sixty-Seventh Brigade's Second Battalion in June 1937 and was published by Ediciones de la 43 Brigada. It was also included in the initial repertoire of the GTP after its take-over of the Teatro Fontalba in September 1936.
13 For the battle for Madrid see Thomas, *Spanish Civil War*, pp.473–87. For the conduct of the war in Aragón see ibid., pp.798–803.
14 *Cuatro batallones*, p.3. Further references are given after quotations in the text.
15 The JSU was formed in 1934 by young socialists and communists. See Cortada, *Historical Dictionary*, p.282.
16 Anon., *Dos divisiones*, p.50. Further references are given after quotations in the text.
17 Aparicio, *Los miedosos valientes*. Further references are given after quotations in the text.
18 Anon., *En las trincheras*, p.12.
19 *Manual del miliciano*, p.14. Further references are given after quotations in the text.

[20] *BOT*, 3 (1938), 7.
[21] Anon., *Nunca falta un Judas*, in *Teatro juvenil*, pp.15–18. Further references are given after quotations in the text.
[22] See 'The Book–the Convalescent's Best Friend' and 'A Loafer is a Fascist', in *The Palette and the Flame*, p.47 and p.53.
[23] Herrera Petere, *Torredonjil*, in *Teatro para combatientes*, pp.17–24 and *Cómo deben comportarse los soldados en los pueblos próximos al frente* (Valencia: Subcomisariado de Agitación, Prensa y Propaganda, [1937(?)]). The edition was printed without page numbers. Further references to the play are given after quotations in the text.
[24] Anon., *Despedida de reclutas*, p.17.
[25] *Lección y escarmiento*, p.36.
[26] Miguel Hernández, *La cola*, in *Teatro completo*, pp.409–15. Further references are given after quotations in the text. Considerable critical attention has been given to Hernández's wartime theatre. See Florence Delay, 'El teatro de Miguel Hernández', in *En torno a Miguel Hernández* (Madrid: Castalia, 1978), pp.109–36 and Francisco Diez de Revenga and Mariano de Paco, *El teatro de Miguel Hernández* (Murcia: Universidad de Murcia, 1981).
[27] Anon., *¡Aplastar a Franco!*, p.9. Further references are given after quotations in the text.
[28] Anon., *Lección y escarmiento*, p.38. Further references are given after quotations in the text.

7. Celebrating the People

[1] See Ramón Tamames, *La República: la era de Franco* (Madrid: Alianza, 1973), p.148.
[2] 'Los campesinos', in Rafael Alberti, *El poeta en la calle* (Madrid: Águilar, 1978), p.102.
[3] See Ramón J. Sender, 'La cultura y los hechos económicos', in Cobb, *La cultura*, pp.191–6 (p.195).
[4] Ramón J. Sender, 'El novelista y las masas', in Cobb, *La cultura*, pp.196–209 (p.209).
[5] See ch.1, pp.58–9.
[6] See Unamuno, 'La regeneración', pp.1,149–54.
[7] Balbontín, *El cuartel*, p.22. Further references are given after quotations in the text.
[8] By the term 'pueblo' I mean all members of the community, both urban and rural, excluding only members of the ruling groups. See *Diccionario práctico de la lengua española* (Barcelona: Grijalbo, 1988), p.787.
[9] See Bradby and McCormick, *People's Theatre*, p.18.

[10] Mussot, *A la orden*, p.21.
[11] Anon., *España no es Austria*, p.45. Further references are given after quotations in the text.
[12] Anon., *Defendemos la tierra*, p.84. Further references are given after quotations in the text.
[13] Mussot, *¡No pasarán!*, p.6.
[14] Anon., *El pueblo fascista*, p.4. Further references are given after quotations in the text.
[15] Hernández, *El refugiado*, p.426.
[16] Anon., *Dos divisiones*, p.51. Further references are given after quotations in the text.
[17] See Mussot, *Mi puesto*, p.1.
[18] See anon., *Cuatro batallones*, p.13.
[19] José Antonio Balbontín, *Pionera* (Madrid: Sociedad General Autores de España, 1936). Further references are given after quotations in the text.
[20] Anon., *Despedida de reclutas*, p.21.
[21] Aub, *Pedro López García*, p.89. Further references are given after quotations in the text.
[22] Bleiberg, *Amanecer*. Further references are given after quotations in the text.
[23] Alberti, *Cantata*, p.191. Further references are given after quotations in the text. Surprisingly, the *Cantata* has been neglected in terms of critical discussion. In her study of Alberti's theatre, for example, Popkin ignores it completely. For an analysis see Hermanns, *Teatro político*, pp.188–94.
[24] Miguel Hernández, *El hombrecito*, in *Teatro completo*, pp.417–23. Further references are given after quotations in the text.
[25] Hernández, *Los sentados*, in *Teatro completo*, pp.431–7 and Aparicio, *Los miedosos valientes*.
[26] See Alpert, 'Soldiers, politics and war', p.218.
[27] Aub, *¿Qué has hecho?*, p.290.
[28] Bleiberg, *Sombras de héroes*, p.127.
[29] See ch.1, p.12.

Conclusion: A Lost Theatre Recovered

[1] Alberti suggested such a course of action in a newspaper interview with *El Imparcial* in April 1933. See Torres Nebrera, *El teatro*, p.142.
[2] See *Un teatro de guerra*, p.6.
[3] See Jesús Izcaray, 'Barcelona: teatro de calle', *Frente Rojo*, 9 March 1938, p.9.
[4] For Lorca's production of *Fuenteovejuna* see Sáenz de la Calzada, *La Barraca*, pp.65–75 and Sandra Cary Robertson, *Lorca, Alberti and the*

Theater of Popular Poetry (New York: Peter Lang, 1991), pp.187–95. For the play's significance in Spain and elsewhere in Europe, particularly during the 1930s, see D.H. Gagen, *Coming to Terms with the Civil War: Modern Productions of Lope de Vega's 'Fuenteovejuna'* (Swansea: University College of Swansea, 1993).

[5] See Aparicio, 'El teatro en nuestro ejército', p.281.

[6] Antonio Machado, 'Sobre los románticos españoles', in *Obras completas de Manuel y Antonio Machado* (Madrid: Biblioteca Nueva, 1984), pp.1,095–8.

[7] See *BOT*, 1 (1938), 5.

[8] Stephen Spender, *The Thirties and After* (Glasgow: Fontana, 1978), p.78.

[9] For information about such groups and other recent radical theatre in Spain, see Eugène van Erven, *Radical People's Theatre* (Bloomington: Indiana University Press, 1988), pp.145–73.

Bibliography

Published Plays

Alberti, Rafael, *Cantata de los héroes y la fraternidad de los pueblos*, in *Teatro* (Buenos Aires: Bajel, 1942), pp.180–201.

——, *Farsa de los reyes magos*, in *Bazar de la providencia: dos farsas revolucionarias* (Madrid: Editorial Octubre, 1934), pp.17–33.

——, *Los salvadores de España*, *Cuadernos Hispanoamericanos*, 485–6 (1990), 11–20.

——, *Radio Sevilla*, *El Mono Azul*, 45 (1938), 6–8; repr. in *El Mono Azul* (Liechtenstein: Detlev Auvermann, 1977), pp.176–8.

Anon., *Cuatro batallones de choque: teatro en la calle* (Madrid: Quinto Regimiento, [1936(?)]).

——, *Guadalajara-Italia* ([Valencia(?)]: Subcomisariado de Propaganda, [1937(?)]).

——, *Nunca falta un Judas*, in *Teatro juvenil* (Madrid: Diana, 1938), pp.15–18.

Aparicio, Antonio, *Los miedosos valientes*, *El Mono Azul*, 46 (1938), 7–8; repr. in *El Mono Azul* (Liechtenstein: Detlev Auvermann, 1977), pp.185–6.

Aub, Max, *Obras completas* (Mexico: Águilar, 1968): *El agua no es del cielo*, pp.230–40; *Juan ríe, Juan llora*, pp.294–8; *Las dos hermanas*, pp.263–5; *Por Teruel*, pp.279–81; *¿Qué has hecho hoy para ganar la guerra?*, pp.285–91.

——, *Pedro López García*, *Hora de España*, 19 (1938), 81–100; repr. in *Hora de España*, 5 vols. (Liechtenstein: Detlev Auvermann, 1975), 4, pp.372–92.

Balbontín, José Antonio, *El cuartel de la Montaña* (Madrid: Sociedad General Autores de España, 1936).

——, *Pionera* (Madrid: Sociedad General Autores de España, 1936).

Bleiberg, Germán, *Amanecer*, *Cuadernos de Madrid*, 1 (1939), 25–34; repr. in *Cuadernos de Madrid* (Liechtenstein: Detlev Auvermann, 1975), pp.25–34.

——, *Amanecer*, in *Teatro de agitación política 1933–39*, ed. by Miguel Bilbatúa (Madrid: Editorial Cuadernos para el Diálogo, 1976), pp.105–32.

——, *Sombras de héroes*, in *Teatro de urgencia* (Madrid: Signo, 1938), pp.97–127.

——, *Sombras de héroes*, in *Teatro de agitación política 1933–39*, ed. by Miguel Bilbatúa (Madrid: Editorial Cuadernos para el Diálogo, 1976), pp.133–64.

Clairac, José Luis, *¡Unidad!, Por qué luchamos (boletín interior de la 38 brigada)*, 24 August 1937, p.2.
Dieste, Rafael, *Al amanecer*, *Hora de España*, 15 (1938), 99–119; repr. in *Hora de España*, 5 vols. (Liechtenstein: Detlev Auvermann, 1977), 3, pp.495–515.
——, *El moro leal*, in *Teatro: 2* (Barcelona: Laia, 1981), pp.95–105.
——, *Nuevo retablo de las maravillas*, *Hora de España*, 1 (1937), 65–79; repr. in *Hora de España*, 5 vols. (Liechtenstein: Detlev Auvermann, 1977), 1, pp.65–79.
——, *Nuevo retablo de las maravillas*, in *Teatro de agitación política 1933–39*, ed. by Miguel Bilbatúa (Madrid: Editorial Cuadernos para el Diálogo, 1976), pp.165–205.
En las trincheras ([Valencia(?)]: Subcomisariado de Propaganda, [1937(?)]) contains the following anonymous works: *El pueblo fascista*, pp.2–5; *En las trincheras*, pp.8–12; *La muerte y la vida*, pp.5–8.
Fuente, Pablo de la, *El café . . . sin azúcar*, in *Teatro de urgencia* (Madrid: Signo, 1938), pp.135–50.
García Narezo, Gabriel, *¡Hacia la victoria!* ([Valencia(?)]: Subcomisariado de Propaganda [1937(?)]).
Garfias, Pedro, *¡Que nos quitan nuestra tierra!*, in *Teatro juvenil* (Madrid: Diana, 1938), pp.7–10.
Hernández, Miguel, *Teatro completo* (Madrid: Ayuso, 1978): *El refugiado*, pp.423–9; *La cola*, pp.409–15; *Los sentados*, pp.431–7.
——, *El refugiado*, in *Teatro de agitación política 1933–39*, ed. by Miguel Bilbatúa (Madrid: Editorial Cuadernos para el Diálogo, 1976), pp.93–104.
Herrera Petere, José, *Teatro para combatientes* ([Valencia(?)]: Subcomisariado de Agitación, Prensa y Propaganda, 1937; repr. Madrid: Editorial Hispamerca, 1977): *La voz de España*, pp.25–31; *Torredonjil*, pp.17–24.
Ontañón, Santiago, *El bulo*, in *Teatro de urgencia* (Madrid: Signo, 1938), pp.17–52.
——, *El saboteador*, in *Teatro de urgencia* (Madrid: Signo, 1938), pp.53–87.
Parrado Vaamonde, Jesús, *¡Guerra, a la guerra!*, *Nueva Cultura*, 12 (1936), 18 and 23; repr. in *Nueva Cultura* (Liechtenstein: Topos Verlag, 1977), pp.214 and 219.
Un teatro de guerra (Madrid–Barcelona: Nuestro Pueblo, 1938) contains the following anonymous works: *¡Aplastar a Franco!*, pp.9–17; *Barco de traidores*, pp.25–33; *Defendemos la tierra*, pp.79–89; *Despedida de reclutas*, pp.17–25; *Dos divisiones de la juventud*, pp.49–59; *España no es Austria*, pp.41–8; *Lección y escarmiento del derrotismo*, pp.33–9; *Pueblos de vanguardia*, pp.71–9; *Tres soldados en una batalla*, pp.89–95.

Unpublished Plays

Mussot, Luis, 'A la orden de la República'.
——, 'La evasión de los flamencos'.
——, 'Mi puesto está en las trincheras'.
——, '¡No pasarán!'.

Other Works Consulted

Abella, Rafael, *La vida cotidiana durante la guerra civil española: la España republicana* (Barcelona: Planeta, 1975).
Abellán, José Luis (ed.), *El exilio español de 1939: Cataluña, Euzkadi, Galicia*, 6 vols. (Madrid: Taurus, 1976–8), 6 (1978).
——, *El exilio español de 1939: la emigración republicana de 1939*, 6 vols. (Madrid: Taurus, 1976–8), 1 (1976).
Alberti, Rafael, *Bazar de la providencia*, in *Bazar de la providencia: dos farsas revolucionarias* (Madrid: Editorial Octubre, 1934), pp.5–15.
——, *Fermín Galán*, in *El poeta en la calle* (Madrid: Águilar, 1978), pp.631–747.
——, 'Los campesinos', in *El poeta en la calle* (Madrid: Águilar, 1978), p.102.
——, *Numancia* (Madrid: Turner, 1975).
——, *Prosas encontradas*, ed. by Robert Marrast (Madrid: Ayuso, 1973).
——, 'Teatro de urgencia', *Boletín de Orientación Teatral*, 1 (1938), 5.
Alejandro, Miguel, 'Antología de los poetas de la revolución: 1. Vladimir Mayakovski', *Nueva Cultura*, 5 (1935), 66–7.
Alpert, Michael, 'Soldiers, politics and war', in *Revolution and War in Spain 1931–1939* (London: Routledge, 1993), pp.202–25.
Alted, Alicia, 'The Republican and Nationalist wartime cultural apparatus', in *Spanish Cultural Studies*, ed. by Helen Graham and Jo Labanyi (Oxford: OUP, 1995), pp.152–61.
Anon., 'Actividad de la Alianza: sección de teatro', *El Mono Azul*, 8 (1936) [n.p.].
——, 'Actuación de la Tribuna', *ABC*, 29 August 1936, p.13.
——, 'Al margen de la guerra: el nuevo teatro', *ABC*, 5 August 1937, p.9.
——, 'Carta de Moscú', *Nueva Cultura*, n.s. 1 (1937) [n.p.].
——, *Como deben comportarse los soldados en los pueblos próximos al frente* (Valencia: Subcomisariado de Agitación, Prensa y Propaganda, [1937(?)]).
——, 'Cómo se está empezando a organizar cooperativamente la vida del teatro', *Mundo Gráfico*, 4 November 1936, p.12.
——, 'El comité del Grupo Teatro Popular se incauta del Fontalba', *ABC*, 26 July 1936, p.32.
——, 'El teatro en España: los actores parados', *Octubre*, 4–5 (1933), 39.

Anon., 'Informaciones y noticias teatrales en Madrid', *ABC*, 5 August 1936, p.35.
——, 'La Barraca', *Pasaremos*, 16 (1937), 4.
——, 'La función para los soldados del frente', *ABC*, 30 July 1936, p.35.
——, 'La guerra contra el analfabetismo', *Ahora*, 22 October 1937, p.6.
——, 'La TEA prepara obras para el frente', *ABC*, 18 August 1936, p.16.
——, *Manual del miliciano* (Barcelona: Editorial Labor, 1937).
——, *Memoria del patronato de Misiones Pedagógicas* (Madrid: [n.pub.], 1934).
——, 'Notas', *El Mono Azul*, 47, 126.
——, 'Para poner el arte al alcance del pueblo', *Frente Rojo*, 18 February 1939, p.9.
——, 'Para recreo de los leales', *ABC*, 29 July 1936, p.30.
——, *Por qué los campesinos están interesados en vencer al fascismo* ([Valencia(?)]: Subcomité de Agitación, Prensa y Propaganda [1937(?)]).
——, 'Por una literatura proletaria', *Octubre*, 1 (1933), 21.
——, 'Por una literatura proletaria: encuesta', *Octubre*, 2 (1933), 32.
——, *Propaganda en los frentes: carteles y rótulos* (Valencia: Subcomisariado de Propaganda, [1937(?)]).
——, 'Teatros, cinematógrafos y conciertos en España y en el extranjero', *ABC*, 4 August 1936, p.43.
——, 'Un teatro del ejército para el ejército', *Boletín de Información y Orientación Política*, 13 (1938), 22-4.
——, 'Una visita al cuartel de Hortaleza', *Pasaremos*, 16 (1937), 4.
——, 'Van a desaparecer la obscenidad y la grosería de los escenarios', *ABC*, 15 August 1936, p.13.
Aparicio, Antonio, 'El teatro en nuestro ejército', *Comisario*, 4 (1938) (repr. Marrast, *El teatre*, pp.279-82).
Araquistáin, Luis, *La batalla teatral* (Madrid: Mundo Latino, 1930).
——, 'Socialismo y poesía', *El Socialista*, 1 May 1925, p.8.
Arconada, César, *Obra periodística: de Astudillo a Moscú*, ed. by Christopher Cobb (Valladolid: Ámbito, 1986).
Aub, Max, 'Piscator y una nueva valoración del teatro', *Nueva Cultura*, 3 (1935), 6-7.
——, *Proyecto de estructura para un teatro nacional* (Valencia: Tipografía Moderna, 1936).
Aznar Soler, Manuel, 'María Teresa León y el teatro español durante la guerra civil', *Anthropos*, 148 (1993), 25-35.
Aznar Soler, Manuel (and others), *València, capital cultural de la República (1936–1937): antologia de textos i documents* (Valencia: Generalitat Valenciana, 1986).
Bentley, Eric, *Seven Plays by Bertolt Brecht* (New York: Grove Press, 1961).
Berenguer, Ángel, *El teatro en el siglo xx (hasta 1939)* (Madrid: Taurus, 1989).

Bhattacharya, Angela 'The social theatre in Spain: 1895–1915' (unpublished doctoral dissertation, University of London, 1975).

Bilbatúa, Miguel, 'La guerra civil y el teatro', *Camp de l'Arpa*, 48–9 (1978), 31–5.

Bilbatúa, Miguel (ed.), *Teatro de agitación política 1933–39* (Madrid: Editorial Cuadernos para el Diálogo, 1976).

Bleiberg, Germán, 'Páginas de un diario: sobre la guerra en el norte', *Hora de España*, 15 (1938), 54–66.

Boland, Roy and Kenwood, Alan (eds.), *War and Revolution in Hispanic Literature* (Melbourne–Madrid: Voz Hispánica, 1990).

Boletín de Orientación Teatral, 1–6 (1938).

Bolloten, Burnett, *The Grand Camouflage* (London: Pall Mall Press, 1968).

Bradby, David and McCormick, John, *People's Theatre* (London: Croom Helm, 1978).

Brecht, Bertolt, *The Measures Taken and Other Plays* (London: Methuen, 1994).

——, *The Messingkauf Dialogues* (London: Methuen, 1977).

Broué, Pierre and Témime, Emile, *The Revolution and the Civil War in Spain* (London: Faber, 1970).

Brown, G. G., *A Literary History of Spain: The Twentieth Century* (London: Ernest Benn, 1972).

Buitenhuis, Peter, *The Great War of Words: Literature as Propaganda 1914–18 and After* (London: Batsford, 1989).

Carr, E. H., *The Comintern and the Spanish Civil War* (London: Macmillan, 1984).

Castellón, Antonio, 'Proyectos de reforma del teatro español 1920/1939', *Primer Acto*, 176 (1975), 4–13.

Cattell, David, *Communism and the Spanish Civil War* (New York: Russell and Russell, 1965).

Cervantes, Miguel de, *El cerco de Numancia*, in *Teatro completo* (Barcelona: Iberia, 1966), pp. 67–133.

Cobb, Christopher, 'El agit-prop cultural en la guerra civil', *Studia Histórica-Historia Contemporánea*, 10–11 (1992–3), 237–49.

——, 'La animación socio-cultural durante la 2a República española', in *Pueblo, movimiento obrero y cultura en la España contemporánea*, ed. by Jacques Maurice and others (Saint-Denis: Presses Universitaires de Vincennes, 1990), pp. 279–87.

——, *La cultura y el pueblo: España 1930–1939* (Barcelona: Laia, 1981).

——, *Los milicianos de la cultura* (Bilbao: Universidad del País Vasco, 1995).

——, 'Teatro proletario–Teatro de masas. Barcelona 1931–34', in *Literatura popular y proletaria*, ed. by Jorge Urrutia (Seville: Universidad de Sevilla, 1986), pp.247–67.

——, 'The educational and cultural policy of the Popular Front government in Spain, 1936–9', in *The French and Spanish Popular Fronts: Comparative Perspectives*, ed. by Martin S. Alexander and Helen Graham (Cambridge: CUP, 1989), pp.240–53.

Cobb, Christopher, 'The Republican state and mass educational-cultural initiatives', in *Spanish Cultural Studies*, ed. by Helen Graham and Jo Labanyi (Oxford: OUP, 1995), pp.133–9.

Collado, Fernando, *El teatro bajo las bombas en la guerra civil* (Madrid: Kaydeda, 1989).

Comín Colomer, E., *El comisariado político en la guerra española de 1936–39* (Madrid: Editorial San Martín, 1973).

——, *El Quinto Regimiento de milicias populares* (Madrid: Editorial San Martín, 1973).

Cortada, James W., *A Historical Dictionary of the Spanish Civil War 1936–1939* (London: Greenwood, 1982).

Cortada Rodríguez, Arturo, *Águilas negras o los misterios de los conventos* (Madrid: Boreal, 1936).

Cox, Geoffrey, *Defence of Madrid* (London: Gollancz, 1937).

Cuadernos de Madrid, 1 (1939; repr. Liechtenstein: Detlev Auvermann, 1975).

Deák, Frantisek, 'Blue Blouse (1923–1928)', *The Drama Review*, 17 (1973), 35–52.

Delay, Florence, 'El teatro de Miguel Hernández', in *En torno a Miguel Hernández* (Madrid: Castalia, 1978), pp.109–36.

Dennis, Nigel, 'Apostillas sobre "El triunfo de las germanías" de Manuel Altolaguirre y José Bergamín', *Revista Canadiense de Estudios Hispánicos*, 3 (1978), 87–9.

——, 'Teatro de agitación política: el caso de José Bergamín (creación y compromiso)', *Camp de l'Arpa*, 67–8 (1979), 21–6.

Diccionario práctico de la lengua española (Barcelona: Grijalbo, 1988).

Dicenta, Joaquín, *Juan José* (Madrid: Cátedra, 1982).

Diez-Canedo, Enrique, *Artículos de crítica teatral*, 4 vols. (Mexico: Mortiz, 1968).

Diez de Revenga, Francisco and Paco, Mariano de, *El teatro de Miguel Hernández* (Murcia: Universidad de Murcia, 1981).

Doménech, Ricardo, 'Aproximación al teatro del exilio', in *El exilio español de 1939*, 6 vols. (Madrid: Taurus, 1977–8), 4 (1977), pp.183–247.

Duchartre, Pierre, *The Italian Comedy* (New York: Dover Publications, 1966).

Erven, Eugène van, *Radical People's Theatre* (Bloomington: Indiana University Press, 1988).

Escolar, Hipólito, *La cultura durante la guerra civil* (Madrid: Alhambra, 1987).

Esenwein, George and Shubert, Adrian, *Spain at War: The Spanish Civil War in Context: 1931–1939* (London and New York: Longman, 1995).

Falcón, Irene and Cobb, Christopher, 'El grupo teatral "Nosotros"', in *Literatura popular y proletaria*, ed. by Jorge Urrutia (Seville: Universidad de Sevilla, 1986), pp.261–79.

Fisher, David James, 'Romain Rolland and the French people's theatre', *The Drama Review*, 73 (1977), 75–90.

Fitzpatrick, Sheila, *'The Commissariat of Enlightenment': Soviet Organization of Education and the Arts under Lunatcharsky. October 1917–1921* (Cambridge: CUP, 1970).

Fola Igúrbide, José, *El Cristo moderno* (Barcelona: Maucci [n.d.]).

Fraser, Ronald, *Blood of Spain: An Oral History of the Spanish Civil War* (New York: Pantheon, 1979).

Frow, Gerald, *'Oh, Yes It Is': A History of Pantomime* (London: British Broadcasting Corporation, 1985).

Fuente, Pablo de la, *Sobre tierra prestada* (Santiago de Chile: Nuestro Tiempo, 1949).

Fuentes, Victor, *La marcha al pueblo en las letras españolas 1917–1936* (Madrid: Ediciones de la Torre, 1980).

Gagen, Derek, *Coming to Terms with the Civil War: Modern Productions of Lope de Vega's 'Fuenteovejuna'* (Swansea: University College of Swansea, 1993).

——, 'Puppets and politics: Rafael Alberti's *Dos farsas revolucionarias*', *Quinquereme*, 7 (1984), 54–73.

——, 'Unamuno and the regeneration of the Spanish theatre', in *Re-reading Unamuno*, ed. by Nicholas G. Round, Glasgow Colloquium Papers 1 (University of Glasgow: Department of Hispanic Studies, 1989), pp.53–79.

Gamonal Torres, Miguel Ángel, *Arte y política en la guerra civil española: el caso republicano* (Granada: Diputación Provincial de Granada, 1987).

García Álvarez, Cristina, 'El teatro durante la guerra civil en la zona nacional', in *War and Revolution in Hispanic Literature*, ed. by Roy Boland and Alun Kenwood (Melbourne–Madrid: Voz Hispánica, 1990), pp.197–209.

García Pavón, Francisco, *El teatro social en España* (Madrid: Taurus, 1962).

Gatti, Armand, 'Armand Gatti on time, place and the theatrical event', *Modern Drama*, 25 (1982), 69–81.

George, David, *'Poor Man's Bread*: a Spanish version of Hauptmann's *The Weavers*', *Theatre Research International*, 12 (1987), 23–38.

Gómez Díaz, Luis Miguel, 'Farsa y esperpento en tiempos de guerra', *El público* (June 1986), 51–60.

——, 'La idea de teatro en la dramaturgia de la guerra civil: algunos ensayos', *Anthropos*, 148 (1993), 35–9.

——, 'Luis Mussot: su labor teatral durante la guerra civil', *Anales de Literatura Española Contemporánea*, 18 (1993), 519–37.

——, 'Santiago Ontañón: escenógrafo y dramaturgo republicano', *Primer Acto*, 232 (1990), 94–101.

Gómez Llorente, Luis, *Aproximación a la historia del socialismo español (hasta 1921)* (Madrid: Cuadernos para el Diálogo, 1972).

González Tuñón, Raul, 'La Tarumba: los títeres al servicio de la guerra', *Ahora*, 12 May 1937, pp.7–8.

Goorney, Howard and MacColl, Ewan (eds.), *Agit-Prop to Theatre Workshop: Political Playscripts 1939–50* (Manchester: MUP, 1986).

Gorelik, Mordecai, *New Theatres for Old* (London: Dobson, 1940).

Grimau, Carmen, *El cartel republicano en la guerra civil* (Madrid: Cátedra, 1979).

Gyseghem, André van, *Theatre in Soviet Russia* (London: Faber and Faber, 1943).

Hall, H. B., 'The working man in late nineteenth-century drama', *Bulletin of Hispanic Studies*, 28–9 (1951–2), 173–85.

Hermanns, Hub, *El teatro político de Rafael Alberti* (Salamanca: Universidad de Salamanca, 1989).

Hernández, Miguel, *Pastor de la muerte*, in *Teatro completo* (Madrid: Ayuso, 1978), pp.441–514.

Hora de España, 1–23 (1937–8; repr. 5 vols., Liechtenstein: Detlev Auvermann, 1977).

Innes, Christopher, *Erwin Piscator's Political Theatre: The Development of Modern German Drama* (Cambridge: CUP, 1972).

Keen, Sam, *Faces of the Enemy* (New York: HarperCollins, 1988).

Kelyn, F. W., 'Literary Spain', *International Literature: Organ of the International Union of Revolutionary Writers*, 6 (1934), 93–105.

Kleberg, Lars, *Theatre as Action* (London: Macmillan, 1980).

L.C., 'Arte de guerra y para la guerra', *Frente Rojo*, 30 December 1937, p.9.

Labanyi, Jo, 'Propaganda art: culture by the people or for the people?', in *Spanish Cultural Studies*, ed. by Helen Graham and Jo Labanyi (Oxford: OUP, 1995), pp.161–7.

León, María Teresa, *Huelga en el puerto*, in *Teatro de agitación política 1933–39*, ed. by Miguel Bilbatúa (Madrid: Editorial Cuadernos para el Diálogo, 1976), pp.55–79.

——, *Juego limpio* (Barcelona: Seix y Barral, 1987).

——, 'La guerra, el teatro, la revolución y la industria', *Boletín de Orientación Teatral*, 3 (1938), 5.

——, *Memoria de la melancolía* (Buenos Aires: Losada, 1970).

López, Estela R., *El teatro de Max Aub* (Barcelona: Uprex, 1976).

Luis Martín, Francisco de, *La cultura socialista en España 1923–1930* (Salamanca: Universidad de Salamanca, 1993).

Machado, Antonio, 'Sobre los románticos españoles', in *Obras completas de Manuel y Antonio Machado* (Madrid: Biblioteca Nueva, 1984), pp.1,095–8.

Marrast, Robert, *El teatre durant la guerra civil espanyola* (Barcelona: Institut del Teatre, 1978).

Marrast, Robert, 'El teatro durante la guerra civil española', *El público* (June 1986), 19–31.

Mayer, David, *Harlequin in his Element* (Cambridge, Mass.: Harvard University Press, 1969).

McCarthy, James, 'Drama, religion and republicanism', in *Contemporary Theatre Review* (London: Harwood, 1996), 7, 47–59.

——, 'Militant marionettes: two "lost" puppet plays of the Spanish Civil War 1936–39', in *Theatre Research International*, 23, 1(1998), 44–50.

——, 'Soldiers as spectators: agitprop theatre and the aesthetics of performance during the Spanish Civil War', *Tesserae*, 2 (1996), 165–79.

——, 'The Republican theatre during the Spanish Civil War: Rafael Alberti's *Numancia*', *Theatre Research International*, 5, 3 (1981), 193–205.

Monleón, José, 'El arte de urgencia durante nuestra guerra civil', *Camp de l'Arpa*, 48–9 (1978), 35–43.

——, *El Mono Azul* (Madrid: Ayuso, 1979).

——, *Tiempo y teatro de Rafael Alberti* (Madrid: Primer Acto, 1990).

Mono Azul, El, 1–47 (1936–9; repr. Liechtenstein: Detlev Auvermann, 1977).

Mundi Pedret, Francisco, *El teatro en la guerra civil* (Barcelona: PPU, 1987).

Nueva Cultura, 1–21 (1935–7; repr. Liechtenstein: Topos Verlag, 1977).

Octubre, 1–6 (1933–4; repr. Liechtenstein: Topos Verlag, 1977).

Oliva, César, *El teatro desde 1936* (Madrid: Alhambra, 1989).

Ontañón, Santiago, 'Francisco Mateos y su arte', *El Mono Azul*, 47 (1939), 107–19.

Orriols, Álvaro de, *España en pie* (Barcelona: Librería Falums, 1937).

——, *¡Máquinas!* (Madrid: Boreal, 1936).

Otero Seco, Antonio, '¡Aquí Madrid, Altavoz del Frente!', *Mundo Gráfico*, 21 October 1936, p.11.

P., 'Las Guerrillas del Teatro: comediantes en las calles, en los frentes, en los pueblos', *El Sol*, 11 March 1938, p.13.

Paco, Mariano de, 'La "nota previa" a *Teatro en la guerra* de Miguel Hernández', in *Estudios sobre Miguel Hernández* (Murcia: Universidad de Murcia, 1992), pp.283–95.

Patterson, Michael, *The Revolution in German Theatre 1900–1933* (London: Routledge, 1981).

Piscator, Erwin, *El teatro político* (Madrid: Cenit, 1930).

——, *The Political Theatre*, trans. by Hugh Rorrison (London: Methuen, 1980).

Popkin, Louise, *The Theatre of Rafael Alberti* (London: Tamesis, 1976).

Prats Rivelles, Rafael, *Max Aub* (Madrid: Epesa, 1978).

Ramos Oliveira, Antonio, *Nosotros, los marxistas: Lenin contra Marx* (Madrid: Editorial España, 1932).

Rico, Francisco (ed.), *Historia y crítica de la literatura española* (Barcelona: Editorial Crítica, 1984).

Robertson, Sandra Cary, *Lorca, Alberti and the Theater of Popular Poetry*

(New York: Peter Lang, 1991).
Rodríguez Alcalde, L., *Teatro español contemporáneo* (Madrid: Epesa, 1973).
Ruiz Ramón, Francisco, *Historia del teatro español: siglo xx* (Madrid: Cátedra, 1984).
Sáenz de la Calzada, Luis, *La Barraca: teatro universitario* (Madrid: Revista de Occidente, 1976).
Samuel, Raphael (and others), *Theatres of the Left 1880–1935: Workers' Theatre Movements in Britain and America* (London: Routledge, 1985).
Sánchez-Barbudo, Antonio, 'Nueva Escena', *El Mono Azul*, 10 (1936) [n.p.].
Santonja, Gonzalo, 'Herrera Petere y el teatro de agitación', *Triunfo*, 2 July 1977, pp.52–3.
Santos, Mateo, *Ensayo de teatro experimental* (Caspe, Nueva Aragón: Consejería de Información y Propaganda del Consejo de Aragón, 1937).
Sarto, Juan del, 'La labor de Arte y Cultura', *Mundo Gráfico*, 22 September 1937, p.10.
Seisdedos, Miguel, 'El teatro socialista. Mi opinión', *El Socialista*, 24 October 1928, p.4.
Sender, Ramón José, 'El novelista y las masas', in Christopher Cobb, *La cultura y el pueblo: España 1930–1939* (Barcelona: Laia, 1981), pp.196–209.
——, *El secreto*, *Nueva Cultura*, 5 (1935), 10–13.
——, 'El teatro nuevo', *Leviatán*, 25 (1936), 45–52.
——, 'La cultura y los hechos económicos', in Christopher Cobb, *La cultura y el pueblo: España 1930–1939* (Barcelona: Laia, 1981), pp.191–6.
——, *Teatro de masas* (Valencia: Orto, 1932).
——, *The War in Spain* (London: Faber and Faber, 1937).
Soldevila Durante, Ignacio, 'Sobre el teatro español de los últimos veinticinco años', *Cuadernos Americanos*, 76 (1963), 256–89.
Speaight, George, *Punch and Judy* (London: Boston, 1970).
Spender, Stephen, *The Thirties and After* (Glasgow: Fontana, 1978).
Stourac, Richard and McCreery, Kathleen, *Theatre as a Weapon: Workers' Theatre in the Soviet Union, Germany and Britain, 1917–1934* (London: Routledge, 1986).
Tamames, Ramón, *La República: la era de Franco* (Madrid: Alianza, 1973).
Templado, José, *Literatura de la posguerra: el teatro* (Madrid: Cincel, 1981).
Thomas, Hugh, *The Spanish Civil War* (London: Penguin, 1977).
Thorpe, Francis and Pronay, Nicholas, *British Official Films in the Second World War* (Oxford: Clio Press, 1980).
Tisa, John (ed.), *The Palette and the Flame: Posters of the Spanish Civil War* (London: Collet's, 1980).
Torrente Ballester, Gonzalo, *Teatro español contemporáneo* (Madrid: Guadarrama, 1968).
Torres Nebrera, Gregorio, *El teatro de Rafael Alberti* (Madrid: Sociedad General Española de Librería, 1988).

Torres Nebrera, Gregorio, 'La obra literaria de María Teresa León (cuentos y teatro)', *Anuario de Estudios Filológicos*, 7 (Cáceres: Universidad de Extremadura, 1984), 379-84.

Tuñón de Lara, Manuel, *Medio siglo de cultura española: 1885-1936* (Madrid: Tecnos, 1970).

Unamuno, Miguel de, 'La regeneración del teatro español', in *Teatro completo* (Madrid: Águilar, 1959), pp.1,129-58.

Vich, P., 'La cultura en los frentes', in Christopher Cobb, *La cultura y el pueblo: España 1930-1939* (Barcelona: Laia, 1981).

Vilches de Frutos, María Francisca and Dougherty, Dru, *El teatro en España entre la tradición y la vanguardia* (Madrid: CSIC, 1993).

Vilches de Frutos, María Francisca, 'Las ideas teatrales de Ramón J. Sender en sus colaboraciones periodísticas', *Segismundo*, 35-6 (1982), 211-23.

Vishnévsky, Vsévolod, *An Optimistic Tragedy*, in *Four Soviet Plays*, ed. by Ben Blake (London: Lawrence & Wishart, 1937), pp.83-179.

Wallis, Mick, 'Pageantry and the Popular Front: ideological production in the thirties', *New Theatre Quarterly*, 38 (1994), 132-57.

Willett, John, *The Theatre of Bertolt Brecht* (London: Methuen, 1959).

———, (ed.), *Brecht on Theatre* (London: Methuen, 1979).

Zambrano, María, *Los intelectuales en el drama de España: ensayos y notas (1936-1939)* (Madrid: Hispamerca, 1977).

Zanetti, V., 'El mural de un batallón', in Christopher Cobb, *La cultura y el pueblo: España 1930-1939* (Barcelona: Laia, 1981), pp.445-7.

Index

A Doll's House 55
A la orden de la República (*At the Order of the Republic*) 67, 149–54, 176, 180, 222n., 225n.
A Man's a Man 25
ABC 11, 35, 40, 41, 42
agitprop 84, 207, 208
Águilas negras . . . o los misterios de los conventos (*Black Eagles . . . or the Mysteries of Convents*) 6, 217n.
Al amanecer (*At Dawn*) xvi, 32, 36, 96–7, 102, 117, 211, 215n.
Alberti, Rafael xiii–xv, xvi, xvii, xviii, 13, 20, 21, 24–5, 27, 29, 30, 36, 51, 53, 54, 56, 63–4, 90–2, 97–100, 101, 102, 103, 109, 116, 138, 178, 195, 207, 208, 211, 212, 213, 231n., 232n.
Alfonso the Thirteenth 107
Alliance of Anti-Fascist Intellectuals 32, 38, 39, 51, 52, 53, 219n., 223n.
Altavoz del Frente 32, 42–3, 49, 56, 64
Álvarez Quintero, Joaquín and Serafín 10
Amanecer (*Dawn*) 88, 95, 96, 103, 110, 137, 138, 193–4, 196, 227n.
An Optimistic Tragedy xv, 215n.
Anarchism, contribution to *teatro de urgencia* xix
Anarchists 132
anticlericalism 6, 183

Aparicio, Antonio 47, 48, 52, 55, 129, 159, 210, 224n.
¡Aplastar a Franco! (*Crush Franco!*) 103, 172–4, 176, 191, 228n.
Araquistáin, Luis 10–12, 58
Aristocrats, The 35
Army of the East 46, 49, 53
Arniches, Carlos 55
Así empezó . . . (*It Began Thus . . .*) 32
Aub, Max 13, 17, 20–4, 26, 27, 29, 30, 75–7, 79, 89–90, 92–4, 101, 125, 185, 191, 208, 210, 213, 222n.
Austria, annexation of 49
autos sacramentales (allegorical religious plays) 24
Ayora, Antonio 41

Badajoz, massacre at 55
Bakunin, Mikhail 48, 132
Balbontín, José Antonio xvi, 32, 59–61, 219n.
Baleares, Nationalist warship 139
Barbero, Edmundo 51, 52
Barco de traidores (*Ship of Traitors*) 67, 74, 139, 225n.
Bardasano, propaganda artist 163
Basque country, dramatic portrayal of 133–7, 202
Bazar de la providencia (*Providence Bazaar*) xviii, 215n.
Bleiberg, Germán xiv, 88, 103, 110, 115, 133, 136, 138, 185, 193, 229n.
Blue Blouse 14–15, 17, 19, 208

Boletín de Información y Orientación Política (*BIOP*) x
Boletín de Orientación Teatral (*BOT*) x, 207
Brecht, Bertolt 1, 8, 13, 60, 61, 83

caciquismo (local political bosses) 148, 178
Calderón de la Barca, Pedro 41, 52
Cantata de los héroes y la fraternidad de los pueblos (*Cantata of the Heroes and the Fraternity of Peoples*) 90–2, 94, 195–6, 227n., 232n.
Carnés, Luisa 32
casas del pueblo (socialist community centres) 86
Casona, Alejandro 55
Cervantes, Miguel de xvii, 210, 213
Chekhov, Anton xii, 51, 52, 53, 54
Chicote, Enrique 40
Christianity, contribution to *teatro de urgencia* 93–4, 136–7, 195–6
Club Anfistora 41
Confederación Nacional de Trabajadores (National Confederation of Workers) (CNT) x, 33, 34, 35, 220n.
Comisario 55
commedia dell'arte 21, 99, 145, 188
Communist Party 34, 42, 44, 215n., 221n.
Cómo deben comportarse los soldados en los pueblos próximos al frente (*How Soldiers Should Conduct Themselves in the Villages Close to the Front Line*) 163, 167, 230n.
Compañía de Variedades Socializadas 34
Compañía Teatro Popular 44, 221n.

Consejo Central del Teatro (Central Theatre Council) (CCT) x, 39, 54, 56, 86, 207, 220n., 225n.
Constitution, Republican 178
Cortada, Arturo 6, 217n.
Council for the Defence of Madrid 148
Cuatro batallones de choque (*Four Shock Battalions*) 44–6, 74, 154–6, 158, 189, 210, 221n.
cuestión social, dramas of 1, 5, 10, 13, 17, 25
Cultura Popular 42, 86

Danton 37
De un momento a otro (*From One Moment to the Next*) 36
defeatism 172
Defendemos la Tierra (*We Defend the Land*) 63, 72, 73, 88, 90, 121, 182, 186, 224n.
deleite y doctrina 143, 154
Despedida de reclutas (*Farewell to the Recruits*) 66, 140, 168, 191, 225n.
Dicenta, Joaquín 4, 179
Dieste, Rafael xvi, 31, 36, 37, 43, 55, 95, 96–7, 99, 101–2, 113–15, 117, 210, 211, 213
Dos divisiones de la juventud (*Two Youth Divisions*) 62, 154, 156–9, 185, 189, 190, 224n.
Duel, The 51

Ebro, military sector of 50, 53, 223n.
Ediciones de la 43 Brigada 220n., 230n.
Ediciones Juventud 54
Ehrenburg, Ilya 55
Ejército Popular de Albacete 224n.
El agua no es del cielo (*Water*

Doesn't Come From the Sky) 21–4, 101, 218n.
El alcalde de Zalamea (*The Mayor of Zalamea*) 35
El Búho 49, 222n.
El bulo (*The Rumourmonger*) xvi, 104–10, 111, 116, 141, 210, 215n., 225n.
El café . . . sin azúcar (*Coffee . . . without Sugar*) 31, 52, 103, 219n.
El cerco de Numancia (*The Siege of Numantia*) xvii, 215n.
El Cristo moderno (*The Modern Christ*) 5, 8, 9, 217n.
El cuartel de la Montaña (*The Montaña Barracks*) xvi, 32, 59–61, 72, 73, 82, 96, 100, 102, 179–80, 189, 215n., 219n., 224n.
El dragoncillo (*The Little Dragon*) 41, 51
Elephant Calf, The 25
El Gil Gil 36
El hombrecito (*The Little Man*) 197–9, 202, 203, 232n.
El Mono Azul xvi, 52, 95, 214n.
El moro leal (*The Loyal Moor*) 113–15, 223n., 228n.
El novelista y las masas (*The Novelist and the Masses*) 179
El nuevo retablillo de las maravillas (*The New Little Tableau of Wonders*) 213
El pueblo fascista (*The Fascist Town*) 70, 103, 116, 182–4, 193, 225n.
El refugiado (*The Refugee*) xiii, 54, 214n., 223n.
El saboteador (*The Saboteur*) xvi, 51, 54, 68, 140–3, 215n.
El secreto (*The Secret*) xviii, 36, 55, 154, 215n., 220n.

El Socialista (*The Socialist*) 10, 11
El Sol (*The Sun*) 62, 63
El toro antifascista (*The Anti-Fascist Bull*) 55
El vengador (*The Avenger*) 41
En las trincheras (*In the Trenches*) 47, 48, 69, 112, 160, 222n., 228n.
entremeses (*interludes*) 24, 117
epic theatre 13
España en pie (*Spain be Ready*) xv
España no es Austria (*Spain is not Austria*) 49, 70–1, 181–2, 186, 190, 191, 192, 222n.
Expressionism, 5

Falangists, dramatic portrayal of 88, 97, 102, 103, 106, 126, 127, 149, 194
Falcón, César 30, 42
Falcón, Irene 18, 30, 51, 207
Farsa de los reyes magos (*Twelfth Night Farce*) 21, 24–9, 101, 208, 218n.
Fascism 88, 109–10, 113, 116, 120, 128, 183, 192, 194
Fermín Galán 146
fifth-columnists 31, 52, 141
Fifth Regiment 44
Fola Igúrbide, José 5
Fortificación (*Fortification*) 47, 86, 129
Fourteenth of July 35
Franco, Francisco 50, 55, 95, 103, 104, 106, 107, 140, 172, 174, 176
Fuente, Pablo de la 31, 52, 103
Fuenteovejuna 35, 36, 209, 232n.

Gandesa, military sector of 63
García Lorca, Federico 209, 210
García Narezo, Gabriel 48, 120, 129, 130

Garfias, Pedro 48, 130, 132
Gatti, Armand 61
Geis, Jacob 17, 217n.
Gemier, Fermin 180
General War Commissariat xix, 46, 65, 70, 114, 124, 125, 147, 149, 160, 163, 215n.
Germans, dramatic portrayal of 112, 113, 128, 135, 194, 206
Golden Age, dramatic forms 209, 210
Gorelik, Mordecai 30, 45
Grupo Teatro Popular (GTP) x, 36, 37, 38, 39, 211, 220n., 221n., 230n.
Guadalajara-Italia 49, 222n.
Guernica 110, 135, 136
¡Guerra, a la guerra! (*War, to War!*) 18–20, 24, 218n.
Guerrillas del Teatro 31, 41, 49, 50, 53, 56, 62, 64, 65, 66, 73, 77, 209, 211, 223n., 224n.
Guerrillas del Teatro of the Army of the Centre 38, 41, 52, 54, 63
Guerrillas del Teatro of the Army of the East 49, 51, 62, 66
guiñol 38

¡Hacia la victoria! (*Towards Victory!*) 48, 68, 87, 120, 126, 133, 137, 176, 222n.
Hairy Ape, The 36
He Who Says Yes 83
Heraldo de Madrid (*Madrid Herald*) 38
Hernández, Miguel xiii, 3, 54, 133, 168, 171, 213
Herrera Petere, José 48, 87, 163
Hitler, Adolf 71, 107, 108, 109, 110, 113, 162
Hora de España (*Hour of Spain*) 215n.
Huelga en el puerto (*Strike at the Port*) xiii, 214n.

Ibsen, Henrik xii, 55
Iglesias, Braulio 43
Imaginary Invalid, The 52
International Brigades, dramatic portrayal of 91, 195, 196
'Internationale' 15, 19, 156
Isaura, Antonio 34
Italians, dramatic portrayal of 94, 108, 112, 128, 135, 206

Jefatura de Sanidad del Ejército 163
Juan José 4–5, 7, 9, 179, 216n.
Juan ríe, Juan llora (*John Laughs, John Cries*) 71, 226n.
Julián, Narciso 33
Junta de Ampliación de Estudios (Studies Extension Council) 14, 217n.
Juventud Campesina (Agricultural Youth) xv, 48, 54
Juventudes Socialistas Unificadas (United Socialist Youth) (JSU) x, 54, 138, 156, 157, 191, 230n.

La Barraca 14, 42, 53, 73, 209, 222n.
La cola (*The Queue*) 168–71, 231n.
La evasión de los flamencos (*The Escapism of the Gypsies*) xvii, 65, 66, 222n.
La llave (*The Key*) 36
La muerte y la vida (*Death and Life*) 95, 116, 226n.
La real gana (*The Bloody Bother*) 55
La regeneración del teatro español (*The Regeneration of the Spanish Theatre*) 179
La retaguardia también es frente (*The Rearguard is also the Front Line*) 168
La Tarumba 38, 110, 220n., 228n.
La tienda de los gestos (*The Shop of Appearances*) 41

Index

La Tribuna 42
La vida es sueño (*Life's a Dream*) 36
La voz de España (*The Voice of Spain*) 87, 89, 226n.
League of Nations, the 19
Lección y escarmiento del derrotismo (*Lesson and Warning about Defeatism*) 50, 75, 139, 140, 168, 172–4, 176, 191, 222n.
lehrstücke xii, 83
León, María Teresa xiii, 1, 2, 31, 42, 53, 66, 207
Ley de Jurisdicciones 146
literacy campaigns 86, 226n.
Living Newspaper, the xii, 15, 20, 27, 45
Lope de Vega 41, 53
Los Faraones Antifascistas 66, 70
Los hombres al frente (*The Men at the Front*) 43
Los marinos de Cronstad (*The Sailors of Kronstadt*) 147
Los miedosos valientes (*The Brave Cowards*) 52, 159–60, 198, 223n.
Los salvadores de España (*The Saviours of Spain*) 32, 36, 37, 38, 51, 102, 103, 139, 219n.
Los sentados (*The Seated Ones*) 133, 198, 229n.
Lunacharsky, Anatoly 10

Machado, Antonio 211
Madrid, battle for 147, 148, 149, 151, 154, 155, 170, 171, 175, 230n.
Maeterlinck, Maurice 54
Manual del miliciano (*The Militiaman's Handbook*) 160, 163, 168
¡Máquinas! (*Machines!*) 7, 8, 18, 217n.

Marqués de Fontalba 34
Martín, Arturo 5
Marx, Karl 48, 132
Meyerhold, Vsevolod 17
Mi puesto está en las trincheras (*My Place is in the Trenches*) 31, 71, 77–84, 86, 120, 188, 208, 219n.
Molina, Miguel de 34
Milicias de la Cultura 147
Ministry of Health and Public Education 49, 54
Miracle of Saint Anthony, The 54
Misiones Pedagógicas 14, 42, 44, 52, 53, 73
Molière 52, 54, 223n.
Montaña Barracks 59, 224n.
Moors, dramatic portrayal of 106, 107, 111, 112, 114, 115, 127, 135, 136
morality plays 143, 163
Morocco, war in 78, 121
mothers, dramatic portrayal of 181, 189, 191, 192, 193, 195, 203
Mundo Gráfico (*Illustrated World*) 35
Muñoz Seca, Pedro 10
Mussolini, Benito 71, 107, 108, 109, 111, 162, 181
Mussot, Luis ix, 31, 34, 43, 46, 49, 61, 65, 77–84, 86, 100, 120, 121, 129, 133, 139, 145, 149, 154, 188, 208

Nationalist soldier, dramatic portrayal of 88–95, 187, 195
National Theatre, Aub's plan for 29
¡No pasarán! (*They Shall Not Pass!*) 32, 36, 37, 60, 100, 121–5, 129, 133, 145, 182, 219n.
Nosotros 17, 25, 40, 42, 51, 57, 83, 207
Nova Galiza (*New Galicia*) 223n.
Nuestra Natacha (*Our Natasha*) 55

Nueva Cultura (*New Culture*) 215n.
Nueva Escena 32, 36, 38, 39, 52, 54, 211
Nuevo retablo de las maravillas (*New Tableau of Wonders*) 95, 100, 101, 117, 210, 227n.
Nunca falta un Judas (*There's Always a Judas*) 161–3, 166, 168, 231n.

O'Neill, Eugene 36
Octubre (*October*) 17, 32, 56, 216n.
Ontañón, Santiago xvi, 20, 68, 104, 109, 116, 140, 210
Orriols, Álvaro de xv, 7, 179, 217n.

Pablo Iglesias battalion 202
pantomime 100
Parrado Vaamonde, Jesús 18–21
Parrilla, propaganda artist 118, 129
Pasaremos 119
pasos (sketches) 24
Pedro López García 89–90, 92–4, 113, 125, 192–3, 194, 196, 203–4, 210, 227n.
Pionera (*Girl Pioneer*) 189–90, 199–202, 232n.
Piscator, Erwin 1, 15, 16, 17, 20, 21, 23, 27, 42, 56, 210
play competitions 224n., 228n.
¡¡Pobres obreros!! (*Poor Workers!!*) 5
Podogin, Nikolai 35
Political Theatre, The 1
Por qué los campesinos están interesados en vencer al fascismo (*Why the Peasants Have an Interest in Defeating Fascism*) 148
Portugal, dramatic portrayal of 109–10, 111, 228n.
Prado, Loreto 40
Prince of Asturias 107
Professor Mamlock 35

Proletarian Theatre, the xii, 15, 19, 56
Proletkult 56
propaganda posters 118, 120, 121, 136, 139, 140, 145, 147, 156, 160
Pueblos de vanguardia (*Vanguard Towns*) 72, 129–30, 226n.
puppetry 99, 109, 115, 117

¿Qué has hecho hoy para ganar la guerra? (*What Have You Done Today to Win the War?*) 75–7, 185, 191, 192, 199, 200, 226n.
¡Que nos quitan nuestra tierra! (*They Are Usurping Our Land!*) 48, 130–3, 229n.
Queipo de Llano 64, 97–9, 109, 225n.
Quintero, Joaquín and Serafín *see* Álvarez Quintero

Radio Sevilla (*Radio Seville*) xiv, 51, 63–4, 97–101, 103, 104, 109, 111, 139, 214n.
Red Megaphones xii
Retablo Rojo 43, 64
Rivas Cherif, Cipriano 41
Rojo, Vicente, Republican Chief of Staff 119, 120
Rolland, Romain 36, 37, 57
romance (ballad poetry) 126, 130, 200, 202
Romillo, José 43
Russlandstag (*Russia's Day*) 15, 20, 23, 217n.

sainete (one-act farce) 116, 210
Sánchez-Barbudo, Antonio xvi
Sender, Ramón xii, xviii, 12–14, 16, 25, 36, 42, 44, 59, 74, 154, 179
Sindicato de Artistas Teatrales 34
Sindicato de Hospitales 161
Singladura roja (*Red Voyage*) 43

Socialist Realism 118
Sombras de héroes (*Shadows of Heroes*) xiv, 88, 110–12, 115, 133–7, 185, 202–3, 229n.
Somosierra, theatrical activity in 32, 40
Spender, Stephen 212
Subcommissariat of Propaganda 48

Tábano 213
Tairof, Alexander 36
Teatro de Arte y Propaganda (Theatre of Art and Propaganda) (TAP) x, 38, 39, 52–4, 104, 138, 211, 220n., 225n.
Teatro de masas (*Theatre of the Masses*) 13, 44
teatro de urgencia, definition of xviii
Teatro del Pueblo of Misiones Pedagógicas 41–2, 44, 73
Teatro Escuela de Arte 41
Teatro Proletario 20
Teatros del Frente, series of plays 48–9, 222n.
theatres
  Alcázar 34
  Español 32, 37, 39
  Fontalba 32, 34, 35, 60
  Lara 32, 42
  Maravillas 32, 59
  Martín 35
  Pavón 149, 154
  Popular 35
  Principal 46

Zarzuela, de la xiv, 34, 38, 52, 138, 220n.
theatres, socialization of 37–9, 82
Toledo, propaganda artist 95
Tomalin, Miles 55
Torredonjil 52, 163–7, 168, 222n.
Trades Union Council of the Moscow Department of Culture 15
Treaty of Versailles 19
Tres soldados en una batalla (*Three Soldiers in a Battle*) 50, 143–5, 222n.
Triunfo de Juliánita y muerte de Don Petimetre (*Triumph of Julianita and Death of Don Petimetre*) 41

Unión General de Trabajadores (General Workers' Union) (UGT) x, 33, 34
Unamuno, Miguel de 14, 179, 208, 209
¡*Unidad!* (*Unity!*) 96, 227n.
Unity Theatre xii

Vishnévsky, Vsevolod xv

Wolf, Friedrich 35
women, dramatic portrayal of 189–99
Workers' Councils 34

Young Pioneers 200

Zanetti 143